A THEORY OF EUROPE

A VIEW OF THE NEW RIGHT

A THEORY OF EUROPE

A VIEW OF THE NEW RIGHT

DARIA PLATONOVA DUGINA

ARKTOS
LONDON 2024

ARKTOS

🌐 Arktos.com 𝐟 fb.com/Arktos ◎ arktosmedia ✖ arktosjournal

ISBN
978-1-915755-94-0 (Paperback)
978-1-915755-95-7 (Hardback)
978-1-915755-96-4 (Ebook)

Translation
Jafe Arnold

Editing
Constantin von Hoffmeister

Layout
Tor Westman

Contents

Part I: The New Right

Part II: Deconstructing French Politics

From the Translator

THE PRESENT BOOK constitutes the third volume of Daria "Platonova"[1] Dugina's posthumously collected works to appear in English, following *Eschatological Optimism* and *For a Radical Life*.[2] As was the case with *Eschatological Optimism*, which brought together the foremost exhibits of Dugina's philosophy, *A Theory of Europe* has likewise been compiled by Dugina's family, friends, colleagues, and admirers out of diverse materials, ranging from lectures and essays to transcripts of interviews, talk shows, and online streams, all of which offer unique insights into Dugina's dearest intellectual, spiritual, and (geo-)political commitments.

In *A Theory of Europe*, we are presented with a rich and variegated picture of Dugina's lifelong engagement with the current of thought that has come to be known as the "European New Right", principally based on what in France came to be called the *Nouvelle Droite*. That being said, what follows is no mere "account" of the so-called "New Right" or *Nouvelle Droite*, as if another monographic study or another paraphrasing manifesto were what is at stake. Instead, in this display of "Dugina and the New Right" or "Dugina on the New Right", we find a

---

1   "Platonova", based on the name of Daria Dugina's philosophical hero, Plato, was the name ("pseudonym" rings utterly unrepresentative) that Dugina donned for most of her works, public appearances, and social media channels.

2   Daria Platonova Dugina, *Eschatological Optimism*, trans. Jafe Arnold, ed. John Stachelski (PRAV Publishing, 2023); *For a Radical Life: Meditations by Daria Platonova Dugina*, trans. Jafe Arnold, ed. John Stachelski (PRAV Publishing, 2024).

young woman and a burgeoning philosopher and activist freely thinking aloud — thinking about the New Right, thinking with the New
Right, and, originally and ultimately, showing what it means to think
proactively and what the New Right furnishes for such thinking. As
Dugina demonstrates to us on the pages that follow, her experience with
the New Right meant thinking through the mosaics of civilisations and
geopolitics, macrocosm and microcosm, the sacred and the profane,
the fateful and the comical, the analytical and the spiritual, the sites,
sights, and powers that be as well as the spaces, visions, and powers that
stand to be affirmed beyond what is immediately present. Therefore,
although this book deserves its place alongside other introductions to
the *Nouvelle Droite*, it is something more, something "meta": it testifies
to the far-reaching, open-ended meaning and resonance of movements
and thoughts above and beyond their coincidental categorisations. After
all, here we find ourselves invited to follow the pathfinding of a young
Russian woman, born in the 1990s and killed in the 2020s, coming to
terms with the impact of a phenomenon that reared its head in France
in the 1960s. This "coming to terms" is not a cold, detached commentary
on people and things afar, nor is it a presumptuous "sentence" passed
upon texts on one's screen; rather, this book is a window into how Daria
Dugina presented — and "re-presents" — a living engagement with
complex and captivating thinkers seeking to commune with the very
spirit of European thinking. Daria beckons us to hear that "European
New Right" or *Nouvelle Droite* names one of the most pressing and
impressive tasks of radical thinking in our days. In Daria's hands and
words, what is concealed behind the name "New Right" comes down
to us as a living experience of the dramatic interplay of continents and
ideas. Therefore, if there is any way to productively leap into the stream
of consciousness that follows, it is to recognise that "life" and "living"
are the crucial words for us, just as they were for Daria in her life, and
just as they are for us in the aftermath of her death.

France and the *Nouvelle Droite* were an indelible part of Daria's
heritage, biography, and bibliography, her thinking, speaking, soul,

and heart. Dugina's father, Alexander Dugin, arguably the greatest philosopher and geopolitician of our age, originally learned French as a dissident in the Soviet underground (following his teachers Yuri Mamleev, Evgeny Golovin, Geydar Dzhemal) along the path of discovering and absorbing some of the essential milestones of modern — but anti-modern — French thought, first and foremost the leading lights of Traditionalism and the *Nouvelle Droite*: respectively, René Guénon and Alain de Benoist. As the Soviet Union was collapsing, Dugin's first travels abroad to Europe were to France, to meet Alain de Benoist and to forge dialogue with the *Nouvelle Droite*, which he in turn translated "into the Russian space", as Daria so often puts it. Readers will soon hear in her own words how Daria Dugina was born into and grew up with this heritage, this legacy, and how she made it her own. In more recent years, as the new-old Russia has emerged out of post-Soviet ruins and compellingly re-posed the question of civilisations in the plural, even by way of war, the young Dugina herself endeavoured to travel to, rediscover, dwell within, and critically interpret the meaning of the *Nouvelle Droite* for France, for Europe, for Russia, for Eurasia, for the dynamics of the world's civilisations along with all the thoughts they invoke and emit. Daria went "back" to the source and became academically, politically, and journalistically involved in France. Back in Russia, as the lectures and interviews reprinted here attest, she was gradually becoming recognised as an interpreter of the *Nouvelle Droite* and an analyst of French politics.

As the foregoing words and the ensuing pages hopefully make clear, Daria's encounter with the France and Europe of the "New Right" is a life story spanning generations, a lived and living history. This story is full of clear-cut thoughts and provocative ambiguities, movements and stops, questions and answers, hopes and dreams, disappointments and daring. Moreover, this story, which is a part of our reality today, is irrevocably marked by the event of Daria's death — which makes this unplanned book something even more dramatic. In being killed as a representative of ideas and trajectories, Daria's death represented an attempt at assassinating the idea of engaging the authentic Europe that she knew, loved, and sought to uncover for others. Daria's death, as the killing of a passionate lover and defender of Europe by the very same forces which her beloved *Nouvelle Droite* identified as the enemies of European identity and well-being, is a microcosm of European fate in the (Post-)Modern age. Daria's life and death are inseparable from the pulse and conscience of European thinking about the past, the present, and the future — including a future Europe where the murder of a young woman means something very different from the imported and exported, hypocritical screeches about "human rights", "democracy", and other epiphenomena that obscure and distract from very real matters of the soul, the souls of countries and peoples, and, indeed, the World Soul. This book, a book brought about by a young woman's death, is not only full of omens, but is itself an omen.

Therefore, like Daria's life and death, this work is no stale "case study", but an animated reminder of the sways, trials, tribulations, and visions of being that a radical human faces in our times and places. Daria treats the *Nouvelle Droite* not as a set of dogmatic concepts, but as a living theorising, a theoretical journey which, like all travel, involves dramatic confrontations and recognitions. We must approach her and her book — and ourselves — accordingly. Thus, when we hear the word "theory" in the title *A Theory of Europe*, we should think not in the modern terms of a hypothesis, concept, or system, but in the ancient Greek sense of *theoria* as a journey, a pilgrimage, a traveling to behold something sacred, something meaningful, something worthy of visiting and returning home to tell of and decipher for ourselves, transformed by the experience of the path, by the sights along the way, and by the visions propelling us forth anew.

When the manuscript of *A Theory of Europe* came into my hands, I knew that it would be a great honour and pledge to publish it through PRAV Publishing, which has hitherto been blessed with becoming the home of Dugina's other works. But I also immediately knew that it would be right, and an even greater homage to Dasha, for her book on the New Right to be published by the first and foremost publishing house of the European New Right, Arktos, where Dugina's volume can rightfully stand alongside the works of her leading light, Alain de Benoist, as well as many of the other authors she draws upon here, whose thinking has been made unprecedentedly accessible to readers and researchers across the world thanks to the historic role to which Arktos has remained unwaveringly committed despite the pressures of censorship and deplatforming. Sincere thanks are owed to Daniel Friberg for recognising the importance of this work and making sure that Daria Dugina's contribution to the intellectual history and spirit of the New Right now finds its rightful place.

As in the case of *Eschatological Optimism* and *For a Radical Life*, my translation of *A Theory of Europe* is worded and intoned in a way that seeks to balance between, on the one hand, the original text, so that Daria's voice might be structurally transmitted in the deeply Russian manner that she thought, and, on the other hand, in the ways I recall knowing Daria's manner of speaking and writing, i.e., how I myself, merely one among her many friends and listeners around the world, heard and interpreted how she spoke and wrote between her unique accentuations in Russian, French, and English. Any idiosyncrasies are my own — but my own as I learned to think with and in the wake of Daria's resounding words. On this front, I wish to thank Constantin von Hoffmeister for his intuitive understanding and generous editing in curating my translation for publication. After all, the words that follow do not belong to just anyone, but to the one and only Daria Platonova Dugina herself, whose life and words became and forever remain symbols of the profundity of the matters at hand. As her writing and her speaking, this book is alive and living. It deserves not only a vital reading, but the most lively responses.

Jafe Arnold
PRAV Publishing
7 October 2024

Daria Dugina's Theory of Europe

Daria against the Degradation of the West

T HIS BOOK by Daria Dugina is dedicated to the New Right. Daria does not even try to hide her "partisanship" here. She does not merely retell or analyse the New Right's views, nor does she simply share her historical knowledge about the origin and development of this European movement; rather, she actively promotes their ideas with which she is fully in solidarity. Her solidarity is not only because of her family's tradition, which she openly refers to in her lectures, livestreams, and interviews reprinted here, but is based on her own philosophical, political, and aesthetic choice. Dasha was an exchange student from Moscow State University at the University of Bordeaux, where she engaged in studying Plato and Neoplatonism. At the same time, she deeply immersed herself in French politics, which she perceived and interpreted through the perspective of GRECE, the Research and Study Group for European Civilisation, which the French press christened the "New Right". Throughout her texts gathered here, Daria describes in detail just how imprecise such a determination was and is, as well as why it was applied to them. Nevertheless, it is important to emphasise that her academic references and historiographic excursions are tied together by her direct life experience, personal contacts, and, most importantly, her ideological kinship with this current in European political philosophy.

The New Right, their ideas, their history, their authorities, and their transformations have been treated in numerous volumes, the information contained in which is often more complete than the broad strokes with which Daria draws a picture of this intellectual phenomenon here. But it is all the more likely that no one other than Daria has so penetratingly, benevolently, and wholeheartedly attempted to present an integral image of the "Theory of Europe" that she recognised in the New Right, which she adopted and to which she swore an oath of allegiance. It is no coincidence that Daria said that if she hadn't been Russian, she would have been French — and not only French, but French of the New Right. In fact, this is how the French themselves saw her. They accepted her as a young passionary of their movement and listened attentively to her clear, almost perfect French, which was at the same time so permeated with Russian meanings that the very combination yielded an explosive effect. Dasha was a beloved favourite of the founders and leaders of the New Right movement, and she was always at the centre of attention, the heart and soul in the company of young French conservatives. She was so, completely independently of her father. Dasha believed in the New Right and was inspired by their views on the need for a great restoration of primordially European values — classical, ancient, and medieval. The very expression "Theory of Europe" belongs to Daria Dugina. Boldly and with Russian openness, with this expression she was perhaps the first to clearly formulate what the New Right existed and acted for over many decades. The matter at hand is the Theory of Europe — not what Europe is now (a shameful, pathetic, impotent and degenerate liberal parody), but the Europe that once was and should arise again. Europe is an idea. The West is matter, decadence, submersion into darkness, and the sunset of decline. Europe is something altogether different.

It is telling that in the autumn of 2023, when the New Right (GRECE) celebrated its 50th anniversary, they dedicated part of the event to the memory of Daria Dugina, whom they sincerely loved, respected, and considered to be an indelible part of them, a heroine, a sister, and a like-minded thinker. To Daria was also dedicated a special issue of the New right's main publication, *Éléments*, on the topic of Russia. This was the very same journal whose pages and old issues Dasha dug into back in her childhood.

Platonova's Analysis: An Epiphany of Deep France

The subject of French politics was very dear to Daria. She studied it with enthusiasm, as she did with everything that genuinely interested her. Where ordinary analysts saw only calculation, benefit, and Machiavellianism, Daria undertook to unveil the deeper patterns which, running far from vulgar and superficial political analysis, lead to political philosophy. In this lies what is foremost in her analysis, which she called "Platonova's Analysis" (the name of her Telegram channel). "Platonova's Analysis" is not simply a combination of two words, one of which was her authorial pseudonym, or better yet, Daria's polynym. "Platonova's Analysis" refers to a conscious, deep approach to matters which at first glance might seem to be rather trivial. Dasha believed that everything depends on one's view, on the way in which one looks at things. A profound view peers into the depths, while a trivial view notices only the surface. The forecasts and assessments voiced by "Platonova's Analysis" on French politics should be perceived in precisely this sense. In some respects, they turned out to be very accurate, while in others, to the contrary, reality refuted them. All the worse for reality! Daria never hid that she analysed French politics from the point of view of deep meanings, from the perspective of seeking grounds and principles beyond the chaos and manipulations seen by ordinary experts and political analysts. What is important from this point of view is that Daria Dugina's texts on French politics retain their relevance, even if they pertain more to the future than to the past.

In "Platonova's Analysis", Daria strove to distinguish the tendencies and vectors of powers at work in the political history of Europe and France, the forces around which current history is unfolding — the history of the depths, the grounds and ideas, not exterior factors. Daria was convinced that, sooner or later, deep France would make itself known — the France of Tradition and the spirit, the France that Dasha knew and loved, that she saw and felt through that nightmarish form of degeneration into which a once beautiful, free, and sophisticated country has been turned over decades of rule by liberal elites.

Macron called France a "hotel". Daria Dugina categorically disagreed. She saw in the country and its people sacred France, rooted in sacred Tradition and full of paradoxes and miracles. In this respect, she was similar to the Romanian philosopher and writer Jean Parvulesco, who extolled "secret France" far better and more deeply than any Frenchman. It is altogether symbolic that Dasha was friends with Parvulesco's grandson, Stanislas — thus, before our very eyes, the physical descendants of European thinkers intersect with their ideological heirs, sometimes in the form of the very same people. After the tragedy that cut Daria Dugina's life short, Stanislas Parvulesco was the first to organise a rally in her honour in Paris, where he gave a piercing, soulful speech in honour of the "Russian Beatrice" and "Eurasian Joan of Arc" who fell at the hands of the enemies of Great Europe. Such a speech would have been so dear to the heart of his genius grandfather as well as his father, who was faithful to the spirit of Tradition (Stanislas' father, Constantin Parvulesco, who some years ago took up monastic life in a Romanian Orthodox monastery, also knew Daria well).

"Platonova's Analysis", if we read it correctly, tells us not of past twists and turns in French politics — so many alliances, opportunities, prospects, unions, positions — but of something much more important: the eternal France, *la France éternelle*, that only barely peeks through before once again disappearing behind the veil of the thickening darkness of the end times.

Moreover, recent events have confirmed the penetrating insight of "Platonova's Analysis": in the June 2024 European Parliament elections, Marine Le Pen's National Rally received 34% of French votes, while President Emmanuel Macron's Need for Europe coalition managed to gather less than half of that — 14.5% in total. This happened despite the fact that all the mainstream media and big financial institutions exclusively supported Macron, while the French right was essentially deprived of access to any broad public tribune. Of course, Marine Le Pen is only an abruption within the liberal, globalist EU in its current catastrophic state, still far from the "Theory of Europe". This is only a reaction, not a project. However, the fact itself is very telling: Europeans are tired of the Europe to which the anti-popular, Atlanticist elites have sworn allegiance. Today, this is felt even more sharply and practically in all European countries than ever before. The New Right's analysis was essentially the only one that foretold this and consciously deliberated alternative strategies, and their analysis coincides in its main parameters with Daria Platonova Dugina's.

The prospect of a fully fledged, continental great Europe — part of Eurasia and the Civilisation of Land — is still far off. However, without trailblazing pioneers who first uphold higher ideals, even at the cost of their own life, a dignified future based on returning to Tradition and synthesising deep cultural identity with demands for social justice will never come. Daria consciously considered herself to be a "human of the future", a future for which Europe is called to return to its spiritual, Platonic, Greco-Roman — and, most importantly, Christian! — roots. This is the Europe she loved. This is the Europe she wished for.

Having imparted her own contribution to the cause of a European Renaissance, Daria will forever remain in the annals of this true Europe. Her personal feat has imprinted upon her ideas, convictions, views, and heraldings the irremovable stamp of heroic sacrifice.

Alexander Dugin

PART I

THE NEW RIGHT

The *Nouvelle Droite* and GRECE: The Name of Great Europe[1]

The *Logos* of Eternal Europe

As a movement and phenomenon, the French *Nouvelle Droite* represents a Traditionalist, cultural, conservative revolution. The New Right might be called the new encyclopaedists or the new European "Enlightenment" — Enlightenment 2.0 — but in the reverse. If you want to know the real Europe and its high intellectual achievements, then it is necessary to get acquainted with the books of Alain de Benoist, the journals *Éléments*, *Kris*, and *Nouvelle École*, and the conference materials of GRECE. These works and publications are key to unveiling the real intellectual heritage of the great Europe that today is under the baton of globalist liberal hegemony, the Europe and its Tradition that are today subject to ostracism.

Reading the French New Right means discovering for yourself the deep Europe that harbours respect for man as a spiritual being, for peoples as living essences, for nature as a source of life and energy, and for tradition as a bearer of genuine knowledge preserved over the

1 Originally published as the foreword to Alain de Benoist and Charles Champetier, *Posledniaia bitva za Evropu. Manifest Novykh Pravykh* [The Last Battle for Europe: Manifesto of the New Right] (Moscow: Slovo, 2023). English edition: *Manifesto for a European Renaissance* (London: Arktos, 2012).

centuries. This Europe has no American recitatives, no BLM, no artificial opposition between "left" and "right", no cultural Marxism, no
Dark Enlightenment, no vulgar materialism, no globalist racism, no
obsession with the economy, no liberal totalitarianism, no universalism, no egalitarianism, no alienated individualism. The New Right is
authentic Europe. Eternal Europe.

The Emergence of the New Right: From GRECE and *Nouvelle École* to *Éléments* and *Krisis*

The emergence of the French New Right is generally associated with
the years 1967–68, when GRECE, the *Groupement de recherche et
d'études pour la civilisation européenne* (Research and Study Group for
European Civilisation), was founded as an ensemble of intellectuals
whose aim was to analyse European civilisation through the prism of
philosophy, anthropology, psychology, political science, and biology,
all for the sake of restoring European intellectual identity. "Give life to
sinking culture!" — such was the idea and aim of this movement.

GRECE began with organising yearly thematic conferences — such
as "The Cause of Peoples", "Left-Right: The End of the System", "The
United States: A Danger", "For a Gramscianism from the Right",
"Against Totalitarianisms — For a New Culture", "The Failure of
Disneyland", and "Europe: A New World" — and its first conference
publications were released in October 1973.

In 1968, Alain de Benoist, the leader and inspirer of the movement,
founded the yearly journal *Nouvelle École*, the first issue of which came
out in February 1968. By 1985, the journal's print circulation reached
10,000 copies. The journal's issues were dedicated to particular personages, such as Friedrich Nietzsche, Vilfredo Pareto, Oswald Spengler,[2]

---

2   Oswald Spengler (1880–1936) was a German historical philosopher best known
     for his influential work *The Decline of the West*, in which he presented a cycli-
     cal theory of civilizations. The book argues that cultures, like organisms, go
     through phases of growth and decay, and he posited that Western civilisation

Ernst Jünger,[3] Knut Hamsun, Georges Dumézil, Pierre-Joseph Proudhon, Konrad Lorenz, and Charles Maurras. The topics included Christianity, paganism, mass culture, the Indo-Europeans, geopolitics, archaeology, political theology, language, demography, biology, psychiatry, the Conservative Revolution, the Greeks and Romans, and the philosophers of the Enlightenment. The publication became the print organ of the new European Conservative Revolution and was distinct from all other publications of the time by virtue of its wide range of topics and personages, its conservative-revolutionary orientation, its going beyond the classical field of left and right (its issues were dedicated to right-wing as well as left-wing intellectuals), as well as its integral and interdisciplinary approach to the study of man, Europe, and Tradition (ranging from religion to zoopsychology). The editorial board of *Nouvelle École* included the philosopher Raymond Abellio, the journalist Louis Pauwels (who at the time was the head of the prestigious newspaper *Le Figaro*), the sociologist Georges Dumézil (until 1974), the philosopher Julien Freund, the zoopsychologist Konrad Lorenz, the historian of the Conservative Revolution Armin Mohler, the scholar of religion Mircea Eliade,[4] the archaeologist and historian Marija Gimbutas, and many other of Europe's most prominent intellectuals of the time.

---

had entered its final phase, marked by materialism, loss of creativity, and decline in cultural vitality.

3   Ernst Jünger (1895–1998) was a German writer, soldier, and philosopher whose works explore themes of war, technology, and existential resilience, notably in *Storm of Steel*, his memoir of World War One. Later in his life, Jünger developed the concept of the Anarch, a figure embodying sovereign independence and inner detachment from external authority, as described in his novel *Eumeswil*. The Anarch represents a self-mastered individual who observes society critically yet maintains autonomy from its political and social forces.

4   Mircea Eliade (1907–1986) was a Romanian religious historian, philosopher, and writer known for his influential works on the nature of religious experience and myth, such as *The Sacred and the Profane*. His scholarship emphasised the concept of the *eternal return* and the symbolic significance of myths and rituals in connecting mankind with the sacred.

In September 1973, the New Right released the first issue of what would become the cult journal *Éléments*, which is still in publication (with varying periodicity, but not less than once a month). *Éléments* features analysis of acute social, political and philosophical topics, such as feminism, economics, the consumer society, ecology, religious crisis, socialism, Islam, corruption, the decay of the political class, populism, globalism, censorship, bureaucracy, immigration, culture, art, gender, etc. A number of intellectuals have collaborated with the journal, such as Michel Maffesoli, Michel Onfray, Marcel Gauchet, Bernard Langlois, Pierre Manent, Patrick Buisson, Christophe Guilluy, Jacques Sapir, Jean-Yves Camus, Serge Latouche, and Jean-Claude Michéa. The publication positions itself as "neither left nor right" and is especially critical of Western liberalism, globalism, egalitarianism, individualism, the Americanisation of France, and the consumer society. Its critiques are bound up with rethinking and reconstructing the fundamental concepts of Tradition and a "New Europe" (a "Europe of Peoples").

In 1988, the journal *Krisis* saw the light of day for the first time and was announced as a "publication for ideas and debates". Oriented to a considerable degree towards "left" audiences, the journal's authors have included prominent left intellectuals like Costanzo Preve, Jean Baudrillard, Régis Debray, and even the left-wing politician Jean-Luc Mélenchon. The issues' themes always pose a question: "Culture?", "Evolution?", "Morality"?, "Society?", "Sexuality?, "Populism?", "Left/Right?", "Paganism?", "Progress?", "Identity?"

A Cultural Revolution — in 1979?

Éléments began to exert tangible influence on French society and politics, and by 1979 the New Right had penetrated the media-sphere: Louis Pauwels, the chief editor of *Le Figaro*, offered Alain de Benoist to maintain a column entitled "Movement of Ideas", and the conservative publications *Valeurs actuelles* and *Le Spectacle du monde* invited a number of New Right authors to collaborate with them. GRECE's 12th congress, titled "The Illusion of Equality" and devoted to critiquing universalist human rights and the mirages of egalitarianism, was held at the Palais des congrès and gathered representatives of French and British academia (the speakers included Thierry Maulnier, a member of the French Academy of Sciences, Henri Gobard, a professor at the Vincennes Institute, and Hans Eysenck, the director of the Institute of Psychiatry of King's College London), as well as politicians (for instance, Julien Cheverny, then a deputy of the Socialist Party). The presence of politicians from the conventional "left" political front and academicians testified to the fact that the New Right's ideas had entered universities and political parties and now posed a threat to the liberal system.

The GRECE movement began to exert an influence not only on politics, science, and the educational sphere, but also on culture. This posed a direct challenge to liberal hegemony, one which the latter was incapable of responding to. In the preface to his book *Les Idées à l'endroit* (which literally means "ideas in the right place" or "the right ideas"),[5] Alain de Benoist remarked that the New Right had effectively carried out a coup. De Benoist openly says: "We managed to overturn and break the table of ideas and the systematisation of concepts and ideas put forth by liberalism. Thus, the New Right succeeded in getting off the plane of hegemony and began developing an autonomous pole of counter-hegemony, a pole for a new culture."

In the summer of 1979, more than 500 articles on the New Right appeared throughout the European and American press. It was at this time that GRECE came to be called the "New Right". For GRECE themselves, such a name was not at all correct, as the movement's members proclaimed a complete rejection of the division into left and right, and instead saw themselves as passing onto the plane of metapolitical struggle, where the real poles are globalism and anti-globalism,

---

5   Alain de Benoist, *Les Idées à l'endroit* (Paris: Libres-Hallier, 1978).

universalism (egalitarianism) and multipolarity. On 5 July 1979, journalists of the left-liberal publication *Libération* wrote that "*la gauche est en retard d'une guerre*" ("the left is late to a war"), and *Le Point* wrote that the left was facing catastrophic defeat. The American *National Review* deemed the New Right responsible for "a cultural *coup d'état*", while the French ultra-globalists Bernard-Henri Lévy[6] and Laurent Fabius[7] promoted a proposal to ban even mentioning the New Right in order to "suffocate them by silence". An active campaign to discredit the movement was launched: the right accused them of "abandoning right-wing economics" and "pointlessly engaging left-wing ideas", while the left blamed them for "masking right-wing ideas under academic concepts".

Thus, the New Right was subjected to critique from all political fronts. Behind this, of course, one can easily detect the strategy of the globalist centre itself, which combines right-wing economics with left-wing politics and uses both the right and left within the system to struggle against its main opponents. The New Right became this main opponent, because they were neither a left-wing nor right-wing

---

6   Bernard-Henri Lévy (b. 1948), a French philosopher and self-styled champion of left-liberal values, has often faced criticism for maintaining an elite, media-focused image while selectively promoting liberal principles that some argue are disconnected from traditional leftist ideals. Known for supporting "human rights", his alignment with liberal capitalism and high-profile presence among France's intellectual elite have led critics to question the depth of his commitment to Marxist critiques of class and economic disparity, viewing his positions as more performative than transformative.

7   Laurent Fabius (b. 1946), a key figure in French politics, has served as Prime Minister, Foreign Minister, and is now President of the Constitutional Council. Aligned with Bernard-Henri Lévy on liberal interventionist policies, particularly regarding the 2011 Libyan conflict, Fabius has drawn criticism for promoting foreign interventions prioritising Western ideals over national sovereignty and regional autonomy. He advances a globalist agenda that compromises France's own autonomy by entangling it in international obligations, while undermining the self-determination of the affected regions by imposing external political structures and ideologies.

flank of the existing system, but instead represented a radical opposition that combined right-wing politics with left-wing economics. In
this lies the power of the *Nouvelle Droite*, the danger it poses to the
globalists, and the explanation for the vital force of the movement that
continues to flourish to this day.

Not a single argument employed by the campaign worked — neither the claim that the New Right are "apologists for totalitarianism"
nor the claims that they are "right" or "left". Instead, from this wave of
criticism the movement gained a name, fame, and stronger influence.

GRECE: The Pole of Counter-Hegemony and the Intellectual Pact with Labour

If we examine them within the intellectual landscape of their time, then
the New Right is genuinely distinguished by its uniqueness, its lack of
any bias, and its break with both left-wing and right-wing movements.
To use the terminology of the Italian philosopher Antonio Gramsci,[8]
the ensemble of GRECE's intellectuals undertook to create a pole of
counter-hegemony, and in so doing they concluded an historic pact
with Labour against Capital.

Gramsci's doctrine is of interest in that it breaks with classical
Marxism by rejecting the absolute determinacy of economic processes
over political ones. For Gramsci, culture (the sphere of civil society
and intellectuals) exerts greater and more tangible influence on
politics than the forces or means of production. Hence, revolutions
take place through the sphere of culture, not through changes in the
balance of the base. Gramsci drew a distinction between "traditional"
(or "conventional") intellectuals (those who justify the status quo and
accept the rules of hegemony) and organic intellectuals. The latter

---

8   Antonio Gramsci (1891–1937) was an Italian Marxist philosopher, journalist,
    and revolutionary, best known for his work on cultural hegemony and the role
    of intellectuals in society. Imprisoned under Mussolini's rule, he developed
    influential theories about power, ideology, and the cultural means by which
    dominant classes maintain their control.

consciously conclude a pact either with Labour (whereupon they take the side of Workers) or with Capital (whereupon they become defenders of the bourgeois system and bearers of bourgeois consciousness, to which class they might not necessarily belong in economic terms). It is through this pact that intellectuals' relation to hegemony is defined. When taking the side of hegemony, the organic intellectual swears allegiance to Capital; by rejecting hegemony and choosing Labour, he becomes a gravedigger of hegemony and a source of vital force for revolution.

Having attentively studied Gramsci's ideas (in 1981 they held a congress devoted to "Gramscianism from the right"), the *Nouvelle Droite* concluded an intellectual pact with Labour, with Anti-Capital. Critiquing the narrow, typically Marxist materialist interpretation of Labour, the New Right reconceptualized the very core of Labour and thus turned an exclusively materialistic phenomenon into an existential category. Labour, along with its bearer, the Worker (Jünger's *Der Arbeiter*), possesses spiritual meaning in that it:

- is opposed to the bourgeois sphere of "mechanical death" which erects a cult of rationalism, individualism, and individual "freedom from" as a self-sufficient form that is void of any content and applicable to any quantity;

- is in a state of total mobilisation, a state of "heroic realism";

- is not something economically determined, and therefore is distinct from the "proletariat."

The intellectual who stands on the side of Labour becomes the Worker and enters into battle against the bourgeois. He is a warrior of counter-hegemony.

In Jünger's opinion, the state of confrontation, war, and primal, elemental force is a manifestation of the divine. Jünger writes: "The Gods love to reveal themselves in the elemental, in the glowing heavens, in thunder and lightning, in the burning bush which the flame does not consume."[9]

For Capital and its bourgeois servants, the main value is security, and it is for this sake that hegemony strives to encourage and reinforce the development of the consumer society. Jünger notes that work always has an "intelligible" character. Work is, above all, tempo and rhythm: "Work is the rhythm of the fist, of thoughts, of the heart, of life by day and night, of science, love, art, faith, religion, war; work is the oscillation of the atom and the gravity which moves stars and solar systems."[10] Jünger clarifies: "The denial of the economic world as life-determining, thus as a power of destiny, is a contestation of its rank, not of its existence."[11] Thus, the economy (the base) should be subordinated to the "higher law of struggle," and the Worker acts not for the sake of changing the balance of the forces and relations of production, but for a total change of hierarchy.

The Rights of Peoples: The New Right's Interpretation of the Foundations of Geopolitics

In addition to their rereading of Gramsci, the New Right also revived European interest in the discipline of geopolitics, which seemed to have flickered out following the Second World War. The New Right's attention was especially drawn to the works of Carl Schmitt.[12] In the 44th issue of *Nouvelle École*, an article by the philosopher Julien Freund expounded Schmitt's ideas in a hierarchical order that is fundamental

---

9   Ernst Jünger, *The Worker: Dominion and Form*, trans. Bogdan Costea, ed. Laurence Paul Hemming (Evanston: Northwestern University Press, 2017), 32.

10 Ibid., 45.

11 Ibid., 18.

12 Carl Schmitt (1888–1985) was a German legal and political theorist known for his critique of liberal democracy and for defining the "friend-enemy" distinction as central to political identity. His works influenced political philosophy by emphasising the role of sovereignty, authority, and decision-making, especially within the context of states of exception.

to the thinking of the New Right. In the first place, the New Right's attention was drawn to analysing the phenomenon of "the Political".[13]

"The Political" (*das Politische*) is the domain of social relations between diverse subjects (states, blocs, etc.) and is based on distinguishing between "friend" and "enemy". This friend/enemy pairing lacks any personal connotations and is instead exclusively connected to the field of groups, i.e. a political enemy is the enemy of the group to which the analysing subject himself belongs. For Schmitt, politics is always a confrontation between different political units (groups and collectives of various scales) and presupposes a permanent multiplicity, which Schmitt calls the "pluriversum". Politics exists only when there are several groups and there is opposition between them. The defining line of Schmitt's concept is that it distinguishes the Political as a separate phenomenon that can precede the state.

Of extreme importance to the New Right is Schmitt's interpretation that the basic principle of politics is "pluriversality". In and of itself, the Political is universal in that the principle and confrontational dyad of friend/enemy is all-encompassing and permeates the whole world, but a multiplicity is necessary for the Political to exist. There must always be relations between political units (parties, states, movements) and the distribution of these relations in accordance with the principle of friend/enemy. The New Right critiques the universalism of globalist politics by highlighting how the West's universalism and egalitarianism harbours the desire to impose the West's own values on other peoples. As Alain de Benoist notes in the *Manifesto for a European Renaissance*: "The Westernisation of the planet has represented an imperialist movement fed by the desire to erase all otherness by imposing on the world a supposedly superior model invariably presented as 'progress'. Homogenising universalism is only the projection and the mask of an ethnocentrism extended over the whole planet."[14] Thus, while it is

---

13   Carl Schmitt, *The Concept of the Political*, trans. George Schwab (Chicago: University of Chicago Press, 2007).

14   *Manifesto for a European Renaissance*, 28–29.

actually waging struggle against its enemy, the modern West masks the pursuit of its agenda under the aegis of "establishing democracy" and "defending human rights" in various regions.

For the New Right, as indicated in the *Manifesto*, the main enemy is liberalism: "In the age of globalisation, liberalism no longer presents itself as an ideology, but as a global system of production and reproduction of men and commodities, supplemented by the hypermodernism of human rights."[15] Liberalism treats politics as a mere technique or technology. For the New Right, inspired as they are by the traditions of ancient Greece, which saw politics as a space of battle, as *agon*,[16] it is of fundamental importance to rehabilitate politics, to de-colonise the symbolic imagination that is enslaved by commercial values. Thus, following Schmitt, the New Right understands politics as an existential phenomenon. Against human rights (which are part of the liberal, de-personified, technocratic interpretation of the Political), the New Right calls for the rights of peoples. "Defend the rights of peoples" — this slogan and call was voiced by the intellectuals of the French New Right back in 1969.

According to Alain de Benoist, the periods of the "three *nomoi* of the Earth" that Schmitt described[17] have come to an end:

The first *nomos* was the *nomos* of Antiquity and the Middle Ages, wherein civilisations lived in a certain isolation from each other. At times there were attempts at imperial unification, such as the Roman Empire, the Germanic Holy Roman Empire, and the Byzantine Empire. This *nomos* disappeared with the onset of Modernity, when modern states and nations appeared in

---

15   Ibid., 19.

16   The Greek term *agon* signifies a contest or struggle, encompassing both physical and intellectual challenges in ancient Greek culture, such as athletic tournaments, dramatic performances, and philosophical debates. It embodies the spirit of rivalry and striving for excellence, reflecting the importance of competition in personal and communal development within Greek society.

17   Carl Schmitt, *The Nomos of the Earth in the International Law of Jus Publicum Europaeum*, trans. G. L. Ulmen (New York: Telos Press Publishing, 2006).

the period that began in 1648 with the Peace of Westphalia and ended with the two world wars — this is the *nomos* of nation-states. The third *nomos* of the Earth corresponds to the bipolar regulation during the "Cold War," when the world divided between West and East; this *nomos* came to an end when the Berlin Wall fell and the Soviet Union was broken up. The question is: what will the new, fourth *nomos* of the Earth be? Here we arrive at the topic of the Fourth Political Theory which is to be born. This is the fourth *nomos* of the Earth that is trying to appear. I think, and I deeply hope, that this fourth *nomos* of the Earth will be the *nomos* of the great continental logic of Eurasia, the Eurasian continent, i.e., a *nomos* of struggle between continental state power and the maritime power and maritime might represented by the United States.[18]

The logic of Eurasia is the logic of defending the "cause of peoples". For the New Right, accordingly, geopolitics is one of the most important sources and disciplines.

It bears dwelling in particular on the geopolitical categories with which the New Right describes the European space: for them, this space is the "middle belt", *Rimland*. In this respect, the European space is close in status to that of the "Third World". It turns out that globalism and Atlanticism[19] have colonised Europe just as the West itself once colonised the countries of the Third World. In 1986, Alain de Benoist released a book entitled *Europe, Third World, One Struggle*,[20] which argues that Europe must return to its roots and traditions and throw off the universalist dictatorship. Defending the Third World means

---

18   Alain de Benoist, *Protiv liberalizma. K Chetvertoi politicheskoi teorii* (Saint Petersburg: Afora, 2009), 18.

19   Atlanticism is an ideology that promotes Western liberal values as universal, enforcing a global system centred on Western political and economic priorities. It imposes a homogenising framework that erodes national sovereignty, prioritising Western interests over the cultural and political autonomy of other regions, often through economic leverage and military alliances that serve to solidify Western influence globally.

20   Alain de Benoist, *Europe, Tiers monde, même combat* (Paris: Robert Laffont, 1986).

standing for non-alignment. This means abandoning the obsession with economics that is characteristic of Western ideology.

De Benoist contrasts contemporary Europe, buried under the heavy slab of economics and human rights, to a "Europe of a thousand flags" in which the pluriverse of different regional cultures can manifest themselves. For de Benoist, the model of a Eurasian Empire is extremely important, and something of its likeness should be created in the space of Europe.

Sacred Ecology

The New Right has also put the topic of ecology at the centre of attention. Continuing and developing the Norwegian philosopher Arne Næss's[21] idea of deep ecology,[22] the New Right proclaims the need to construct an ecological philosophy beyond the context of capitalism. The superficial ecology that liberalism promotes sees nature exclusively as a "resource", and the main task of this ecology (of a universalist bent) is to extract as much profit as possible out of finite natural resources. Conserving nature is necessary only in order for nature to yield more resources. Such an approach is unacceptable to the New Right, as anthropocentrism and the capitalist approach destroy the world surrounding us and the world as an integral whole. De Benoist writes: "Sound ecology calls us to move beyond modern anthropocentrism towards the development of a consciousness of the mutual coexistence of mankind and the cosmos. This 'immanent transcendence' reveals nature as a partner and not as an adversary or object."[23]

---

21 Arne Næss (1912–2009) was a Norwegian philosopher best known for advocating intrinsic ecological values beyond human utility. His work emphasized a holistic approach to environmentalism, promoting the view that all living beings have the right to thrive, a principle which greatly influenced environmental ethics worldwide.

22 Arne Naess, "A defence of the deep ecology movement", *Environmental Ethics* 6(3) (1984): 265–270.

23 *Manifesto for a European Renaissance*, 46.

The deep ecology movement has pointed to how indigenous peoples do not exploit their surrounding environment and instead preserve a stable society over the course of millennia. The anti-capitalist agenda of deep ecologists, and the New Right following them, points to the danger of megalopolises as gigantic spaces of de-personified cities. In the New Right's opinion, every city should bear its own uniqueness. Universal containers and faceless cages destroy the human being and nature. This interpretation of ecology and urban spaces is in many respects a development of German Romantic thought, which highlighted "life" as the central force: "life" is a self-sufficient ontology dictating its own logic of energy and health. The "will to life" must be allowed to come about both within us and in our surroundings.

Conclusion

Across their numerous works and publications, the New Right, the new encyclopaedists of alternative Europe, have offered assessments of all the acute topics manifest in today's social, political, ecological, and philosophical spheres. One can find in their works an answer to virtually any topic — from pandemics to gender. The New Right's *Manifesto for a European Renaissance* presents the axis and framework of their ideas, the main vectors of their struggle, and the foremost themes of their reflections and deliberations. Acquaintance with this manifesto is your acquaintance with the real Europe.

Throughout the pages of this dense and fine-tuned manifesto, you will find a definition of the precise place of our era in its historical context as well as orientations for the future. These pages awaken mind and feeling, and they provoke debates. They are roads and starting points for reflective thinking.

A Theory of Europe and the New Right[1]

I T'S A GREAT PLEASURE that so many listeners have turned out for a lecture on the New Right, because this is an incredibly important topic, one that has been left completely understudied in Russia. In the Russian media space and in Russian philosophical discourse, the very term "new right" is often misunderstood, or understood differently than in Europe. In Russia, the term "new right" is sometimes applied to classical right-wing groups with somewhat revised ideological positions. Therefore, I would like to draw clear boundaries around the New Right and clarify how they are distinct from other "rights" and "lefts" (with some of whom, no matter how strange this might sound, the New Right has much in common) as well as from other metapolitical systems and ideologies which exist in Russia and Europe today.

Today, the emphasis will be on the European space. We will dwell on and in France, and at the centre of our attention will be the movement that is habitually called the "New Right" or *Nouvelle Droite*.

The phrase "New Right" appeared in 1979, when it was applied to an ensemble of intellectual movements that took shape around GRECE, the *Groupement de recherche et d'études pour la civilisation européenne* (Research and Study Group for European Civilisation). The GRECE movement itself, the main basis and focal point of everything that in 1979 came to be called the "New Right", arose in 1968.

---

1   Lecture delivered at the Listva bookstore in Moscow in July 2022.

To be even more precise, it emerged around the winter of 1967–68, in December-January.

Overall, it is a mistake to presume that the New Right took shape as a response to the events of May 1968, and that it was a forced reaction to the left-wing, or rather "new left" coup that was carried out in France then. It is more correct to say that GRECE as it emerged in 1967–68 was a movement that took shape in parallel to the "new left", in parallel to the "May French Revolution". This testifies to the fact that there was already a definite ideological crisis in French society that was not overcome — a split into right and left non-conformists. While the left ceased to be real non-conformists after 1968, as they signed onto and fit themselves into the bourgeois liberal system, the New Right remained real non-conformists. This remains the case to this day.

In 1968, French society was definitively divided into "left" and "right", and this division was closed unto itself and didn't develop into anything. The "left" lost its ideological and philosophical positions and dissipated into the liberal pole. The "right" shut itself off in nationalism and rejected any dialogue. Hence, the proponents of European identity, the followers of many of the authors whose works are on this bookstore's shelves — including Evola,[2] the Jünger brothers, the non-conformist circles of the 1930s and the Conservative Revolution, the various 20th-century sociological schools ranging from Weber, Sombart, Durkheim, and Spengler to Lévi-Strauss and Marcel Mauss, as well as diverse other atypical 20th-century philosophers — found no place for themselves.

---

2   Julius Evola (1898–1974) was an Italian philosopher and esoteric writer who started his career in avant-garde art, particularly Dadaism, before shifting his focus to Traditionalist philosophy. His major works, such as *Revolt Against the Modern World*, present a vision of society based on spiritual hierarchy and transcendental values, critiquing modern egalitarian and materialist ideologies. While some of his ideas influenced far-right groups in Europe, Evola maintained an independent stance, criticizing both the fascist and National Socialist movements for lacking true spiritual foundations.

GRECE was a reaction, a blast of energy that broke out of the midst of the intellectually suffocating, cloying "gaucheist" France of 1968. It is worth noting that nothing more significant and more colorful in the intellectual sense has appeared in France since GRECE. Everything that is now unfolding in France on the level of ideas, in the space of the "wars of the mind", is happening within the space of the New Right, in the movements, publishing houses, journals, and initiatives connected to this group in one way or another.

And so, what did GRECE initially present? What did it look like? From the very outset, GRECE wielded all the characteristic signs of a fully fledged social movement — an official registration, membership, leading organs, and budget. Each year, and increasingly frequently, it held colloquiums, conferences, and symposiums, following which small blue booklets were printed with the texts of the speeches, articles, debates, and roundtables. As a general rule, these events and publications were dedicated to serious topics: the end of the world, the cause of peoples, human rights, the rights of peoples, multipolarity, problems of the modern world, the crisis of democracy, socialism, liberalism, the delusion of the ideology of individualism, the US as a parody of society, planetary Disneyland, etc.

The Press' First Reaction: Criticism and Silence

When it comes to the formula "New Right" itself, it was first applied to GRECE in 1979. In the preface to his book *Les Idées à l'endroit*, Alain de Benoist recalls that it was on the summer solstice of 1979 that the term "New Right", and his movement itself, suddenly became a hit.[3] More than 500 articles came out within half a year. Everyone started writing about them, from ultra-liberal to ultra-left and ultra-right publications in France, Europe, and even the *National Review* in the US.

How did they characterise the "New Right" and what were they writing about at this initial stage? First, on 5–6 July 1979, the left-wing publication *Libération* released a series of sensationalist articles and claimed that the left was lagging behind and losing the war of ideas: "*La gauche s'attarde.*"[4] The point was that the New Right had infiltrated the space of politics and thought to such an extent that left-wing discourse had irrevocably lost. Then followed a flurry of other publications with approximately the same content. This is how the New Right became famous.

The situation changed in 1979, when the former left-wing philosopher, Bernard-Henri Lévy, — who went on to become one of the criers of right-wing liberalism, globalism, and Atlanticism — and Laurent Fabius wrote that the best way to treat the New right would be to completely pass them over in silence. When Alain de Benoist met Bernard-Henri Lévy at a public event in 1979 and tried to shake his hand, Lévy pulled back his hand and said: "I won't shake your hand, I hate you." De Benoist later wrote of this delicately in his memoir that it was at that moment that he, as a person who had never hated anyone, as a Traditionalist and as a representative of the New Right who was ready for dialogue with any political spectrum (besides pure liberals), understood that Bernard-Henri Lévy was nothing more than a liberal, because he hated him with every fibre of his being. His hatred was the best proof that he was not a left-winger, but a liberal. This later became obvious to everyone, although in that period Lévy was still considered a classic anti-liberal, anti-capitalist leftist.

Despite the silent treatment in France itself, where Bernard-Henri Lévy became extremely influential and capable of influencing media policy, the media wave on the New Right persisted abroad — in *The Times*, *Der Spiegel*, and *The New Yorker*. The *National Review* in the US wrote that the New Right phenomenon was a real, fully fledged cultural coup, a revolutionary ideological model that was destroying the hitherto culture of France.

---

4   "The left is stagnant."

All of the media wrote about the New Right from three positions. On the one hand, the New Right were interpreted to be the "old right" merely under a new guise, as if everything was merely a strategy to mask Gaullism, Poujadism,[5] and nationalism, as if the whole intellectual shell, and all of their typically non-right-wing positions, were only words meant to hide a radical, nationalist ideology of a "brown tint". This is what the majority of left and left-liberal publications believed. A number of articles with this sort of content came out abroad and on the pages of *Libération*. On the other hand, the classical right denied that the New Right had anything to do with the right: as if the New Right were being completely honest that, in fact and deed, they represented a complete betrayal of ordinary right discourse, and therefore the movement should be banned for mixing up all the cards and confusing flanks. GRECE spoke of the need to overcome the schism of left and right and upheld serious opposition to communism and migration, but they deprived the right of the possibility of winning the ideological war. In any case, it seems to me that the main strategy that the liberal (concentration) camp armed itself with in the media and on the information front in general was Lévy and Fabius' strategy: the strategy of silence. The New Right were not to be spoken of, and instead everyone should pretend as if they didn't exist or as if they were an utterly marginal phenomenon.

Of course, GRECE's ideas themselves were not destroyed by this. The people proclaiming their ideas did not suffer in legal terms or from other forms of persecution, but henceforth they were consistently subjected to the most fundamental ostracism. Moreover, it needs to be said that the outcome of this first media wave was that, on

---

5   Poujadism was a populist political movement in 1950s France, founded by Pierre
     Poujade, the founder of the Union for the Defence of Tradesmen and Artisans.
     The movement primarily represented small business owners, shopkeepers, and
     rural interests. It emphasised opposition to high taxes, centralised bureaucracy,
     and perceived government indifference to the economic struggles of the "little
     man", resonating with a mix of anti-elite, anti-tax, and nationalist sentiments
     that later influenced other populist movements.

the one hand, the New Right got out of the basement and became a real force, while, on the other hand, after being "hyped up", they were silenced — silenced fundamentally.

If we examine the history of the New Right movement, then we see periods in which it was more famous and periods when it was less well-known. For example, ahead of the 2017 French presidential elections, *Éléments* once again showed up in kiosks and their colloquiums in Paris and other cities gathered upwards of 1,000–2,000 people, which are rather high numbers in France. They had a certain upswing. At the same time, however, they naturally tried to deplatform GRECE and deprive it of the right to have its voice heard. Naturally, only channels like TV Libertés want to hear their positions, while the New Right itself to this day does not have its own broadcast.

If we examine the articles published in *Libération* starting in July 1979, we find them writing to the tune of "we need to fight against all the New Right's ideas — even ethology and ecology". The authors try to explain everything that is bad and intolerable, but do so altogether superficially.

The New Right's breakthrough into the media-sphere in 1979 was also significant. When they finally did make it, they made it to the extent of having a column in *Le Figaro*. Alain de Benoist curated a whole column: "Movement of Ideas". This could only cause worry. It is also of interest that the chief editor of *Le Figaro* at the time was Louis Pauwels, the co-author of the interesting book *Morning of the Magicians*.[6] What a time — the author of *Morning of the Magicians* was also the authority who could decide whom to let write columns in such a popular, major French publication as *Le Figaro*. It's astounding.

We might be wondering: Why did they start writing about the New Right in 1979? If we systematise and analyse the context, then we see that, firstly, by that time GRECE had already exerted a fairly strong

6   Louis Pauwels and Jacques Bergier, *The Morning of the Magicians: Secret Societies, Conspiracies, and Vanished Civilizations*, trans. Rollo Myers (Rochester: Destiny Books, 2009).

influence on intellectuals. More than a thousand people came to the New Right's congresses, such as the 12th congress on the "Illusion of Equality" in the Palace of Congresses. Among the speakers were conventional left-wing as well as right-wing representatives of the French Academy, a number of professors, including the head of the Institute of Psychoanalysis, the director of the King's College London's Institute of Psychiatry, and other prominent scholars. Secondly, the New Right succeeded in the hitherto unthinkable: gathering ensembles of authors from the whole political spectrum, which is to say they were coming close to breaking the logic of the "System". They were starting to overcome the *clivage*, the schism between left and right. Naturally, this couldn't be to the System's liking: the System understands that as soon as a unification of the poles that habitually fight and oppose each other takes place, the System is already living out its last days, for such an intellectual movement could at any moment simply sweep away the "great manipulator" and come to power. The System now had to pay attention to the New Right in order to find the most precise way to destroy them. Direct criticism did not succeed, and in the era of their newfound hegemony the left got lazy at waging ideological struggle, especially under the new rules which they themselves didn't dictate. Therefore, they adopted the strategy of silence and marginalisation.

Main Influences: The German Conservative Revolution

Alain de Benoist and the GRECE movement were greatly influenced by certain atypical intellectuals, the majority of whom were from the right (but not the classical right), but also some left ones. On the whole, there was no strict classical model in the New Right movement. They boldly took all of the best from any and all sources: we find references to the conservative Catholic Carl Schmitt, an admirer of de Maistre and Cortes, to the anarchist Proudhon, to the Traditionalists René Guénon[7] and Julius Evola, as well as to the communist Gramsci.

The strongest influence on the New Right were the Conservative Revolutionaries, a German ideological movement from the 1920s-'30s.[8] The Conservative Revolution was a special position that matched neither the established left nor right. The Conservative Revolution was strictly anti-liberal and had certain sympathies for conservatism and Traditionalism as well as socialism and nationalism. In relation to the National Socialism of Hitler, the Conservative Revolutionaries as a general rule kept a critical distance. Many of them became active participants in the anti-Hitler underground (Harro Schulze-Boysen, one of the leaders of the Red Orchestra,[9] Ernst Niekisch,[10] etc.). In Germany, the Conservative Revolution was associated with such names as Arthur Moeller van den Bruck, Oswald Spengler, Carl

---

7   René Guénon (1886–1951) was a French philosopher and metaphysician who became a leading figure in the Traditionalist movement, which emphasises a universal spiritual truth underlying all religions. Born in Blois, France, he studied Western philosophy before turning to Eastern metaphysics, eventually converting to Islam and moving to Cairo, where he lived out his life immersed in Sufi practices.

8   Armin Mohler and Karlheinz Weissmann, *The Conservative Revolution in Germany, 1918–1932: A Handbook*, trans. F. Roger Devlin, ed. Nina Kouprianova (Whitefish: Washington Summit Publishers/Radix, 2018).

9   Harro Schulze-Boysen (1909–1942) was a German Luftwaffe officer and a leader of the Red Orchestra (*Rote Kapelle*), an anti-Nazi resistance group that provided intelligence to the Soviet Union and spread anti-fascist literature. Arrested by the Gestapo, he was tortured and executed by hanging in 1942 for his involvement in these activities.

10 Ernst Niekisch (1889–1967) was a German intellectual and political activist who sought to forge a unique path for Germany through a synthesis of socialism and nationalism, a perspective known as National Bolshevism. His ideas emphasized the importance of cultural independence, anti-capitalism, and alignment with Russia as a counterbalance to Western influence, aiming to create a strong, self-reliant Germany. Niekisch's anti-Nazi stance led to his imprisonment from 1937 to 1945, and his legacy remains significant for its influence on later intellectual circles that value cultural independence and anti-liberal thought.

Schmitt, Othmar Spann, Werner Sombart, and Friedrich Hielscher. Ernst Jünger and his brother, Friedrich Georg Jünger, also played a significant role among the Conservative Revolutionaries. Some people count the great philosopher Martin Heidegger among them. Ernst Niekisch, the founding theoretician of German National Bolshevism, was also associated with them.

The Conservative Revolutionaries' main idea (and here Niekisch especially seriously influenced de Benoist) was anti-capitalism from the right, or an organic, folkish, non-Marxist and non-dogmatic socialism, plus a non-chauvinistic, non-bourgeois, imperial nationalism. Their strategy of synthesising left and right discourse was atypical and revolutionary in its time. In some sense, we could consider GRECE to be a continuation of the Conservative Revolution. The Conservative Revolutionaries and the German National Bolsheviks proclaimed total nonconformism and the need to fight against the capitalist system. They considered orthodox Marxists to be part of this system insofar as they shared faith in the mechanical necessity of capitalism, whereas the Conservative Revolutionaries advocated struggling against capitalism here and now.

The philosophy of one of the most brilliant Conservative Revolutionaries, Ernst Jünger, manifested a new element which Alain de Benoist took for the New Right's armoury: the confrontation of two types of human beings. On the one hand there is the proletarian, the worker, who is doomed to slavery in the materialist system; on the other hand, there is the labourer, the Worker (*der Arbeiter*), the national revolutionary who has a connection with Tradition and revolts against the whole system, against the materialism and determinism of political-economic formations. If the first, the proletarian, the Marxist element, the impersonal subject, is devoured by the city, destroyed and enslaved by the capitalism by which he is spawned, then the Worker rejects the very foundations of this system — he doesn't wait for the system to become total before he launches an uprising against it. The uprising against capitalism should be launched at all times and in all conditions. Capitalism is not destiny, but is historically arbitrary. Jünger's anti-capitalist orientation was a formidable influence on Alain de Benoist.

In addition, the New Right greatly appreciated the works of Oswald Spengler. They fully shared his theory of the decline or end of Europe.[11] They agreed with him that, at the present time, Europe is undergoing a period of deep degeneration, its Culture turning into "Civilisation" (culture comes to its end when the era of atheism and materialism sets in). Then comes its hysterical, aggressive colonial expansion, as the dying civilisation tries to preserve itself by desperately exporting and spreading itself outwards. It also bears mentioning that Spengler advocated a non-Marxist, Prussian, conservative socialism, an idea which was also dear to Alain de Benoist.

Young Europe: Jean Thiriart

Besides the Conservative Revolution, the second essential influence which we should highlight in particular is Jean Thiriart (1922–1992). Thiriart was a famous Belgian politician, intellectual, and geopolitican who passed through a number of political clans over his life. He started on the left, then had sympathy for National Socialism, then, after the Second World War, he took up the position of integral Europeanism. From this point, Thiriart had a decisive influence on Alain de Benoist's "theory of Europe". In the 1960s, Thiriart organized the *Jeune Europe* movement, in which many of the older generation of GRECE members who are still alive today once participated.

For Thiriart, unlike other representatives of the nationalist front of the time, it was "Europe above all" — not Belgium, not France, but Europe. "Long live Europe!" and "Europe is the highest value, the Empire!" — Thiriart proposes to think in terms of this potential

---

11 Oswald Spengler, *The Decline of the West*, 2 vols. (London: Arktos, 2021).

Empire.[12] The main enemy of this Empire is the Anglo-Saxon, capitalist, liberal-globalist West. First and foremost, he associates the West with Americanism. Meanwhile, Thiriart saw more of an ally in the communist system, because the Soviet Union was to a certain extent fighting capitalism and the hegemonic impulse emanating from the West.

Thiriart, like Alain de Benoist after him, fiercely opposed the classical right, against whom he declared that the profit economics that the old right defended is murderous, for it kills man and culture. Marxist economics was also unacceptable to Thiriart as a utopia. In turn, he developed a theory of economic potential that focused on the natural development of regional economic possibilities.

Thiriart advocated federal nationalism. We find in his works a development of the topic of the "autarchy of great spaces". He speaks of the need to create a grand, centralised geopolitical entity out of Europe, one that would be economically and ideologically independent.

Thiriart wrote of himself: "I am a European National Bolshevik in the tradition of Ernst Niekisch, inspired by the historical examples of Joseph Stalin and Friedrich Hohenstaufen II."

Jean Thiriart also significantly influenced de Benoist in another sense: on the question of accepting the Soviet Union. Thiriart put forth the ideological formula "Great Europe from Dublin to Vladivostok". This very same formula which our President as well as other politicians are now often uttering is in fact a deep experience of thinking through the role of Europe and the role of anti-liberal forces, both left and right, in the anti-globalist struggle against Anglo-Saxon imperialism and Atlanticism. Therefore, when you hear the formula "Russia and Europe from Dublin to Vladivostok", you now know that we find ourselves in the space of the discourse of the New Right or its sources.

One might often encounter the point of view alleging that the New Right was anti-communist. Yes, they partially were, but they also

---

12   Jean Thiriart, *Europe: An Empire of 400 Million*, trans. Alexander Jacob (London: Arktos, 2021).

adopted anti-capitalism, which they shared with communists. Alain de Benoist even said that he prefers the Soviet cap to the American beret. This phrase shocks the ordinary right, who disagree with such a position and consider opposition to the left to be the main task instead of opposition to capitalism.

The Jeune Europe movement was active in the 1960s across Europe (especially in Italy) and even in some countries of the Middle East, particularly in Saddam Hussein's Iraq. Jean Thiriart planned to create a "European Liberation Front" and spoke of the need to get rid of all the American bases in Europe. He began to gather rather large collectives of his supporters and tried to unify them into a pan-European party of direct-action anti-American European Brigades intended to attack American bases and liquidate pro-American politicians. The movement was fairly popular in the 1960s. Thiriart himself interacted with Nasser, Tito, and Zhou Enlai. But he received no support from the USSR, and Moscow at one point even signalled to its satellites not to collaborate with Thiriart. In so doing, he was virtually cut off from all the opportunities that he had tried to use to form his European Liberation Front in the pro-Soviet regimes.

Thiriart was in Russia only once, in 1992, not long before his death. He died in November of the same year. He was in Moscow in August. During his trip he met with Zyuganov,[13] Prokhanov,[14] Dugin, Baburin,

---

13 Gennady Zyuganov (b. 1944) is a Russian politician who has been the longtime leader of the Communist Party of the Russian Federation, which he has headed since 1993. He is known for his staunch promotion of Soviet-era policies and nationalist rhetoric, positioning himself as a key figure in Russian opposition politics.

14 Alexander Prokhanov (b. 1938) is a Russian writer, journalist, and political figure, often described as a leading voice of Russian ultranationalism. He is the editor of the newspaper *Zavtra* (Tomorrow) and has written extensively on Russian identity, geopolitics, and his vision of a powerful, sovereign Russia.

Alksnis, and even Geydar Dzhemal[15] (they disagreed upon literally everything).

The Legacy of Carl Schmitt

Yet another source of defining influence on the New Right was the political philosophy of Carl Schmitt, a German thinker who specialised in constitutional law. This is, firstly, Schmitt's theory of the partisan, the irregular fighter who is tied to the earth, to Land.[16] This is the telluric character. The partisan is faithful to the land (as Nietzsche beseeched: "Brethren of mine, be loyal to the earth"). The partisan is the guardian of Europe. For de Benoist, the theory of the partisan is the theory of the one who shall preserve European identity in the end times.

Also important to de Benoist in Carl Schmitt's theory is his concept of war. According to Schmitt, there is total war and there is war of forms.[17] War of forms is war that is waged according to definite rules, which has clear specifications, limitations, space, laws, and is waged temporarily and then turns into a concluded peace. Total war, meanwhile, is the war of all against all that is waged permanently and incorporates all of society.

Schmitt says — and Alain de Benoist follows him and develops this topic — that the presence of terrorism in the world in general means that we are in a situation of permanent war. War no longer has a strictly defined territory for combat operations (the Twin Towers can be blown up, a terror attack can be organized anywhere). Thus, we find

---

15 Geydar Dzhemal (1947–2016) was a Russian Islamic philosopher, political activist, and founder of the Islamic Renaissance Party, known for his critiques of secular Modernity and advocacy for Islamic political thought. Dzhemal was one of Alexander Dugin's early teachers in the Soviet-era dissident Yuzhinsky Circle, although their philosophical and political views later diverged significantly.

16 Carl Schmitt, *Theory of the Partisan: Intermediate Commentary on the Concept of the Political*, trans. G. L. Ulmen (New York: Telos Press Publishing, 2007).

17 Carl Schmitt, *Four Articles, 1931–1938*, trans. Simona Draghici (Washington, D.C.: Plutarch Press, 1999).

ourselves in a space of constant war. Alain de Benoist says that liberalism leads to such constant war, to total war, as it rejects the idea of war
of forms and deceitfully claims that there should be eternal peace and
human rights. Such demagogy and double standards lead only to the
bloodiest and cruelest wars.

Also important for Alain de Benoist is Carl Schmitt's concept of
friend/enemy as the essence of the Political. When you say that you
have an enemy, you are forming your own identity; a certain self-
determination is formed on the basis of this contrast.

These are the key points that Alain de Benoist's political philosophy
takes from the Schmittian model.

Traditionalism

With respect to Traditionalism, the influence of Julius Evola, René
Guénon, as well as Mircea Eliade, on the New Right was rather strong.
Julius Evola's works were especially of interest, although Alain de
Benoist only started referencing them in his later works, in which he
proposed a reading of this Traditionalist's ideas that critiqued some
aspects while agreeing with others. But according to de Benoist's own
admission, Evola's ideas had a decisive impact on him in his youth. In
Evola, he discovered an intense intellectualism and a sense of the significance of ideas and generalising theories in an author attributed to
the right. At a time when the ordinary right called primarily for maintaining the status quo and used emotional arguments, Evola subjected
modern civilisation to merciless critique and fought for recreating the
ancient ideal. This is yet another source of the "Theory of Europe".

De Benoist also took an interest in Guénon, although he did not
fully adopt the structure of Traditionalist philosophy. More appealing
to him was the critique of European Modernity and liberalism. On
some fundamental positions, the New Right adhered to a different
standpoint — in particular, they were optimistic about technological

development and modern science, which the classical Traditionalists completely rejected.

Let's note that Evola's influence was especially strong among Italian Traditionalists. In France, the majority of Traditionalists strictly followed Guénon. Yet the New Right preferred Evola. One telling case is that of the Italian Traditionalist Claudio Mutti, whose works can now be read in Russian. Mutti is a Traditionalist who recognizes the authority of both Guénon and Evola. In his youth, he participated in the Italian section of Thiriart's Young Europe, and on a number of positions he is close to the New Right.

Mircea Eliade, the renowned historian of religions, and his main train of thought on the importance of the sacred also served as a source of inspiration for GRECE. Eliade was a member of the scientific committee of the New Right's *Nouvelle École*.

Nietzsche and Heidegger

In the realm of philosophy, the New Right turned most of all to Nietzsche and his philosophy of life. The heroic ideal of the cold thinker who is not afraid of clashing with the darkest and most dangerous sides of knowledge became a guiding star for GRECE.

The works of the German philosopher Martin Heidegger also had a huge influence on the New Right. Developing his ideas was at the core of their "philosophical paganism". This meant constructing an immanent ontology which had a sacred core at its centre. Heidegger became a philosophical orientation for GRECE, who built their philosophical programme on the existential principles he established. They paid special attention to the dialogue between Heidegger and Ernst Jünger.

The Sociology of Holism

From the very outset, the New Right also paid great attention to sociology and cultural anthropology. In particular, they highly appreciated the works of Marx, Weber, Sombart, and other sociologists.

They especially singled out the works of Louis Dumont, who offered a substantiation of social hierarchy and subjected all forms of individualism to harsh critique.[18]

Dumont says that what is most important is a correct resolution of man's relationship to society. If we proceed from society being primary (as in the sociology of Durkheim, Mauss, etc.), then we arrive at holism. The fullest and most complete form of holism is a hierarchical society. Dumont studied hierarchical society in his programmatic work *Homo Hierarchicus*, which treats the caste system of Indian society.[19] Dumont notes that Indian culture also knows the principle of the individual, which is even elevated to the absolute as Atman, but the realisation of the absolute "I" in no way violates the holism of the castes. It is simply the case that a certain type of people, or even people of a certain age, at some point leave society and concentrate on the inner world. This does not at all damage the whole. According to Dumont, this was also the case in the European Middle Ages, where monks who concentrated on the inner world in no way destroyed the social hierarchy of estates.

The problem began with Protestantism, which destroyed the doctrine of the Church, ever since which individualism started gaining momentum in the West — the individualism which Dumont, and the New Right in his wake, unabashedly critique.[20] Dumont categorically rejects egalitarian theories that violate holistic organicism and replace it with purely mechanical equalising, which, as in the case of outright individualism, leads to the destruction of the whole.[21]

18   See *Eschatological Optimism*

19   Louis Dumont, *Homo Hierarchicus: The Caste System and Its Implications*, trans. Mark Sainsbury (Chicago: University of Chicago Press, 1974).

20   Louis Dumont, *Essays on Individualism: Modern Ideology in Anthropological Perspective* (Chicago: University of Chicago Press, 1986).

21   Louis Dumont, *Homo aequalis I: Genèse et épanouissement de l'idéologie économique* (Paris: Gallimard, 1977).

Philosophical Anthropology

A major role in shaping the New Rights' ideas was played by the anthropologist Arnold Gehlen.[22] Gehlen says that man is the only species among animals that has the following problem: it cannot cope with its psychological load. Liberalism denies collective identity and proclaims abstract human rights, which leads to focusing only on the isolated individual. This destroys community and deprives man of psychological recharging. In my view, this is an absolutely genius defence of holism: man's psyche simply can't stand solitude. Therefore, in order to cope with this psychological load, man needs a collective. This excessive load is resolved through culture. Thus, Gehlen argued for the necessity and importance of society against individualistic theories and concepts. Culture, according to Gehlen, turns out to be a strategy for survival.

Gehlen also believed that the modern city is a toxic environment for man. The modern city can't let man be alone, nor does it give him connection with a collective, with an organic community. Man falls into collapse, into a state of absolute internal implosion. There is no community that would remove this tension.

This situation and the significance of society, along with Gehlen's critique of the differentiated subject, would be taken up in the arsenal of Alain de Benoist. On the whole, from sociology and in anthropology the New Right drew arguments in support of "communitarianism", community, and sociality, and refuted the individualism that constitutes the essence of liberal philosophy.

---

22 Arnold Gehlen, *Man: His Nature and Place in the World*, trans. Clare McMillan and Karl Pillemer (New York: Columbia University Press, 1987).

Konrad Lorenz and Ethology

Alain de Benoist was also influenced by the Austrian zoopsychologist Konrad Lorenz.[23] The New Right's interest in deep ecology can be traced in the case of their engagement with Lorenz's doctrine. Lorenz called his theory "ethology". According to it, animals also have social interactions and relationships, hence the principle of the collective is extremely important to determining individual behaviour in the animal world. A full analogue of society exists among animals, and the many parallels between humans and animals shed light on the general laws of sociality. This is the main thesis of ethology, the science of animal behaviour.

Konrad Lorenz also severely criticised capitalism and argued that overpopulation is extremely harmful to the planet. The desertification of living spaces and the high tempo of life is killing mankind.

This perspective influenced the entirety of the New Right's ecological worldview to a significant extent.

The Left: Proudhon and Gramsci

In addition to sociologists, anthropologists, philosophers, and the atypical right, GRECE was also influenced by a number of left-wing authors, particularly the French anarchist Pierre-Joseph Proudhon. De Benoist agrees with Proudhon's critique of capitalism: "property is theft". But he is against the dogmatic generalisation of this in the communist spirit. According to Proudhon, life should be organised on the principle of mutual exchange and solidarity between autonomous workers' collectives and, above all, farmers. This fully corresponds to rural traditionalism.

Even more influential on the New Right was the Italian communist Antonio Gramsci. Gramsci opposed liberalism and fascism and

---

23   Konrad Lorenz, *Behind the Mirror: A Search for a Natural History of Human Knowledge*, trans. Ronald Taylor (New York: Harvest/Harcourt Brace Jovanovich, 1978).

spoke of the need to construct a counter-hegemonic ideology. Gramsci understood hegemony as, above all, the expansion of the capitalist, liberal-democratic cultural paradigm. Fascism and semi-closed Eastern societies are partially protected from this influence in maintaining their sovereignty, but they partially let in this hegemony—which is, in essence, liberal ideology and the practices founded on it (above all the market). Gramsci called this "Caesarism", or half-baked resistance to global liberal hegemony. But Caesarism is not effective in the long term. Only a fully fledged alternative ideology—and, above all, its cultural formation and expression—is capable of prevailing over hegemony. The New Right agreed with this, but unlike Gramsci himself, they take "counter-hegemony" to mean not Marxism, but their own synthesis, their own "Theory of Europe".

Nouvelle École

One of the main platforms of the *Nouvelle Droite*'s intellectual activities is the publication *Nouvelle École*, which appeared in 1968. The journal had an altogether impressive editorial board featuring some of the stars of European philosophy, sociology, anthropology, geography, cultural studies, ethnology, history, etc. Among them figured: Georges Dumézil, Mircea Eliade, Konrad Lorenz, Marina Gimbutas, Jean Haudry, Roger Peyrefitte, Louis Pauwels, Paul Sérant, Jean Varenne, Raymond Abellio, Julien Freund, Vintilă Horia, Pierre Gripari, Hans Eysenck, Thomas Molnar, Stéphane Lupasco, Armin Mohler, Franz Altheim, etc. At the head of the journal stood the main figures of the New Right.

As a general rule, each issue of this high-professional and carefully conceived academic publication is dedicated to one topic. The issues' themes could be extremely broad, for example: "The Greeks", "The Enlightenment", "Political Theology", "Geopolitics", "Christianity", "The 1930s", "Tradition", "Economy", "Mass Culture", "Darwinism", "Ethology", etc. In some cases, an issue would be devoted to a specific author, such as Knut Hamsun, Georges Sorel, Oswald Spengler, Friedrich Nietzsche, Vilfredo Pareto, etc. In 2013, for example, one issue was devoted entirely to Carl Schmitt. It included excerpts from Schmitt's works, a general survey written by the leader of GRECE and the editor-in-chief, Alain de Benoist, and articles by various scholars connected with the New Right. The issue drew together various authors from both the "left" and "right" flanks, published new studies, as well as republished old texts with extensive commentary.

Alain de Benoist: The Founder and Irreplaceable Leader

The GRECE movement and the very category of the "New Right space" are unthinkable without Alain de Benoist, the French philosopher and intellectual who considers himself more of an "historian of ideas" and rejects any labels whatsoever, including the "New Right". He doesn't wish to be recognised as a sociologist or anthropologist, although he has deeply and seriously engaged these disciplines; instead, he simply says: "I am only an historian of ideas."

Alain de Benoist was born on 11 December 1943. He studied, law, philology, philosophy, archeology, linguistics, political science, and sociology. He has written more than a hundred books. When you work with and read his books, you really see a definite scholarly modesty gracefully covering his encyclopaedic knowledge.

In fact, Alain de Benoist has one of the biggest private libraries in Europe — 250,000 volumes according to some counts. He has a large home near Versailles with an incredible number of books. The entire space of his giant basement is filled with books.

Alain de Benoist's work is, above all, about systematising the European heritage, its boundless array of extremely interesting theories, schools, and teachings, both classical and avant-garde. He attentively dissects concepts that have been left and bequeathed to the European man who doesn't want to follow the path of liberal globalisation and universalism, who is set on seeking out his own identity. De Benoist's works are very useful if you really want to get acquainted with European culture. By reading him, you'll become familiar not only with his own ideas and views, but also Konrad Lorenz's perspectives on animal and human societies, how Oswald Spengler saw the history of the West, what Georges Dumézil, Émile Benveniste, Jean Haudry, and Vyacheslav Ivanov thought about the homeland of the Indo-Europeans. You'll also learn of the tendencies among the followers of Carl Schmitt and how his theories can be interpreted from the right (Piet Tommissen, Julien Freund, etc.), as well as from the left (Giorgio Agamben, Chantal Mouffe, etc.).

Thus, Alain de Benoist is a true modern European encyclopaedist. He is a bearer of the genuine spirit that the Enlightenment should have been in principle. Each of Alain de Benoist's works is a separate encyclopaedia. And he has written more than a hundred books. He has a wonderful book, my favourite one, that is a complete bibliography of Carl Schmitt. Alain de Benoist is the incredible, energetic centre of the whole GRECE movement. Without him, it would most likely have never come to be.

Europe and the Third World: Ties of Solidarity

Among de Benoist's many works, it's worth highlighting *Europe, Third World, One Struggle*. This book is important because de Benoist draws a connection between Europe and the Third World and says that "we are united in our common revolt against the hegemony of the West." Unlike the old, classical right, de Benoist says that we are not simply Europe, but all the peoples who have been driven out of the agenda of international politics. This includes all those peoples who have been subjected to the hegemonic violence of the System, of the big empire (meaning the US).

De Benoist takes the side of the Third World and says that Europe is also the Third World, and together we must oppose hegemony. This position is completely uncharacteristic of the conventional right, who in France are ordinarily fixated on fighting migrants, anti-communism, and have nothing against the capitalist model, colonialism, or Atlanticism, that is, American hegemony.

Right Ideas: The Imperative of Inequality

De Benoist expresses the foundational principles of the New Right in his book *Les Idées á l'endroit*. De Benoist writes: "The main enemy is egalitarianism, which denies and reduces the whole richness of the world."[24] For de Benoist, egalitarianism is the idea of artificially equalising people regardless of their inner qualities, capacities, and cultural level. He identifies the source of this egalitarianism, which he fights against, in the Great French Revolution of 1789. A similar idea was held by the Conservative Revolutionaries. De Benoist believes that it is necessary to get rid of this myth, this ideology of egalitarianism, because this egalitarianism leads to even greater inequality and imbalance. For de Benoist, the fundamental position can be formulated as Nietzsche put it in *Thus Spake Zarathustra*: "I do not want to be mixed in with and mistaken for these preachers of equality. For thus justice speaks *to me*: 'humans are not equal.'"[25] If de Benoist considers equality to be a "myth", then with even greater reason he recognises the "ideology of progress" to be a "myth".

De Benoist rejects both liberalism and Marxism. From his point of view, liberalism and Marxism are opposite poles of the same system of economic values, and both of these doctrines are built on economic grounds. Liberalism is always on the side of those who oppress and exploit, while Marxism is on the side of the oppressed. But they have the exact same understanding of reality. The New Right has a different one. Alain de Benoist does not recognize the thesis that economics is

24   Benoist, *Les idées á l'endroit*, 66.

25   Friedrich Nietzsche, *Thus Spoke Zarathustra*, trans. Adrian del Caro (Cambridge: Cambridge University Press, 2006), 78.

fate or that the capitalist phase of development and changes in historical formations are inevitable. The concurrence of liberalism and Marxism is based on prioritising the domination of the economic over all spheres of life. The New Right adheres to a principally different point of view: the primacy of life and idea in the flesh, the structures of the soul, and the ontology of communities and collectives.

The Eternity of Tradition

Also in *Les Idées á l'endroit,* Alain de Benoist expresses some important considerations on Tradition. He writes: "Tradition is not the past: this should be unceasingly repeated over and over. It has nothing to do with the past, the present, or the future. It is beyond time. It is connected not with what is old, what is 'behind us', but with what is constant, what is 'within us.'"[26] Tradition means searching for and finding the point of eternity within ourselves.

Against Racism

Let's take note of an important point: the New Right consistently opposes racism. Along with this, they oppose anti-racism. To be more precise, there are two kinds of anti-racism.

On the one hand, there is universalist anti-racism, which says: "No, racism is bad, we should make way for a universal, anti-racist acceptance of everyone and everything." In de Benoist's opinion, this anti-racism in fact leads once again to inequality, which is once again proclaimed to be the priority of either Western white man or, for instance, black man. De Benoist says that if you stand for "black power", then you should also stand for "yellow power", "white power", and "red power". That is, if you say that you are for black power, then you need to add the other three powers if you are a consistent anti-racist. If you only take black power and denigrate the rest of mankind, then you are an incorrect anti-racist, a hypocrite. This is the totally (in)correct

---

26 Benoist, *Les idées á l'endroit,* 118.

strategy of liberal totalitarianism, and it needs to be fought. "Race". in de Benoist's opinion, is not a zoological unit, but a certain kind of community that upholds a common history, culture, and fate.

"I condemn without exception all forms of racism, including those which are masked by anti-racism", de Benoist writes, and cites Raymond Ruyer: "Anti-racist and egalitarian ideologies are just as responsible for genocide and ethnic cleansing as are racist theories."[27]

Besides this anti-racism, there is a real alternative: recognising the differences between peoples and cultures without introducing any hierarchy between them. In order to achieve this, it is necessary to discard the universalism typical of the West first and foremost. At the present time, this is, above all, liberal universalism. Instead of human rights, de Benoist proclaims the rights of peoples. Instead of universalist doctrine, he proclaims pluriversalism.

Éléments

The journal *Éléments* has been published primarily in French, but it has also come out in other European languages. Starting in 1992, it was also published in Russia, its full title being *Elements: Eurasian Survey*. It was published by my father, Alexander Dugin. It represented the resonance of the New Right's ideas in Russia.

In France, *Éléments* appeared in 1973. Each issue is a thematic edition. It exists to this day. At present, issues come out every two months. Recently, the issues have been increasingly dedicated to the current political agenda. This is connected with *Éléments'* growing influence on the political life of France. One of the recent issues covers the "yellow vest" phenomenon in detail.

To this day, *Éléments* covers theoretical issues as well as the topical problems of the day. Not too long ago, *Éléments* started to appear for sale in French kiosks again. You can be walking around Paris and suddenly discover that, alongside such publications as *France Soir* and *Le*

---

27 Benoist, *Les idées á l'endroit*, 147.

Figaro, behind the kiosk window will be the pleasant sight of *Éléments*. The design of the issues is rather interesting: there are pop-art collages and classical motifs, while the presentation of *Nouvelle École* is predominated by graveur style and traditional designs.

I would like to draw your attention to the *Manifesto for a European Renaissance* that was written in 2000 and which has now been translated into Russian. I was invited to help with the editing, to check the translation against the French original and to write the foreword. This manifesto is a programmatic work, and if you want to know about the New Right and get to know their position, then I recommend you turn to it.

The Chief Editors of *Éléments*

Let's briefly look at the profile of the chief editors of *Éléments*. This might be needed for a more detailed study of this publication.

Originally, in 1968, when the publication was only beginning to take shape, Alain de Benoist took on the position of chief editor. But he signed his editorial columns under a pseudonym, "Robert de Herte". I'll give you a small hint: in order to find your way around any given issue (or if you don't have the time to read a whole issue), it's enough to read Alain de Benoist or Robert de Herte's column. Everything will become clear on the whole. These columns are important for understanding the essence of what is described in the given issue, they are like abridged transcripts.

Alain de Benoist has had many pseudonyms. His initial activities were under the pseudonym "Fabrice Laroche", then under Robert de Herte. He now works under his real name, but his old friends that crossed paths with him in their youth and started their path of war against the modern world and liberalism together back in the '60s-'70s still endearingly call him "Fabrice".

You might also have heard of or come across the name Michel Armand. He is a film critic, one of the most well-known figures besides

Alain de Benoist. He spent some time as the chief editor of *Éléments*. In 2013, he became the founder and one of the sponsors of the re-information channel TV Libertés, which is dedicated to bringing an alternative to the global agenda to French audiences.

At another point, the editor-in-chief was Charles Champetier, the co-author of the New Right manifesto and a student of de Benoist. Since 2017, the editor-in-chief has been François Bousquet, a rather interesting philosopher who studies Nietzsche. Bousquet is educated in philosophy and for a long time worked at right-wing conservative publications like *Le Figaro*, *Valeurs actuelles*, and *Le Spectacle du Monde*. If you follow the information agenda in France, you might recall that that it was *Valeurs actuelles* that around 20 April 2022 published a letter by French generals who spoke out against a "civil war" supposedly being set up by Macron and against the migration disorder that is being created in France today. At the present moment, *Valeurs actuelles* is a platform for expressing right-wing conservative ideas.

Now Bousquet also heads a bookstore, *La Nouvelle Librairie*, which is located across from the Jardin du Luxembourg. It opened in 2018 and over the past few years has been subject to numerous attacks and acts of aggression. Its windows are constantly broken, because the left, anarchists, and liberal anti-fascists of a globalist bent don't like the works that are shown in the windows. The bookstore's owners believe that this might symbolise the following: "If they break shop windows, then that means there's a reason. And if there's a reason, then that's good, that's something."

How the "New Right Movement" Was Born

Naturally, the New Right did not come out of one or another left or far-right circle. They did, of course, have ties in one way or another with the old right, although originally these ties were quite peculiar. Even among the classical right, these close ties were with atypical intellectuals, the followers of the "non-conformists of the '30s", and critics of liberalism and global capitalism. Narrow nationalism, chauvinism, and xenophobia were foreign to the New Right as a movement from the beginning.

The New Right largely attracted scholars, professors, students and youth who were revolutionarily attuned on the one hand, and completely unsatisfied with gaucheist ideas and practices on the other.

At the first stage, the New Right was close to organisations like Europe-Action, which was created by the writer Jean Mabire and the philosopher Dominique Venner. Europe-Action itself existed for only four years, from 1963 to 1967, and the New Right absorbed most of its members.

The New Right also came to be seen as the way forward by disparate movements of "left nationalists" as well as a significant portion of the pan-European "Young Europe" movement (Jeune Europe) founded by the Belgian political philosopher Jean Thiriart.

There were also attempts to shape the New Right movement into a political structure, Le Mouvement nationaliste du progrès, which appeared in 1966–1968 and was organized by the Rassembelment Européen pour la Liberté. Its representatives tried to participate in elections, but they faced a rather big failure in this field. Afterwards, they regrouped and concentrated on intellectual activity, on what they would later define as "metapolitics". Metapolitics is not politics by other means, but work in the field of changing hegemony, work in the field of the superstructure. According to Marx, there is the base and there is the superstructure, but Gramsci argued that the superstructure now determines who rules the world. Whoever controls the superstructure, controls the base. This superstructure is now dominated by liberalism and bourgeois ideology, and therefore the situation and the balance of forces can only be changed on the top. Only if influence can be exerted on culture, on the superstructure, will it be possible to seize the reins of governance from liberal and bourgeois hegemony. Then it will be possible to change the balance of forces against universalism. This is the strategy of metapolitics (or "Gramscianism from the right") that the New Right chose.

Many of the people who have been with GRECE since the early days are now 70–80 years old (born around the 1940s), which means that they joined the New Right around the age of 20. They originally came from these movements. When you talk with them personally, they'll often let the joke slide that "yes, we were once young and un-educated and took part in various nationalist circles and movements, but then everything changed, we got smarter, learned a lot, and became different".

The Old Right Is Dead

In the period when the New Right was born, the old right-wing ideology in Europe was in a deep crisis. Especially in the intellectual sense. Everyone repeated the old, pointless anti-communist formulas. GRECE clearly recognised their complete break with the old right. In 1979, in one of his fundamental programmatic works, *Les idées á l'endroit*, Alain de Benoist wrote: "*La vieille droite est morte. Elle l'a bien mérité.*"[28] What does this mean? "The old right is dead, and it deserved it."

Indeed, at that time, the French right was represented by rather narrow-minded, chauvinist groups who were against the idea of a united Europe, against communism and socialism, and thought exclusively in terms of local French nationalism. Naturally, this was not welcomed by Alain de Benoist; it drew only a negative reaction from him and his associates.

The old right were bound up with the Poujadists or the residual structures of Action Française. The agenda that the National Front under Jean-Marie Le Pen would later take up was tantamount to the one that the New Right harshly criticised. The old right defended the formula "right-wing economics + right-wing politics". The New Right

---

28   Benoist, *Les idées á l'endroit*, 57.

constructed an even more nuanced and ideologically revolutionary model. For Alain de Benoist and the intellectuals of the New Right, combining right-wing economics and right-wing politics was unacceptable, above all by virtue of their deep revulsion towards capitalism, liberalism, and globalism, that is to what is regarded as economically right-wing. The New Right argued that a market can exist in society, but a market society, that is a society where all values are expendable, sold, and bought, has no right to exist. GRECE raised serious questions to right-wing politics: they rejected Western European racism, ethnocentrism, the exclusivity of the Western path of development, and nationalism, chauvinism, and xenophobia along with such. They considered immigrants to be victims of capitalist exploitation, not the source of all evils as the "old right" habitually believed. Thus, a radical break took place between the New Right and the old right.

Gramscianism from the Right

GRECE gradually came to completely reject and condemn nationalism. The phenomenon of nationalism was recognised to be a characteristic trait of the bourgeois capitalist civilisation which the New Right opposed. Therefore, whenever we talk about the New Right, it needs to be understood that they were not simply continuers of the preceding right-wing currents and organisations. They were not simply a "reformatted right" that allegedly tried to hide its real ideological orientation under the guise of nuanced intellectual constructs. Rather, this was a real, radical break with the old right ideology. Above all, this break consisted in revising the key element of traditional right ideology, that is in rejecting capitalist economics. In de Benoist's opinion, this complete rejection of liberalism pierced not only the left, but also the new right movements of the time.

For GRECE and Alain de Benoist, creating an alternative to left-liberal hegemony in Europe and the whole world is of the greatest importance. For Alain de Benoist, political victory and political agenda is not as important as cultural victory. He believed that the New Right would not be able to win if it acted only politically, because the whole discursive space, the space of political thought, had been seized by left-liberal hegemony. On this note, Alain de Benoist draws on the ideas of the left-wing anti-capitalist philosopher Antonio Gramsci, who believed that hegemony, that is the monolithic and monopoly rule of the global bourgeoisie, is based first and foremost on control over culture, science, education, the press, information, and the epistemological field. Only then does this hegemony descend onto the level of politics and the economy. Therefore, without winning the epistemological war against hegemony on the level of ideas, any political struggle will be deliberately doomed. Therefore, it is first and foremost necessary to create a counter-hegemony that can pose a decisive fight against capitalism as an idea. For Gramsci, this counter-hegemony was Marxism. Alain de Benoist shares this analysis of hegemony, but he believes that Marxism, which previously claimed to be the fight against capitalism, has gradually become part of the liberal paradigm. This gave rise to the phenomenon of left liberalism, which then became the dominant force. So, Marxism cannot play the role of counter-hegemony. The New Right set the goal of developing a different ideological paradigm for the lethal struggle with liberalism and capitalism. This became the main goal of GRECE. Thus, the New Right proclaimed a Gramscianism from the right.

The Axial Themes of the New Right

Immediately following its founding in 1968, GRECE's founders engaged in active intellectual politics — seminars, congresses, debates, publications, interviews, symposiums, colloquiums, conferences. All of their activities revolved around several central themes which allow us to trace the intellectual map or ecosystem of the New Right movement and understand their main orientations.

In this lecture on the New Right, I would like to build our exposition along the hierarchical levels of "theory", "concept", and "notion". I will try to systematize what out of the whole mass of the New Right's topics is a genus, what is a species, and what is a more individual notion.

All of the topics which the New Right has developed constantly intersect with each other. At first glance, it'd be difficult to say what is first and foremost in Alain de Benoist's thought — the theory of Greater Europe, overcoming the left-right schism through a common anti-liberal platform, metapolitics, geopolitics, ecology and organicism, the legacy of the Conservative Revolution or the non-conformists of the '30s, or futurist technocracy, etc. All of these topics are intertwined. It will be difficult to distinguish the main one, but over the course of this lecture and, I hope, in a follow-up course, we plan to busy ourselves with this complex process of distinguishing the main concepts of the New Right and the theories based on them.

Here are the titles that the GRECE movement's colloquiums and conferences had: "Against all forms of totalitarianism", "For a new culture", "For a Gramscianism from the right", "The failure of Disneyland", "The US: a danger", "Europe: a new world", "the End of the World" (the content of which isn't so much about eschatology as it is about critiquing liberalism and the thesis of the end of history), "The cause of peoples", "Left and right", "The end of the system". These titles themselves help us take note of certain key points in the ecosystem of the New Right. We can clearly see that, firstly, the enemy is declared to be the US, and the highest value is Europe, free from the United States of America. Peoples are recognized to be the main subjects of history (hence the "rights of peoples", not "human rights"). Here we can recall Greimas' semantic quadrant, in which the positive content of a thesis is clarified only once it has been compiled along with the concrete content of an antithesis. Here, the people as a value means collective identity, and is contrasted to the separate human being, to the individual, to individual identity. For GRECE, this is fundamental: the concrete whole is above the abstract part. Hence their radical rejection of liberalism in all of its forms and, to the contrary, their sympathies for socialism and organic democracy.

As for the other topics, like "Left and right" and "The end of the System", GRECE believes that the division into left and right is a completely artificial construct that prevents people from breaking through to meaning and leaves them working within the space of an artificial collision between alienated concepts, a kind of "duel of fakes" intended to keep mankind in ignorance and divide people into two categories on different fronts so that they destroy each other over utterly secondary matters. This division into right and left artificially divorces healthy ideas into two fronts so that they never unite. The New Right speaks of the necessity of passing from politics to metapolitics. They argue that in order to save European identity, we must pass from war over momentary political interests, from war within the existing political system, to war for minds, war for consciousness, and war for culture. The goal is to break the System, to abolish it as such. In essence, the goal is a European Revolution.

The confrontation between right and left only plays into the hands of the liberal centre, which, in pitting anti-fascists and anti-communists against each other, ensures its domination over the whole political spectrum. This is the System, the model of liberal-capitalist hegemony. This is what "Gramscianism from the right" takes aim against.

The First People

When it comes to the founders, the people who first participated in GRECE, they numbered around 40 people.

There was Alain de Benoist, whom we've already discussed.

The philosopher Dominique Venner, who became famous when he ended his own life in 2013 at the altar of the Cathedral of Notre-Dame in Paris in a symbolic act of protest against left-liberal, globalist dictatorship.

The Italian philosopher, sociologist, and writer Giorgio Locci. Although he is not often mentioned, he had a big influence on shaping the New Right's ideas.

The writer Jean Mabire, an author of historical and adventure novels, including one about Baron Ungern-Sternberg.

The famous French journalist and director of prestigious *Le Figaro*, Jean-Claude Valla.

Pierre Vial, who later left the movement and launched the identitarian publication *Terre et Peuple* ("Land and People") and inspired a wide circle of youth who organised summer camps, trips around the French provinces, and music festivals.

The famous French film critic and specialist in the field of audiovisual art, Michel Marmin.

The French linguist and medievalist Jean-Claude Rivière.

The historian Jean-Jacques Moreau.

Expanding Cooperation

GRECE gradually expanded its circle of authors. A broad spectrum of French and, more broadly, European intellectuals began collaborating with the New Right's publications. The spectrum of philosophers, intellectuals, historians, and social anthropologists who actively cooperated with the New Right is no coincidence. This array once again convinces us that the New Right cannot be deemed a mere rebranding of the ordinary right or a cover for the left's infiltration of a right-wing segment of politics. For GRECE, there is no such division. Hence the very cases of those who began to actively interact with the New Right and who became regular authors and columnists in their publications. For instance:

- Michel Maffesoli, a professor of the Sorbonne and a student of the renowned sociologist and founder of the sociology of imagination, Gilbert Durand.

- The left-wing political scientist, sociologist, and journalist Michel Onfray, whose *Treatise on Theology* is now a bestseller. This despite the fact that Onfray is an atheist, counts himself a member of the far-left clan, and supports Mélenchon.

- Marcel Gauchet, a French historian who is often cited in de Benoist's book *Beyond Human Rights*.[29] He says that human rights is a completely artificial, manipulative concept, since law and rights cannot be individual but, after all, are fundamentally something collective. Accordingly, human rights is nonsense inasmuch as it is built on appealing to two incompatible terms.

- Bernard Langlois, an alter-globalist journalist who founded the journal *Politis*.

- Pierre Manent, another alter-globalist journalist.

- Patrick Besson, a political scientist who was an advisor to Sarkozy from 2007 to 2012. He is a follower of Charles Maurras. He was also an advisor to Philippe de Villiers, a right-wing conservative politician and the founder of the Puy du Fou historical park (a wonderful, patriotic alternative to the colonial, globalist Disneyland). This park is located near Vendée and has a square with 10 enormous stages which host reenactments of various events from the history of France. For example, there is an exhibit about Jean of Arc. All of this is presented in the format of a content-rich, highly artistic spectacle with numerous elements of entertainment, including birds, salutes, special effects, etc.[30]

- Christophe Guilluy, a geographer who in 2017 actively advocated revising the foundations of the European Union.

---

29   Alain de Benoist, *Against Human Rights: Defending Freedoms*, trans. Alexander Jacob (London: Arktos, 2011).

30   Daria Dugina visited the Puy du Fou park in 2017 on the personal invitation of its founder and owner, Philippe de Villiers.

- Jacques Sapir, a left-wing critic of liberalism known in Russian media as an economist who is critical of liberal doctrine.

- Jean-Yves Camus, a journalist and specialist on the far right who is also a critic of immigration.

These names don't need to be especially remembered. The New Right is Alain de Benoist and his close circle. But this list of names goes to show that the New Right is a very heterogenous movement. There are both left-wing and right-wing figures, former advisors of Sarkozy as well as supporters of Mélenchon, atheists and pagans, Orthodox (for example, Christophe Levallois is a priest serving in the Church of St. Seraphim of Sarov) and Catholics. It is a multifaceted movement which has no strict political orientation.

A Merciless Critique of Liberalism

But what unites them? When it comes to the staples unifying this collective of authors gathered around *Éléments*, then we see, firstly, the position that they are neither left nor right, the very division between which they reject, and secondly, a radical and merciless critique of liberalism.

Liberalism is critiqued as a universalist doctrine that proclaims abstract human rights, which is essentially a myth and falsification in that the very idea of law and rights (according to de Benoist and rights theory as such) means arranging justice in a collective, and this requires that the collective be recognised as primary in relation to the individual. Therefore, law regulates and arranges the proportions between the citizens of the *polis*. It is an instance of authority that thwarts injustice. At the same time, the rights of the individual are proclaimed to be innate. From de Benoist's point of view, this understanding is illegitimate because law cannot be placed outside of the context of the interaction between people. Therefore, for Alain de Benoist and the whole GRECE movement, "human rights" are a myth.

The Rights of Peoples
and a Europe of a Thousand Flags

What do they propose in turn? The New Right says that it is necessary
to recognise the rights of peoples. The rights of peoples, as the rights of
collective identities, should be proclaimed and ensured. The rights of
peoples should become the guiding star of the new movement for the
rebirth of European identity. In critiquing liberalism, the New Right
is critiquing not so much the economic theories of liberalism as the
deep philosophical foundations of liberalism. In general, for the New
Right, liberalism is by no means only an economic phenomenon. For
them, liberalism is above all a philosophical phenomenon. It began to
take shape in the era of Modernity and was marked by the progressive
separation of man from his context, from his tradition, from religion,
from his roots.

Accordingly, the New Right stand opposed to liberalism as a philosophical movement. Without a doubt, they do not accept economic
liberalism, but the priority of their fight against liberalism is the critique of the new European subject itself as it is nominally regarded to
be separate from everything and completely independent and autonomous. Thus, for de Benoist, human rights and the abstract elevation
of man as an individual into a cult lead to society being undermined
and its very pillars collapsed. Culture and civilisation as a whole are
destroyed, replaced by the consumer society. This is the logical continuation of the doctrine of individualism and liberalism.

So, the New Right affirms the principle of a "Europe of peoples"
against the universalist "Europe of individuals". This Europe of peoples,
as we have seen, was extolled by Thiriart. On the one hand, this is a
united Europe (a continental identity that is opposed to the West and
the civilisation of Sea), and, on the other hand, a Europe of a plurality
of cultures and regions. De Benoist calls this "Europe of a thousand
flags".

Exposing the American Neoconservatives

Alain de Benoist has numerous works dedicated to analysing American neoconservatism. He draws attention to the fact that the neoconservatives are entirely based in liberalism. In other words, this "conservatism" does not conserve differences and cultural identities, but instead destroys them.

Yet another characteristic trait of the neoconservatives, according to de Benoist, is their reconceptualisation of St. Augustine's concept of a "just war". St. Augustine considered a "just war" to be a "war of good against evil, against the forces of the devil", American neoconservatives identify the "good" with the US, the liberal, globalist world order, that is the alliance of the international capitalist elite with the US deep state. Globalism is based on the ideology of human rights, liberalism, and extreme individualism, which destroy any and all communities and organic collectives. That is, this "conservatism" is not conservatism at all; on the contrary, it is the most aggressive form of the planetary destruction of differences, traditions, and communities.

The New Right and Philosophical Paganism

One of the important orientations of the New Right's whole strategy is their special attention to Tradition. The majority of them tend not towards Christianity, but to a kind of "philosophical paganism". This rather original current is the subject of Alain de Benoist's book *On Being a Pagan*.[31] When I undertook to distinguish the main idea of the New Right, I came to the conclusion that it is a "theory of Europe". "Philosophical paganism", as an elevated attention devoted to the traditions, myth, and sacrality of European peoples, can be considered a subsection of this theory.

There are rather many neo-pagans among the New Right, practically 90% of the movement. But on this point, let us warn ourselves

---

31   Alain de Benoist, *On Being a Pagan*, trans. John Graham (North Augusta: Arcana Europa, 2018).

that we shouldn't immediately fall into extremes and say that since they are pagans and we are Orthodox Christians, we should be skeptical of their ideas. Among the New Right there are also Christians, even Orthodox ones. Christophe Levallois, for example, in his search for sacred tradition, came from this milieu to the Orthodox Church and became an Orthodox priest.

In general, the topic of the New Right's paganism is very interesting. For instance, I gave a lecture at the Listva bookstore in Saint Petersburg, and listeners proposed a response to the question as to why philosophical paganism is organic for the New Right in France but in Russia, to the contrary, is completely inappropriate. Listeners explained this in the following way. Orthodox Christianity absorbed a rather large mass of ancient East Slavic beliefs. We have tighter ties with Indo-European tradition than Catholics do. Moreover, Orthodoxy is closer to Hellenic culture as it was preserved in Byzantium up to its latest eras. Accordingly, the opposition to Christianity that the New Right sometimes declares is only directed against the Catholic Church, which in the broader context is not equivalent to and cannot automatically be applied to the [Orthodox] Christian Church. This response is interesting in that Orthodoxy has in fact preserved sacrality, the collectivity of *sobornost'*, and fidelity to Tradition. Alain de Benoist criticises Western Catholicism, to the contrary, for its cultivation of individualism. Let us recall that this was also the idea of Max Weber, who said that the Protestant ethic is the source of the spirit of capitalism.[32] Werner Sombart discovered the sources of individualism and the capitalist system even earlier than the Reformation, in Catholicism itself.[33]

Alain de Benoist argues that the Catholic Church facilitated the idea that man needs to communicate with God individually, and

32 Max Weber, *The Protestant Ethic and the "Spirit" of Capitalism*, trans. Peter Baehr and Gordon C. Wells (New York: Penguin Books, 2002).

33 Werner Sombart, *Traders and Heroes: Patriotic Reflections*, trans. Alexander Jacob (London: Arktos, 2021).

therefore man is torn out of the collective, and religion is turned into a private affair. In his earlier works, especially from the 1970s, de Benoist is highly critical of the Catholic religion. On this point, he is in many respects following the Italian Traditionalist Julius Evola.

Deep and Superficial Ecology

A separate bloc among the topics covered by the the New Right is ecology. This is an interesting, complex topic about which little has been written.

While preparing for this lecture, I found in the New Right's works a distinction between "deep ecology" and "superficial ecology". The New Right says that there is so-called "deep ecology", *écologie profonde*, and there is "superficial ecology", *écologie superficiel*. The latter operates in the capitalist topography and is focused on minimising threats posed to nature, including physical threats posed by production, and finding a compromise between nature and production which is harmful to the environment. In other words, this ecology works within the existing, given paradigm.

Deep ecology, meanwhile, tears apart the idea of seeking compromise with capitalism and acts against the very approach of treating nature like an object of exploitation. Whereas superficial ecology says "let's cause a little less harm to nature", the fundamentalist, integral ecologists, and other representatives of deep ecology, say that it is necessary to reconsider man's place in nature, to abandon the conviction that man is the master of nature, and instead acknowledge that man is only one element of nature. Man should no longer be perceived as the centre of the world, as the manager of nature. Man must protect and watch over nature.

This is a very interesting direction which we won't dwell on in detail for now. What is important is the very distinction between "deep" and "superficial" ecology.

The New Right Today

Now a few remarks about the New Right's platforms today, where you can listen to and read them.

Earlier we mentioned François Bousquet, the chief editor of *Éléments*. We also mentioned his bookstore, La Nouvelle Librairie. If you're in Paris, this is a place you need to visit. To this day, you'll see the shop windows broken by aggressive liberals. The store has two floors: on the first floor they sell new books, on the second they have books for collectors and used books. When this bookstore with such an orientation opened, there was a real agitation campaign waged against it. In principle, it is comparable to Listva, but it has a much bigger selection of books. The orientation is similar.

TV Libertés is a re-information channel that was conceived as an alternative to the globalist media and was formed in 2012–2013. It is now one of the largest serious YouTube platforms in France, which covers predominantly everything from the New Right and ordinary right-wing positions. On the whole, the channel belongs more to the classical sector (if we stick with the old division into right and left), but it has a programme called *Les Idées à l'endroit*, which is hosted by Alain de Benoist himself and bears the same name as his programmatic book from 1979. The channel also has a special programme with the editorial team of *Éléments*, "*Le Plus d'éléments*" ("More Elements"). It is often hosted by the director of *Éléments,* François Bousquet, himself.

One interesting project which has turned into a serious intellectual centre is *L'Institut Iliade*, which was created with the support of GRECE, Alain de Benoist, and authors like Jean-Yves Le Gallou (who was also a member of GRECE until 1974, when alongside Yvan Blot and Henry de Lesquen he joined the schism that split off into the Club de l'Horloge, whose positions are more in line with the classical right). The Iliade Institute (which is not an institute in the direct sense, but rather a community of like-minded thinkers, an association of intellectuals of New Right bent) describes itself as an "institute for the study of long European memory", that is of European heritage. It regularly holds congresses and publishes books. The emphasis here is on younger researchers, not from the 1947 generation but from the '80s-'90s, my age group. I myself have spoken there.

One of the Iliade Institute's events was "*Au-delà du marché*", "Beyond the Market", with the subtitle "The Economy in the Service of Peoples". Another event has been devoted to ecology. On the posters of their colloquiums we find a characteristic inscription: "Proud to be Europeans". Or from one of their first events: "*Transmettre ou disparaître*", which can be translated as "Pass along [heritage] or disappear". In a word, "Tradition or death" — on the one hand Tradition, on the other the abyss, non-being.

The New Right in Russia

Now a bit about whom the New Right has crossed paths with in Russia. We already mentioned the founder of Young Europe, Jean Thiriart's visit to Russia 1992. Also in 1992, in March, Alain de Benoist visited Russia along with Robert Steuckers, one of his comrades in the New Right movement — Steuckers was also a member of GRECE and de Benoist's secretary, but he later left the movement and joined a schismatic group. This group organized an alternative New Right movement, *Synergies européennes*, but they couldn't compete with GRECE. Back in 1992, de Benoist and Steuckers visited Moscow together on the invitation of Alexander Dugin and the newspaper *Den'* ("Day"), and they held a number of conferences there. They met with Prokhanov and a number of colourful figures from the anti-Yeltsin and left-right opposition. The New Right was greatly impressed by the patriotic front that was then coming together, and they gained sincere sympathy for Russia.

At the present time, in Russian bookstores you can find Alain de Benoist's essay "Beyond Human Rights", which I recommend you read, in his Russian anthology *Against Liberalism: Towards the*

Fourth Political Theory, published by Amfora in a good translation
by Alexander Kuznetsov. Overall, pay attention to translations, verify
the terms, especially if you have the possibility to look at the original.
Unfortunately, translations of the New Right are at times done hastily,
and somehow some editorial addition gets thrown in, like at the end
of the Russian edition of de Benoist's *On Being a Pagan*. De Benoist
himself was disappointed by it. So I don't recommend that edition. The
original is better.

Given that Alain de Benoist also professes the Fourth Political
Theory, which was developed jointly by him and Alexander Dugin,
Dugin's book *The Fourth Way* and a number of his other works can
help you understand the New Right.[34] In principle, contemporary
Eurasianism,[35] that is neo-Eurasianism, is a Russian reception of the
New Right's ideas.[36] So, I recommend getting acquainted with works
on the Fourth Political Theory, or in the very least with the materials
that have been put in open access. They will clarify a lot and help you
enter the New Right's space of thought.

---

34 A. G. Dugin, *Chetvertyi put'* (Moscow: Academic Project, 2014); Alexander
Dugin, *The Fourth Political Theory*, trans. Mark Sleboda and Michael Millerman
(London: Arktos, 2012); *The Rise of the Fourth Political Theory*, trans. Michael
Millerman (London: Arktos, 2017).

35 Eurasianism is a geopolitical philosophy that advocates a multipolar world
centred on the cultural, political, and spiritual unity of the Eurasian continent,
opposing Western universalism. It promotes the idea that each civilisation
should retain its unique values and governance, viewing the alliance of Eurasian
nations as a counterbalance to Western influence and as essential to preserving
different cultural identities and traditional societies.

36 Alexander Dugin, *Eurasian Mission: An Introduction to Neo-Eurasianism*
(London: Arktos, 2014).

Questions and Answers

Listener: It's unclear what the sources of law are for de Benoist. If it's not natural law, and not positively descended from above, and not *ius civile*,[37] then what are its sources?

Dugina: For de Benoist, law is not transcendent, but immanent, i.e., law is an arrangement reached in the name of carrying out justice, a kind of pact.

Listener: Concluded by whom and on what basis?

Dugina: As in who pronounces the decision? The community. Tradition. Tradition not in the transcendental view as though a conviction descended from God or a mythical legislator, like the Laws of Manu. Law[38] is given by Tradition. A people always has its law and needs to uphold and preserve it. It defines and demarcates interactions between people; it is directed towards fixing relations. Law cannot be individual; it is collective. This is described in detail in the book *Beyond Human Rights*, which examines the etiology of this understanding of law.

Listener: How does the Belgian philosopher Chantal Mouffe's dissensual model, which calls for aggravating contradictions rather than seeking consensus, relate to the New Right's idea of abolishing the difference on the political front between right and left? Or has she at least said anything about this?

Dugina: I don't think that Chantal Mouffe, even given all her interest in Carl Schmitt, one of the most important authorities of the New Right, would agree to a common illiberal front like some others on the left have in the past, such as Jean-Edern Hallier, Michel

---

37 *Ius civile* refers to the body of civil law in ancient Rome that governed Roman citizens, forming the basis of legal principles in the Roman Republic and Empire and later influencing modern legal systems.

38 The Laws of Manu, or *Manusmriti*, is an ancient Hindu legal text that outlines religious, moral, and social duties, providing a comprehensive code of conduct that governed aspects of life such as caste, justice, and daily behavior in traditional Indian society.

Onfray, Jean-Claude Michéa, Costanzo Preve, Diego Fusaro, etc. She insistently counts herself on the extreme left wing. For example, she is positive about migration processes and doesn't condemn the migration crisis like the New Right. Alain de Benoist and *Éléments* defend European identity. This is not something dear to Chantal Mouffe, who wages polemics against them, although she is in dialogue with them. They have a common broadcast on Arte France, "Alain de Benoist with Chantal Mouffe", where they sit together in the studio, express their points of view, smile at each other, and say, "Well you're a Schmittian, so you can't be completely wrong." In 2017, de Benoist and Mouffe had an interesting and substantive radio show on populism.

It is very important to mention the theory of populism, because Alain de Benoist has been unpacking this topic in connection with the 2018 elections. He published the book *The Populist Moment*, which says that the schism into left and right is no longer legitimate.[39] Instead, the schism between populists and elites is making itself known. What is this? Populism is a movement of the people, which takes account of the elite's abandonment of the people. This phenomenon comes about whenever the people understands that its interests are no longer represented in power. Then the revolt begins. Then we have the "Yellow Vests" and movements like Matteo Salvini's, especially the collaboration between Salvini's Lega Nord and and the left-wing Five Stars Movement. For de Benoist, such phenomena are signs of the onsetting "populist moment".

In 2018, at the 60th anniversary of GRECE, Alain de Benoist said, "Look, everything I've said about the populist moment, everything we've written, is coming true. The 'Yellow Vests' movement marks the overcoming of the right-left opposition, when different wings of the political spectrum come together in a unified protest against capitalism and against the powers-that-be."

---

39 Alain de Benoist, *Le Moment populiste. Droite-gauche c'est fini!* (Paris: Pierre-Guillaume de Roux, 2017).

Listener: Why were they called the "New Right" instead of, for example, the "New Left"? They aren't as much on the right insofar as they actually take over some common orientations, including left-wing ones. Why the skew to the right? Why did they decide to be called right?

Dugina: I've already said that this wasn't their choice. This is how they were christened by their ideological opponents, by liberals. This was likely done for the sake of demonising them. This label was applied to them in 1979. Eleven years had passed since 1968, and by that time the liberal party had been working out a strategy for opposing the movement. At that moment, it was more convenient to use a right-wing label for demonisation. Moreover, there were associations with fascist movements and the beginning of an anti-fascist, anti-racist wave. Therefore, it was easier to discard their opponents as right-wing, as "racists" (which they never were), than as left-wing. Plus, the left front, the "New Left", was already taken. The movement of May 1968 emerged and they couldn't share any space with them, because they disagreed on fundamental positions.

Listener: Does the New Right's critique of Christianity only show up in regards to the modern Catholic Church, or are there any more fundamental things here?

Dugina: Pierre-André Taguieff, an historian of the New Right, writes about this. There is a line of critique of Judeo-Christianity as a whole. This is especially clear-cut in the '70s, but then the New Right somewhat departed from it. The point of this critique is that the Christian model (unlike the pagan model) tears man out of the collective context, out of living community. Christianity individualises man, and in so doing lays open the path to liberalism and Modernity — this is how Alain de Benoist sees it. At the same time, however, he's never had any critique of Orthodoxy. He's said several times: "If I were a Christian, I definitely wouldn't be Catholic, but Orthodox." But he makes a point to emphasise: "But I'm not a Christian." So, Alain de Benoist has a general critique of Christianity that is radical when it comes to Protestantism and Catholicism, but, while being a pagan, he has some clear sympathy for Orthodoxy.

Listener: On the one hand, the movement has a critique of Catholicism and even a critique of Christianity. On the other hand, traditionally, the French conservative tradition is strongly connected to the Catholic Church ever since the time of the royalist movement of Joseph de Maistre, Chateaubriand, etc. How does the New Right relate to this conservative tradition? Do they reject it on the whole and propose to start everything over from scratch?

Dugina: No, it is not completely rejected, although it is substantially reconceptualised. For example, in the GRECE movement, there are Orthodox and Catholic priests, clerics, as well as ordinary believers. In central Paris, there is the Saint-Paul Centre — a Catholic traditionalist centre.[40] The majority are Catholics who are against the Pope, who have gone into "schism", a kind of Old Believers in their own way. These types of "catho-trads" really like GRECE; they often organise events with Alain de Benoist and gather with members of the New Right. They don't face any harsh opposition, and the point is not that the New Right has dismissed the conservative ideas of Joseph de Maistre. To the contrary, they often cite him and treat him as a figure of interest. The New Right has a critique of the Christian-Catholic tradition to the extent that it manifests individualism and a break with holism. So, it's completely incorrect to say that they are in some kind of permanent war against Christianity. They do not discard European heritage; they try to find a certain compromise. They are intellectuals, and you won't find very sharp-cut formulas among them. It's more about an encyclopaedic overview. They underscore their orientation by the very fact of their analysis of traditions, Indo-European traditions, including by appealing to paganism, but they do not insist on

---

40 The Saint-Paul Centre in Paris is a cultural and religious hub connected to traditional Catholicism. It offers services such as traditional Latin masses, catechism classes, and Gregorian chant courses, promoting a space for spiritual, cultural, and liturgical activities that emphasise classical Catholic practices.

anything. Some members who have distanced themselves from de Benoist, like Pierre Vial for instance, have a much harsher style. Pierre Vial can allow himself to produce more outright propagandistic texts in favour of paganism. But the people who join in solstice celebrations include those who represent the Catholic point of view. I attended one of them once, although I am a deeply Orthodox person, and there were no disagreements. When you start to talk about how we, Orthodox, in many respects share the holism and communal quality that they like in paganism, and when you discuss our sacred traditions, its spirit, its life with them, then you're often met with absolute solidarity.

Listener: What is the New Right's opinion of Islam? After all, the migration question has become increasingly acute in recent time. Not everything is determined here, the cause isn't obvious, but still as a consequence we have a radicalisation of Muslims.

Dugina: The European New Right doesn't like migration, but they have much sympathy for migrants. Alain de Benoist writes that migrants are people who have become victims of economic liberalism. They no longer have a homeland back home (because their homeland has been destroyed either physically or through certain economic instruments of pressure), nor do they have a homeland here (because France rejects tradition and is no longer a homeland for anyone). That is, migrants come to some kind of anonymous hotel. For the New Right, migrants are unfortunate victims, but migration itself is part of the criminal, murderous process of liberal globalisation. There are some more radical elements on the New Right who are closer to the classical right agenda. They agree with the idea that the global elites want to implement a "Great Replacement". This theory, for which the French journalist Renaud Camus is so sharply criticised, is supposed to lead to the fact that at one fine moment the European population will be completely replaced by migrants and simply wiped off the face of the earth. Supporters of this theory fear the ascendancy of "Islamo-fascism" in Europe. This line has been mostly developed by Guillaume

Faye.[41] For those who think the "Great Replacement" plan really exists, this process is, of course, negative and fatal for Europe. But this is the more right wing of the New Right, the more classical right. The National Front (now the National Rally) and all those who share classical right theses adhere to similar ideas. But Alain de Benoist himself treats this topic in a complex and subtle manner, always emphasising that the responsibility for migration lies entirely with liberal hegemony, American dominance, and that it is not migrants that need to be taken care of (in the sense of sending all of them back), but liberal hegemony itself which is the main source of this negative process that is destroying Europe.

Listener: Does the New Right appropriate Dugin's notion that there are not strictly national or racial divisions, so people can integrate into another culture regardless of their origin?

Dugina: Of course, they by all means reject biological racism. They have a solid critique of National Socialism, and they say that the strategy of dividing people in biological terms is a fatal form of totalitarianism. Not only do they reject biological racism, but they insist that the human being completely depends on the culture in which they are nurtured. Identity is a cultural notion, not a biological or racial one. There is no predetermining biological fact that completely defines identity. On this point Dugin and de Benoist's thought is identical. They are similar in many respects as thinkers, but Alexander Gelyevich [Dugin] has more metaphysics, more metaphysical coverage of the history and tradition of Europe. De Benoist has more analysis and sociological and anthropological theories, but there is also an element of Heideggerianism in de Benoist that once again brings these

---

41 Guillaume Faye (1949–2019) was a French New Right intellectual and fierce advocate for European revival, envisioning a new order rooted in strength, identity, and civilisational unity. His imperial concept of "Eurosiberia" proposed a grand alliance between Europe and Russia as a cultural and ethnic bulwark against global homogenisation, while his philosophy of "Archeofuturism" called for a synthesis of ancient virtues and advanced technological progress.

two thinkers close to each other. We also find a turn to Heidegger among other thinkers of the New Right. For example, Yvan Blot, one of the inspirers of the Club de l'Horloge created in 1974. This club is oriented towards national liberalism, which in de Benoist's eyes is a definite deviation from the main line of the New Right. But an interest in Heidegger is present in both places. Yvan Blot, in his last interview given in 2017, said "Macron is the *Gestell*", using the Heideggerian term for the "enframing of technology". This understanding of the nature of modern politics and society is shared by the majority of the New Right. The foremost problem of the modern West is its inauthentic existence, its forgetfulness of Being, its alienation. This is engendered by the enframing, the *Gestell*, that substitutes technology for politics. Both Alexander Gelyevich Dugin and Alain de Benoist think in sync on this point. Their position on most questions is identical, although in the religious sense and in the sphere of metaphysics they have gone down different paths.

Listener: A question on the topic of the nation: there is no single French political nation. In France there are Bretons, Occitans, the cultures of Provence, the inhabitants of Île-de-France — what is the New Right's approach to this?

Dugina: They are for organic pluralism. For example, they have a centre in Aix-en-Provence, in the south of France, not far from Marseille. It's called "*Domus*", that is "home" or "house", and since the 1970s they've been hosting celebrations of the solstices, school trips, and symposiums and colloquiums there. It is a building with three floors, where every room is a miniature hotel with the flag of a particular region. If you end up in the Brittany room, you walk around calling yourself a Breton, and if someone gets lucky and stays in the room representing where they were born, then there is boundless joy. The value of the multiplicity of regions is manifest even in such seemingly elementary things as accommodation, as a house. From the point of view of the New Right, Europe is a plurality of regions with their own cultures and peculiarities; they should all be unified into a common front and they are called upon to become one whole "great space". This is a great, enormous Europe "from Dublin to Vladivostok" as per Jean Thiriart. So, they have an interest in regions, which they really love. In fact, they take pleasure in singing Breton songs.

Listener: If for the New Right all people are very similar and can be replaced by one another, which means that there is essentially nothing bad in migration, then from where do we derive the idea that the multipolar world and the diversity and pluralism of cultures is one of our values?

Dugina: Excuse me, but have you even been listening to what I've been saying? For the New Right there is much that is negative in migration processes. On the whole, these processes are absolutely negative. If a person leaves their cultural space, moves to a different city, a different province, a different region, then this is already something negative. The New Right call this *déracinement*, that is literally "uprooting". They fight against this by all means. If a person ends up in a different culture, they can become a receptacle for it and adopt it if they choose in favour of this new identity. In this case, they acquire new roots. But this doesn't always happen, and not even often. Instead, a person is usually broken. Man loses his roots and doesn't gain anything in return. He is left *déraciné*, "rootless". Therefore, migration is a negative process. For the New Right, the main point is that every person should remain where they were born. They should be raised in their own culture and remain within it. If a person by dint of circumstances ends up in a different culture, then, of course, they can and should appropriate its configuration, adopt it, and become its bearer. There are no racial or biological obstacles to this. De Benoist emphasises the pluriverse, the multiplicity of cultures and civilisations and the dignity of every one of them. There is no hierarchy between peoples — there are neither superior nor inferior peoples, races, cultures, or economic systems. But migration, to the contrary, Alain de Benoist and his supporters perceive as negative. Of course, he is an opponent of migration, as is Dugin.

Listener: So a person with his roots is a value in and of himself?

Dugina: Yes, this is very important. This is what needs to be cultivated and developed. These roots first need to be found, discovered, and affirmed in the case of every society. De Benoist says that hierarchy, tradition, courage, and heroism are Europe's roots, but everyone has forgotten and discarded this today, while those who stand for the roots of European man are subjected to ostracism. The problem which contemporary migrants face when they come to France is that they don't see what Europeans' values are. Europeans themselves have betrayed their values and roots. Then all sorts of atrocities break out — terrorist attacks, riots, theft, clashes, and other misunderstandings. According to de Benoist, this is not a result of contact between two cultures, but a situation in which one culture (Islamic, African, albeit in a fragmentary state) clashes with something unclear, with some other "non-culture" (with what was once European culture but has denied itself).

Listener: Very well, so we beat liberalism, but the migrants are still here. Does the New Right somehow work with migrants? Let's presume that the left in Europe (anarchists, communists) try to do some kind of social work with migrants, like libraries, concerts, football matches. They show them: here is Europe, this is how people live, let's try to develop and integrate somehow. Does the New Right set any such tasks for itself?

Dugina: The left in Europe doesn't engage in integrating migrants. They are committed to multiculturalism and only facilitate the blurring of the collective identity of Europeans as well as migrants. The New Right works with the victims of migration as a globalist strategy of the European liberal elites. They help and give shelter to those who have been thrown out onto the street by the terrible totalitarian machine. For example, in France there is the Bastion Social movement that has organised a network of shelters for French people who have for one reason or another, including due to the migrant crisis, lost their homes. These aren't even the traditional clochards — today, any university teacher who has been kicked out and ruined only because his point of view disagrees with liberal dogmas can end up in this situation.

Listener: So only a Frenchman can get in?

Dugina: Anyone who is ready to call themselves French and be French can get in. A migrant who says "I've come to France from Syria, this is my fate, and I want to learn French culture" can get in, receive shelter and food. They have no strict ethnic criteria. The problem is: what culture does the left show to these migrants? If a library, then what books? A textbook on gender? Football matches — what's European about that? The problem is that the New Right is probably the only force in Europe that is capable of assimilating migrants, the only force that is capable of showing them culture. The left is simply incapable of this. The left turns them into perverts. These migrants simply become unhappy as they lose their own culture and gain nothing in turn. This is what the New Right's social work is about. There are volunteers who are busy with this, but the emphasis, of course, is on supporting indigenous French people. For example, if in Moscow you had the choice of helping an old Moscow professor who has been kicked out of his home, or a migrant who doesn't speak Russian and has no plans to, who would you choose? Everyone needs to be helped, but there would likely be more attention given to the Moscow professor, because there would be understanding of how this happened.

Listener: What about multinational or multicultural families? If someone doesn't want to choose "only here or only there", then what territory, or what people, should they be counted as in this system? Who will choose for them if the rights of multiple peoples include them?

Dugina: Belonging to the cultures of multiple peoples is, in general, a miraculous option if one is lucky enough to manage it. This would't be anything bad for de Benoist. The problem is only how would someone of two cultures not forget their sources, their origin? It'd be a catastrophe if he forgets that his father is from there, and his mother from there — then this person loses his identity. Remembering that his mother is from one place and his father is from another, receiving these two cultural traditions and acknowledging them and oneself as a person on the border of these cultures, in both directions at once — this is something very valuable. This is the identity of the frontier. To have two cultures does not mean having neither. If someone doesn't decisively choose in favour of only their father or their mother, then they'll be a happy wielder of a dual heritage.

Listener: Is it correct to say that the New Right sees allies in some migrants? Alexander Andreyevich Prokhanov recently wrote an article about how some migrants from Central Asia are not as much immigrants in relation to us as they are people returning to the homeland that left them. Could it be that migrants of this kind return to the civilisation that was taken from them (in our case, the Soviet civilisation)?

Dugina: The New Right doesn't have such a meta-understanding of migration processes. They stay within the classical interpretation that migration processes are a result of the liberal capitalist model of exploitation and egalitarianism, which needs to be got rid of.

Listener: A friend who is a writer is now writing a novel (more of the fantasy genre) about a Karelian-Murmansk People's Republic. If we go back to the thesis of Europe "from Lisbon to Vladivostok", then it turns out that he is developing this topic. If this happens, and Russia is divided up into several parts that will be separate national republics...

Dugina: Who's dividing Russia up?

Listener: Let's say Europe, if Russia were to join the EU.

Dugina: No one will divide us. And Russia isn't going anywhere. We are a civilisation unto ourselves. Moreover, there's the Eurasian Union under our leadership. In any case, for the New Right, the EU is not the Europe that they want and thirst for, but an anti-Europe, Europe's negative double. Just as there is Christ and the Antichrist, so for them is there Europe and anti-Europe. The EU is the anti-Europe. There are no traces of any full rights of peoples. There is the atomisation and dismemberment of organic societies. Moreover, liberalism and atomism are not European ideas, but something imposed from the outside. The New Right wants to reconsider this source. It is interesting that back in the 1970s they advocated creating a unified European Union, but a completely different one, founded on the rights of peoples, not what we see now, not one based on economics and individualism, which leads only to political, social, and economic crises.

Listener: Has the New Right dealt with political questions in America? If America was founded by people who weren't yet torn out of European culture, or the culture that was also traditional for the American territory up to colonisation, then how should politics in America look according to the New Right?

Dugina: When it comes to foreign policy, a positive strategy for America would, for the New Right, first and foremost be the realist vector. This is what Trump tried to proclaim and do. Trumpism is the principle of the autonomous existence of Americans in a certain isolationist mode that stops the expansion of the liberal worldview. This realism in international relations is fully consonant with paleo-conservatism, with traditional politics and the worldview of not only Republicans, but even Democrats up to a certain point in American history. When Alain de Benoist dissects American politics, he sees the main threat in American neoconservatism. The main principle of neo-conservatives, whose ideology came out of the milieux of American Trotskyists, ardent internationalists, and virulent Russophobes, lies in that the American idea of democracy and liberalism should dominate the whole world. This is not simply the choice of Americans, but the fate of all mankind, and therefore the American Empire's task is to im-pose it on a planetary scale even without taking Americans themselves into consideration. This is globalism. This thesis does not stem directly from classical American politics. It is an expression of the most nega-tive side of liberal hegemony.

De Benoist shows that the American neoconservative world-view took shape under the influence of the political philosophy of Leo Strauss, which is distinct for its cynicism and the legitimacy it recognises for outright deceit and double standards in politics. The masses are told tall tales about democracy, while power is concentrated in the hands of a narrow circle of the global liberal elite, oligarchs and monopolists, which works behind the back of peoples and states. This America under the power of the neoconservatives is not to the liking of de Benoist and the New Right. The America that the New Right likes is Trumpist-style America, but only if Trump were the one we saw ahead of the first elections which he won, not the politician squeezed between the Deep State and his own extravagant madness. If only Trump consistently followed the Trumpist path…

Listener: The inner, pragmatic *logos*?

Dugina: Yes, the pragmatic *logos* of America's roots. The philosophy of pragmatism is not at all what we might rush to conclude based on its name. It contains an interesting ontology, or more precisely a complete absence of subject-object ontology. The whole of reality consists in the moment when an indeterminate object (without any prescriptions) collides with an equally indeterminate subject. Then it either works or doesn't, and that's it. The correct pragmatist course of America is when there won't be any politics of expansion or desire to broadcast their own point of view of the American dream to other worlds, to other spaces.

Listener: The idea of Europe "from Dublin to Vladivostok" — do I understand correctly that the point is a political unity that still preserves cultural parochialism?

Dugina: Parochialism isn't the right word. The point is the plurality of cultural communities united into a whole geopolitical identity. A continentalist, tellurocratic bloc is formed that also preserves the identity of each people. In this space, the peoples of Europe say a decisive "No!" to globalism and liberal expansion; they fiercely oppose the ideology of individualism and "uprooting" (*déracinement*). The New Right has not worked out a concrete plan for how this is supposed to be implemented (whether as a political union or not). For now, it is a philosophical proclamation of principles. Looking through the geopolitical prism, this means recognising Europe's continentalist identity, Europe as the Civilisation of Land. Europe stands on the side of Rome and breaks with the thallasocratic civilisation of Carthage, that is liberalism and globalism. The New Right has not devised any kind of rigid political model (how the structure of cooperation between regions would come together, what the European Federation would be based on). The details of such a political project are also missing in Thiriart, for whom this was more of a philosophical model, a kind of thought experiment, a fore-concept (to use the expression of Carl Schmitt).

Listener: What, then, would the European community — but not the part of Asia that belongs to Russia — be based on if every people will de facto defend its own interests? For example, Catalonia or Alsace might break away. Everyone will break away. Also, if we take into consideration that Russia is a multinational state, how will the rights of peoples be defended within this framework if not everyone lives only in their own territory?

Dugina: The New Right would probably respond to you in the following way: for all the peoples located in this geographical European and Eurasian space, there is some kind of common value. This is the priority of the common over the individual. To speak in other terms, there is the priority of the community (*Gemeinschaft*) over the socius consisting of atomic individuals (*Gesellschaft*). These terms were coined by the sociologist Ferdinand Tönnies. The individual is a concept that isn't originally intrinsic to European culture or the Russian mentality. It is a product of the Anglo-Saxon Modernity that destroyed classical European culture and today claims universality (the ideology of human rights, etc.). In order to ground this commonality of different peoples, there should be some kind of meta-language, some kind of meta-links, that unify everyone. How were multiple peoples united within the single space of empire in the past? This is how it is necessary to act in the future.

Who will regulate disputes? No concrete answers will be found in de Benoist or in Thiriart. But, presumably, there are certain configurations of the Indo-European type: firstly, holism, secondly, a certain hierarchy in society, not necessarily a caste hierarchy, but a hierarchy of values. At the peak of this structure of values will be religion or philosophy, that is spiritual authority (*l'autorité spirituelle* per Guénon). The martial element will be under the governance of this spiritual group. Only then will space be set aside for the economy, for what Plato called the "lustful" element (ἐπιθυμία) associated with pleasure, goods, and comfort. The economy will be under the control of warriors and philosophers.

The New Right would also respond to this question by referring to the meta-values that unite all of these pluralities, emphasising that any kind of unified association could come about on the basis of these meta-values. Individualism, liberalism, and universalism are alien to the traditional peoples of Europe and Eurasia. This unites them beyond languages, customs, and history.

This is perhaps how they would respond. They don't have a clear-cut strategy worked out with respect to the practical technique and organisation of the future united Europe or a concrete political solution intended to constitute all of this. But this is not a minus. Whenever ideas are mastered and new elites are cultivated, applying principles to situations is not always a difficult undertaking.

A History of the Ideas of the New Right[1]

"New Right" and the *Nouvelle Droite*

DEAR FRIENDS, first of all, I sincerely thank you for coming to this lecture, which is devoted to a topic that is insufficiently studied in Russia. Moreover, there are problems with interpreting the phenomenon of the New Right in Russia. For example, you might have seen the film *The New Right in Russia*, whose initiator was Ksenia Sobchak.[2] It showed various materials, including about the Listva bookstore in Saint Petersburg, as well as figures like Svetov and his enotourage. Some feminists also showed up on film and gave their commentary. When I saw this film, I understood that there is no such notion as "New Right" in Russia, in our terminological array. We're simply not ready for it; we don't yet know it in sufficient measure.

First and foremost, I would like to say that the New Right is not simply the classical right that has arranged some kind of rebranding while remaining within one and the same classic Western paradigm of right and left, or which has merely updated its theses to suit the

---

1 A lecture at the Sun of the North (*Solntse Severa*) cultural space in Saint Petersburg in 2022.

2 Ksenia Sobchak (b. 1981) is a Russian television personality, journalist, and political figure known for her liberal views regarding democratic reforms and "human rights". She is the daughter of Anatoly Sobchak, a prominent oligarch and former mayor of Saint Petersburg.

contemporary situation. Not at all. If we turn to the notion of the "new right" in the American/English context, including the academic context, we find ourselves faced with a completely different phenomenon defined by the term "new right". This movement is associated with the American neoconservatives, Margaret Thatcher, and the new liberal order. This "new right" is utterly unrelated to the New Right that I will tell you about today. Therefore, in order to immediately demarcate notions, it bears emphasising that there is the Anglo-Saxon "new right" and there is the French, and more broadly, European *Nouvelle Droite*. When I'm talking about the New Right today, I'm sticking to the context of French political terminology as it has taken shape since 1968.

My lecture today includes a brief overview of the history of the New Right. I see that there are some people here who have attended my lectures on the New Right before. This is now the third lecture that I've given on this topic. So, I ask for forgiveness in advance, gentlemen and professors, that you'll be compelled to once again listen to this wonderful history, but I believe that this is a way for this history to be remembered and, moreover, you can then reproduce it.

We'll start with an historical introduction. I won't dwell on too much detail. Then we'll move on to the main publications and works of the New Right, and we'll conclude by examining their concepts and influences that are of interest not only because of their paradoxical and unordinary character or their representativeness of European thinking, but because they are a certain guiding star for the development of a Russian ideology, a pan-Russian ideology, including that which today is manifest most fully in Eurasianism. Given that I'm also close to this ideational current, and specifically to neo-Eurasianism, the topic of the New Right is, without a doubt, very important for me, as it has a direct relation to my own worldview. The New Right significantly influenced the formation and ideological development of Alexander Gelyevich Dugin, who in the 1980s visited Alain de Benoist in Paris, made acquaintance with him, his associates, and intellectual networks, and became a friend and frequent guest, as well as an author for the journals *Éléments*, *Krisis*, etc. An interview with him came out in *Éléments* in the early 1990s, so he began to collaborate with this cultural and ideational milieu back then.

The New Right themselves emerged — well, now I'm interested if you, dear professors, could please say what you think: in what timeframe did they emerge? I already mentioned this in passing today.

Voice from the audience: The late '60s...

Dugina: Yes, the end of the '60s, but in what year do you think?

Voice from the audience: '68, an iconic year...

Dugina: In the '60s, right, but do you think they emerged after or before '68?

Voice from the audience: Probably afterwards.

Dugina: You see, when I started studying the New Right, when I had just got to know them personally in France, I also thought that they emerged as a reaction to the events of 1968, that they were an attempt to think through an alternative to the left-liberal intellectual hegemony that established itself in May 1968, and that they were a kind of desperate attempt to save France from the New Left. But, in fact, no. The New Right took shape as a movement and tendency in late 1967 and early 1968, a few months before the events of May 1968, before the so-called "Revolution of the New Left" took place. Thus, the New Right phenomenon appeared in the very same "epoch", at the very same moment, that the New Left movement appeared. It is not, therefore, a reaction, not a response, but a parallel movement that finally took shape just before and cannot be seen as merely a reaction, as merely a direct response to the challenge of the new left-liberal forces. Yes, without a doubt, these New Left forces exteriorly positioned themselves as anti-liberal, but in fact, and in this sense we can draw on the brilliant analysis of Alain de Benoist himself, it was in May 1968 that the agenda that would become the direct expression of the left-liberal doctrine was formed. Its main features were: individualism against holism, revolting against tradition, radically protesting against all kinds of hierarchy, and a deep fusion of cultural Marxism and purely liberal theses.

The Appearance and Publications of the New Right

And so, in France in late 1967-early 1968, there appeared a group under the name GRECE, which in French is literally read as *Grèce*, that is Greece. This analogy is intentional. They took on this name in order to have a connection with the Greek *logos*. The *Groupement de recherche et d'études pour la civilisation européenne*, that is the Research and Study Group for European Civilisation, was an ensemble of intellectuals who were united by the common goal of learning, developing, assembling, and "encylcopaedicising" the foremost European intellectual achievements and, on the basis of developing this European model, on the basis of the traditions and cultures of Europe not only of earlier eras, but also their own, including the 20th century, opposing the dominant liberal version. In essence, the idea was to create an institute for the rebirth of Europe. Their main thesis is that the civilisation of Modernity (they use this term, "Modernity", in both the historical and sociological sense) is a civilisation heading towards its end, a civilisation that is obsessed with the false idea of progress, individualism, one that puts the empty, substance-less individual in the place of traditional man, who, to the contrary, was conceived as being in an inextricable bond with hierarchy and was one part of an immense world. Traditional man, the man of traditional society, is immersed in an integral totality, an ordered social structure, and is in this respect *homo hierarchicus*; on the other hand, he is inwardly free, because tradition presents him with the possibility of revealing himself. The civilisation of Modernity, the civilisation that is contemporary to the New Right, declaratively rejects this *homo hierarchicus*, instead asserting *homo aequalis*, that is a human who has been completely equalised, equated with everyone, and thereby devoid of any collective identity. This egalitarianism, this equalising, this leveling, this egalitarian liberal democracy which proclaims the ideology of human rights, while taking the human to be an abstract individual who has nothing to do with cultural earth, with where he is born — all of this is outrageous to the New Right. Accordingly, their goal is to restore European thinking in all its fullness, to reconstruct it not merely as some kind of encyclopaedic model, but to live by it, to live by these tendencies.

They founded the publication *Nouvelle École*, which translated from French means "New School". It appeared in 1968. Each yearly issue is a big, thick, A4-sized volume which dissects different themes. They have issues dedicated to various topics ranging from the Indo-Europeans, Greeks, and Germans to Jünger, Nietzsche, Schmitt, and even zoopsychology. Running ahead a bit, I'll tell you right away that GRECE and the New Right movement are distinct for their attempting to encompass the unencompassable. On the one hand, you can find them referring to diverse avant-garde philosophers of their time; on the other hand, they turn to the classics, to Plato and Aristotle. At the same time, completely incomprehensibly to others, you'll find Proudhon, seemingly an author who shouldn't at all be incorporated into right-wing doctrines, or the communist Gramsci, crossing paths with the theoreticians of the Conservative Revolution in Germany in the 1920s-'30s. The topics of their publications are so atypical and provocative that they tore the rug out from under critics and left a lasting effect.

Later, in 1979, when the intellectual community of France, permeated as it was by left-liberal tendencies, saw what was happening, they raised the alarm: as it were, some kind of cultural revolution is going full speed ahead in the country and needs to be resisted! After all, this wasn't classic right-wing discourse, nor was it classic left-wing discourse, but something completely new and revolutionary. As Alain de Benoist said in one of his foremost works from 1979, *Les Idées à l'endroit*, everyone started to react to them as soon as they understood that the New Right had simply flipped over the "table of ideas".

Accordingly, in overturning the table of ideas, all the concepts that on this table were typically "right-wing" or conventionally "left-wing" were shuffled. Thus, in overturning the table of ideas, the New Right mixed and looked into all the concepts that were out there and, metaphorically speaking, chose the best of what they saw.

Nouvelle École was their print organ, and it is very important for understanding the New Right's views on any given problem, but also for delving into European culture in general. I insistently recommend that you turn to the issues of *Nouvelle École*, the whole collection of which is available on the website of the journal *Éléments*. You can find issues on the Greeks, the Indo-Europeans, Ernst Jünger, Carl Schmitt, Konrad Lorenz, Spengler's decline of Europe — you can find everything there.

The third print organ that is important for understanding the phenomena of the New Right in its entirety is the journal *Éléments*. I have several issues with me here. This time I brought mostly issues from 1992, my birth year. In fact, on the photo on the cover here is a photograph of my mom, my father, and Alain de Benoist in Moscow in 1992 — I just noticed this, completely coincidentally. In fact, I've never seen this photograph before.

Needless to say, I know the New Right not only from journals, but from my personal experience and acquaintance with them. Of course, back in 1992, I poorly understood who they were, but now, in the very least, I'm trying to carry out a certain reconstruction of their thought. This is difficult at times, because when you grow up in a family which back in 1992 was meeting with Alain de Benoist, it's very difficult to have any distance. But for me as an adult reading de Benoist's books, my personal experience is one of completely accepting all of their theses and even being somewhat astonished. Without a doubt, this is the case. How could it be otherwise? This is to say that this is something "native" to me, so if there is anything that is organically intelligible to me by origin, but which in today's lecture isn't clear, then please, don't hesitate to ask questions. I might consider something to be self-evident, but if something isn't clear to you, then let me know and I'll try to articulate it as much as possible.

And so, among the New Right's publications there is also the journal *Études et recherches*. And here is one of the first issues of *Éléments* from 1974 — the journal itself came out in 1973. And here are some other issues. And this is the 85th issue, which is dedicated to the 18th anniversary of the founding of GRECE, that is the 18th "birthday" of the New Right. Here you can see an article surveying their activities. And here is a dossier, the young Alain de Benoist, and materials of this type that accumulated over 20 years of working to bring about a European renaissance.

And now a brief historical note: How did the New Right emerge? Who were their forerunners? Was there anyone who fundamentally influenced them? How much were they connected to other ideological or political groupings? Without a doubt, the New Right brushed shoulders with right-wing movements in one way or another. This would be the Europe-Action movement, which was founded in 1963 by Dominique Venner, the Jeune Europe movement of Jean Thiriart, which became substantially influential in the late '60s, the *Fédération des étudiants nationalistes* ("Federation of Nationalist Students") that was active mainly in the '60s until 1967, and the *Mouvement de progrès nationaliste* ("Nationalist Progress Movement"), etc. But by the time the New Right was constituted, these movements were already shrinking and the best of their representatives, the most talented and colourful, joined GRECE.

Opposite Voltaire: The Conservative Enlightenment

De Benoist himself participated in the *Fédération des étudiants nationalistes* in his youth, when he was studying at university. Alain de Benoist is the central figure of our lecture because he is the key personage that shaped the entire conceptual apparatus of the New Right.

Alain de Benoist is, in essence, the "opposite Voltaire", that is an ency-clopaedist who meticulously works through the European heritage that he has before himself, which he examines and systematises, but in the opposite direction from the enlightened encylopaedists of Modernity. He restores and brings back to the fore everything that the material-ists and progressists discarded, condemned, turned down, mocked, and marginalised. This is the grandiose project of a "Conservative Enlightenment".

Alain de Benoist's works also have a particular style. As a general rule, he frequently cites the works of other authors and offers detailed overviews of the schools and currents to which he refers. Instead of putting forth his own formulations, he often quotes authors who im-pressed him and with whom he completely agrees. In so doing, his articles and books take on a genuinely encyclopaedic character.

Take, for example, his work *Beyond Human Rights*, which has been translated and published in Russian, which you might have seen on sale or read. There you'll find constant allusions to Marcel Gauchet, references to anthropologists, to Levi-Strauss and Louis Dumont. Here, in the mode of living thinking, there is a constant, ongoing confirmation of the main theses of the great intellectuals of European culture. Accordingly, I would describe Alain de Benoist precisely as an "encylcopaedist". It seems to me that the main thing he's done is not contributing some kind of new, avant-garde theories and concepts to European culture, but rather the systematisation, ordering, and hierar-chisation of the already existing heritage, and on this basis discovering the core that is inherent to European culture but which has been lost sight of. Accordingly, the New Right was born on the principles of these great thinkers of Europe, their schools and theories.

The Great European Space

What was around in the moment when it was born? What was happen-ing in France? Without a doubt, there was a deep crisis of right-wing ideology. At that time, the right couldn't intellectually pose any alternative to the left-liberal discourse that was developing. Moreover, the right closed itself off too tightly in nationalism and thought exclusively of France — "thinking in terms of France" in the spirit that Trump "thinks in terms of America", that is in the sense of isolationism, yanking America out of context. If this is a rather good strategy for America, then for France, which is part of the European cultural space, such an artificial operation makes itself felt more negatively in culture, artificially tearing France away from Europe and its classical tradition.

Therefore, the first thing that the New Right did, following Jean Thiriart, who inspired them in many respects, was to reject the then widely accepted French nationalism and to instead advocate European nationalism. They turned to the geopolitical ideas of Carl Schmitt on "great spaces" and the "rights of peoples".[3] They developed Jean Thiriart's idea of the autarchy of great spaces. This theory was originally formulated by the German economist Friedrich List[4], who applied it to Germany and neighbouring countries of Central Europe, but Thiriart revises it and projects it onto Europe as a whole. Thiriart, himself Belgian, understood well that a small space cannot survive on its own or ensure its sovereignty. In order to wage war, in order to effectively oppose Americanisation, universalisation, and globalism — both physically and ideologically — it is necessary to form a European great space. Accordingly, the influence of Jean Thiriart is very important, and unlike the ordinary right of the time, the New Right said that it is necessary to "think Europe" or "think in terms of Europe". This distinguishes them from, and puts them at odds with, the old right. For example, who was the right at the time? There were the so-called Poujadists, followers of Pierre Poujade. Jean-Marie Le

---

3   Carl Schmitt, *Völkerrechtliche Großraumordnung mit Interventionsverbot für raumfremde Mächte. Ein Beitrag zum Reichsbegriff im Völkerrecht* (Berlin: Duncker & Humblot, 1991).

4   Friedrich List, *The National System of Political Economy*, trans. Sampson S. Lloyd (London: Longmans, Green and Co., 1909).

Pen and his National Front later grew out of this movement. Le Pen
had ties with Poujadism. There was also the right-wing movement
of monarchists and nationalists in the spirit of Charles Maurras, the
founder of Action Française. GRECE decisively broke with all of this.
As the New Right would later write about themselves, particularly
Alain de Benoist in 1979, when he formulated the first reflections on
GRECE's 11th anniversary: "We felt a complete break with the old
right, especially on the front of ideas." As he wrote in his *Les Idées à
l'endroit*, an important guidebook for analysing the New Right, "The
old right was dead."[5] The old right put itself to death, and it deserved
this in principle. Accordingly, GRECE found itself in a certain rupture
between the right, whom they didn't accept, and the left, which disagreed with them in one way or another, because, as de Benoist put it,
the left remained within the *topos* of the economy, and for them the
human being is first and foremost conditioned by economics. For the
New Right, the human being is conditioned not by economics, but by
culture and the sphere of the spirit. Therefore, the left doesn't accept
GRECE in that it puts the economy's influence on human life in second
place, or rather denies that human life is conditioned by the economic
sphere. They reject this, and so they really did end up in a certain rift.

Among the first members of the New Right, we can highlight the
foremost figure, Alain de Benoist, as well as Dominique Venner, and
a number of other figures, such as Jean-Claude Valla and Pierre Vial,
whom you might have heard of. All the rest are not so famous, their
works haven't even been translated into Russian. Under the rubric of
GRECE, in 1968, the New Right started organising annual symposiums
and conferences — "*les colloques*". In French, "*colloque*" is something
in the likes of "congress" or "symposium". In fact, we also use this
word in our language: *kollokvium* ("colloquium"). The typical topics
of these colloquiums included: "Gramscianism from the Right", "The
Cause of Peoples", "The Left", "The Right", "The End of the System",

---

5   Benoist, *Les Idées à l'endroit*, 57.

"The End of the World", "Europe", "The New World", "The US: The Danger", "Against Disneyland", etc. Accordingly, these are the points in which the New Right sees the nodal points of their intellectual life. Here's one example: the anthology of the 15th GRECE colloquium, *Le cause des peuples* ("The Cause of Peoples"), where the main speeches are published. The left-wing newspaper *Le Monde* was frightened by how the New Right "took aim at the Western-American system for erasing differences in personalities and turning everyone into robots". This critique of American hegemony and global liberalism in no way fit with the old right, who, as a general rule, defended such. No less shocking for the left was the praise for Gramscianism that could be heard at one of their other colloquiums.

In 1988, they released the special publication *Krisis*, which was aimed at left-leaning audiences and worked primarily on the left front, where key topics were examined predominantly from a left (although always anti-liberal) position. Accordingly, their publishing base was *Éléments*, *Nouvelle École*, and *Krisis*.

Now that we've covered the history and main figures, let's move on to influences. Here, everything is very interesting. These influences will probably take up the greater part of my lecture, because, as I said, the New Right are a kind of encyclopaedists. When we talk about who influenced them, we are essentially getting acquainted with their main theses and concepts.

First and foremost, the New Right was strongly influenced by the Conservative Revolutionaries — on all fronts. This includes the left-wing National Bolsheviks in the spirit of Ernst Niekisch and the right-wing Conservative Revolutionaries like Oswald Spengler, Carl Schmitt, as well as left-wing Conservative Revolutionaries like Ernst von Salomon or Harro Schulze-Boysen. This whole layer of German non-conformist culture in the 1920s-'40s entered the French context and was integrated into the New Right's structure of thought. They popularised this milieu. They really like Ernst Jünger. De Benoist himself met Jünger, was friends with his secretary, Armin Mohler, and maintained a regular correspondence with him. He was inspired by Jünger's ideas like the "forest passage", which means leaving the civilisation of Modernity, radically opposing it, and returning to the sphere of Tradition, to the sphere where the spirit is dominant over the economy.[6] His ideas on war also fascinated Alain de Benoist — above all his deep description of the very spirit of Kshatriyanism.[7] This also runs throughout the New Right like a guiding line.

Moving on, also important is the influence of Jean Thiriart, the theoretician of a united Europe from Dublin to Vladivostok.[8] This formula was first proclaimed by Jean Thiriart. Today it is often used by many, including Russian politicians. The thesis of establishing a Greater Europe from Dublin to Vladivostok (or another version: from Lisbon to Vladivostok) was Jean Thiriart's idea. He speaks of the necessity of creating a single European space, the integration of the European continent, which includes European countries as well as Russia. Thiriart's conclusion is that the geopolitical identity of this bloc is that of Land, tellurocracy. It is anti-globalism and anti-universalism, the antithesis to Anglo-Saxon, Atlanticist geopolitics. This region of Great Europe, this pole, should become the platform for the rebirth of Tradition, a coup against egalitarianism and universalism, the restoration of the traditions that have been lost.

It follows that when the New Right looks at the phenomenon of Europe and speaks of the need for a rebirth of European civilisation, they are in many respects following Thiriart. It is important that they

---

6   Ernst Jünger, *The Forest Passage*, trans. Thomas Friese (Candor: Telos Press Publishing, 2013).

7   Ernst Jünger, *Storm of Steel*, trans. Michael Hofmann (New York: Penguin Books, 2016). The Kshatriya is a member of the warrior and ruler caste in traditional Hindu society, responsible for protecting and governing, embodying values of courage, strength, and honour.

8   Yannick Sauveur, *Jean Thiriart et le national Communautarisme européen. mémoire présenté devant l'Institut d'études politiques de l'Université de Paris* (Charleroi: Editions Machiavel, 1983).

also include Russia in this vision as one important part of the European space.

The New Right Isn't "Right"

Another point on the history of the New Right: What's going on with the very term "New Right"? The point is that the New Right rejects this name and formulation, because they believe that they break with the right just as they break with the left. What do you think — shall we delve deeper into this?

This formulation appeared only in 1979. That is, the New Right had already existed for 11 years, but only in 1979, as de Benoist writes, did the New Right become phenomenon number one in the press.[9] Why did this happen? By that moment, the New Right had already "infiltrated" nearly all of the intellectual movements in France. Both left and right were more frequently referring to them — because they completely shattered the ideological map that divided everyone into right and left. They attracted biologists, psychoanalysts, zoopsychologists, philosophers, anthropologists, sociologists, historians, linguists, scholars of religion, archaeologists, etc. The movement's diversification of topics and approaches, as well as their rising and growing influence on the intellectual and, indirectly, political processes in France undoubtedly started to frighten the entirety of conformist, liberal society and drew envy from the steadily marginalised old right. The left-wing *Libération* wrote in panic that the left was losing and behind in the war of ideas. Bernard-Henri Lévy and Laurent Fabius together declared that it would be better to never raise the topic of the New Right, better to keep the silence over them. This strategy of silence subsequently turned out to be maximally effective. It was applied by left liberals and, in fact, the liberal establishment continues to act in the same way towards the New Right to this day. They're simply silenced. They're nowhere to be found on the main TV channels. If they have their own

---

9   Benoist, *Les Idées à l'endroit*, 11.

platform, then it's alternative media in the spirit of TV Libertés, Radio Courtoisie, etc. This course proposed by Bernard-Henri Lévy back in 1979 is still being replicated today. The New Right de facto has no fully fledged opportunity to express itself in media to the degree that Bernard-Henri Lévy, who never leaves French TV, or Laurent Fabius do.

At this first stage, however, the foreign press outside of France constantly ran analyses of the New Right's ideas, albeit casting them in a negative light and demonising them. The media space of the West, including the US, saw sensational statements to the tune that the New Right had accomplished a coup d'état, an intellectual revolution.

So, the term "New Right" appeared in 1979, yet Alain de Benoist still utterly rejects it and points out that it is inaccurate because the "New Right" is beyond right and left. Whenever he speaks of himself and his own identity, he says: "I'm an historian of ideas, not a new rightist." Instead of "New Right", they prefer the term "Gramscianists from the right" or some other formulations, such as "people engaged in metapolitics", "independent intellectuals", "scholars and defenders of European culture". For them, "New Right" is an extraneous label. To this day, it still harbours the very same semantic traces of the persecution that was unleashed against them in 1979.

It is an interesting point that the New Right came to be criticised from different fronts. The old right said they "betrayed France" for advocating some kind of singular European space, as if they discounted a strictly French mission. Moreover, there also appeared conspiracy theories that the New Right was possibly linked to some Israeli groups and that the New Right was a special strategy for destroying and destabilising right-wing movements in France. The left said that they were a "brown plague", in line with which there appeared conspiracy theories that they were a special operation by the French intelligence services.

In principle, at least on the basis of my own analysis, not a single one of these definitions is correct or has any grounds to it. They are neither one nor the other. It is impossible to reduce them to being right, left, or some kind of mythical project by one or another intelligence service. Any given intelligence services are much lower in intellectual level than the New Right and by definition aren't capable of having originally generated such a formidable, profound, and at the same time paradoxical and avant-garde movement.

The New Right themselves proclaimed that they broke all ties and burned all bridges with the right-wing movements that existed earlier, including those with a neo-Gaullist agenda. In 1972, they rather harshly opposed the National Front. Recently, however, during the French presidential campaigns, when Marine Le Pen opposed the liberal globalist Macron, the New Right nevertheless came a bit towards Le Pen as she started the process of moving her party towards the left. Classic right-wing politics originally predominated in the party, but through the line of Florian Philippot[10] (who, it's true, was later excluded from the party) they began to move in the direction of left-wing economics. Hence, much of the French working class voted for the National Front. Then, after losing the elections, Marine Le Pen cancelled this tendency and, accordingly, the New Right partially withdrew their support. In some cases they also support the Republicans, for instance.

In general, their position is reflected in Alain de Benoist's formulation: there must be something else, some alternative between the "fascist ghetto" and "liberal swamp". That is, the New Right advocates creating an alternative.

I'd like to once again emphasise the importance of distinguishing the New Right from the old right. The old right stood for nationalism, chauvinism, territorial sovereignty, and against migrants. The New Right says that this needs to be abandoned in favour of turning Europe

---

10 Florian Philippot (b. 1981) is a French politician known for his Eurosceptic views, initially rising to prominence as a key strategist for Marine Le Pen's National Front, where he influenced the party's shift towards economic protectionism and opposition to the European Union. He later founded The Patriots party, promoting a "Frexit", or exit from the EU, and championing policies focused on economic independence and resistance to globalist influence.

into an anti-globalist, anti-liberal pole, a kind of empire that is allied
with Russia and hostile to the US and Britain. The old right stands for
liberalism. The New Right is categorically against liberalism and stands
for radical anti-liberalism. The old right proposes political action and
talks about the obligatory necessity of showing oneself in politics. The
New Right insists on metapolitics, on the intellectual sphere. They
believe that political work is insufficient because as soon as we're
swallowed up by party and electoral vicissitudes we cease to devote
attention to culture, and culture and ideology are the superstructure
through which the main changes in society are carried out. The New
Right insists that political processes are influenced by metapolitical
processes, by culture, and therefore a political revolution cannot possibly be carried out without first making changes and renewals in the
cultural layer. The old right had a very strong, sharp anti-left tendency,
whereas the New Right was overall friendly towards the left. *Krisis*, as
I've already mentioned, was aimed at reconciliation with the left.

Splits in the Movement: The Club de l'Horloge

This sharp rejection of liberalism and frontal opposition to the left
brought a certain imbalance into the New Right movement already
at its first stage. In 1974, the Club de l'Horloge movement, founded
by Jean-Yves Le Gallou, Henry de Lesquen, and Yvan Blot, broke
away from GRECE. These three came out of the GRECE movement
and proceeded to develop a doctrine similar to the system of the New
Right, only in the context of national liberalism. They were softer on
liberals and harsher on the left. In many ways, they were oriented
towards Hayek's neoliberalism, albeit interpreted in a peculiar way.
Some of them, first and foremost Yvan Blot, followed Heidegger just
like Alain de Benoist. The Club de l'Horloge started to head out for
the political domain. Yvan Blot, for instance, was for some time an
advisor to President Nicolas Sarkozy. So, there were also splits within
and among the New Right.

The Club de l'Horloge also split with GRECE over the religious factor, as they tried to draw on Catholicism to a greater extent, to identify European identity with Catholicism, whereas GRECE held on to pagan positions, defending pagan culture and sharply critiquing Catholicism as a religion that was the stimulus and cause for the emergence of European individualism. For the New Right, Catholicism and Christianity represent a serious problem. This problem, according to the New Right, is that Christianity establishes an autonomous axis for man's communication with God, which thereby cuts man out of his community. This religious component is the most difficult point in the New Right's doctrine for myself, because GRECE based its judgments on the works of Weber and Sombart, where the discourse is about deconstructing specifically Western Christianity, while de Benoist does not analyse Eastern Christianity. The point is that if de Benoist had some kind of immersion and life experience in Russia, any experience of acquaintance with Orthodoxy, then it is possible he would be inspired by how elements of ancient Slavic tradition have been synthesised with Christianity within Orthodoxy. Perhaps he would adopt Orthodoxy as a possible variant of religious identity. I can tell you that there are Orthodox priests in the GRECE movement, and one of them, Christophe Levallois, a priest who served in the Church of Seraphim of Sarov in Paris, not far from Gare Montparnasse, was a member of GRECE from, if I recall, 1970 or 1972. That is, there are cases of Orthodox Christians participating in GRECE that are documented and confirmed. Therefore, I'll leave aside the question of the opposition between Christianity and paganism. I won't cover it today and, in principle, I think that whenever we talk about this topic, it is necessary to understand that the New Right is talking above all about Western Christianity. Drawing any unambiguous conclusion to the effect that de Benoist is unacceptable to us as a person because he is a pagan simply isn't an argument and shouldn't exist. Such an argument would be out of context, anachronistic, and doesn't have even a bit to do with analysing de Benoist's thought and the intellectual space in which he works.

Critiquing Liberalism with Louis Dumont's Sociology

We were talking about influences. We mentioned Jean Thiriart and the Conservative Revolution (its partial influence). Among the important figures who influenced Alain de Benoist and the formation of the GRECE movement, it bears highlighting the philosopher and anthropologist Louis Dumont, the author of the works *Homo Hierarchicus*, *Homo Aequalis*, and *Essay on Individualism*. "Hierarchical man" and "equal man" (man outside of hierarchy) are the two basic social types of human. In *Homo Hierarchicus*, Dumont formulates a thesis that was of the greatest importance in shaping the doctrine of the New Right. In India and in the East, there exists a certain hierarchical model of society in which man, on the one hand, has a strictly fixed social place in the caste system and, as it were, is not free insofar as he is within a closed, sealed structure; on the other hand, he wields an inner freedom, because the tradition in which he finds himself liberates him. Despite the fact that he is locked within a social framework, he is nevertheless spiritually free, because he always retains the possibility of leaving this space spiritually or even physically. In analysing the periods of human life in Indian culture (*ashrama*s), Dumont encounters what lies beyond the periods of social integration into the caste hierarchical system: the phase of the disciple (*brahmacharya*) and the phase of the householder (*grihastha*) — these are phases of moving away from society, of liberation. Once the householder raises children who are able to take care of themselves, he can enter the third phase of being a renunciate, a hermit (*vanaprastha*), who goes off on his own or with his wife into the forest. Finally, he can even renounce his simple hut in the forest and leave his wife to become a wandering ascetic (*sannyasa*) who has nothing in common with and is independent of society. Dumont shows that this forest dwelling, this forest passage, the third stage of human life, presents man with freedom, the culmination of which is the status of being a *sannyasi*. Thus, the strict hierarchy in Indian society does not contradict the full freedom of one's personhood in its self-concentration, but harmoniously synthesises with it on different, non-intersecting levels or orbits.

Homo aequalis as analysed by Dumont is the man of modern Western civilisation. European man of the era of Modernity is free on the outside in that he is not placed within a clear-cut caste structure of subordination, but he is absolutely unfree on the inside. For de Benoist, it is this type of person whose rights are what liberalism upholds and defends. "Human rights", for de Benoist, are an error, because "human rights" are for an "equivalent" person, one who is a slave on the inside while free on the outside. Against "human rights", Alain de Benoist puts forth the theory of the "rights of peoples". This is a much more complex notion. To use Louis Dumont's formulation, we can speak of the "rights of *homo hierarchicus*". "Hierarchical human rights" would also be correct.

Louis Dumont also says that the economy of Tradition presupposed a society in solidarity. Sure, inequality, subordination, and a system of hierarchical relations (lord, vassal, peasant) existed in such a model, but there was also the cohesion and coherence of all layers of society. Only in Modernity did a different system take shape, one dominated by alienation. In this alienation, man breaks his ties and destroys his cohesion. Henceforth, everyone understands that they need to work more in order to earn more money — they become detached from their community. A rift in the cohesion takes place, and this rift in the cohesion of society precipitates the process of individual material accumulation and the destruction of hierarchy. Excessive products, the so-called "accursed share" (Georges Bataille[11]), are not eliminated, and this "accursed share" (*likhva* in Russian) has grown exponentially since

11   George Bataille, *The Accursed Share*, 3 vols., trans. Robert Hurley (New York: Zone Books, 1988–1993).

the Middle Ages. This accumulation reaches the point of oversupply and leads to collapse. This collapse spills over to man himself who, in Tradition outwardly unfree but held together by community, becomes innerly unfree. This is the new "religion," the "religion" of egalitarianism, the "religion" of the individual. Man, as it were, can freely move around, have a certain freedom of opinion, and can change his material situation, but at the price of a complete rift with surrounding people, de-socialisation, atomisation, and ultimately, de-humanisation.

For Dumont, the transition from *homo hierarchicus* to *homo aequalis* marked the shift from the society of Tradition, from the society of the European Middle Ages, to Modernity. In Dumont, Modernity is perceived as negative. What is its goal, what is its project? Dumont (unlike the Traditionalists) is more engaged in describing a certain model rather than proclaiming imperatives or sturdy principles. He has no declaration or theses in the likes of a call for a New Middle Ages or the revival of *homo hierarchicus*. But the New Right, drawing on Dumont's works and analysing his views, proposes such a project: to restore *homo hierarchicus* and destroy *homo aequalis* as the very concept that destroys the essence of man by depriving him of what is most imoprtant, his inner freedom. This influence is very important for Alain de Benoist, and he regularly cites Louis Dumont. This is one of the main lines of influences under which the New Right's critique of liberalism took shape.

The New Right was also greatly influenced by geopolitics. When we spoke of Thiriart, I mentioned how the European space is identified with Land. This is a direct reference to geopolitics. Alain de Benoist has deeply studied the works of Carl Schmitt. His generalised analysis has been published in the book *Carl Schmitt Today*.[12] He is in solidarity with Schmitt's position that all types of wars can be divided into "war of forms" and "total war". Schmitt supposed that modern civilisation, which exteriorly rejects war in general, denies war the right to have

---

12   Alain de Benoist, *Carl Schmitt Today: Terrorism, 'Just' War, and the State of Emergency*, trans. Alexander Jacob (London: Arktos, 2013).

any legitimate forms, and therefore in fact leads to total war. The more liberal democracy stubbornly insists on world peace, the more it leads to the colossal, bloody way. Developing Schmitt's ideas, de Benoist says that terrorism is an important testimony as to how war has become total.

I'll remind you of Carl Schmitt's distinction between the types of wars. War of forms is war waged according to certain rules, in certain borders, with certain codes. It has a beginning and an end. Total war is war that appears when the legitimacy of war is completely denied. Politicians claim "that's it, there are no more wars" — and then whoever starts a war is not even an enemy but a criminal, a non-human, a monster, and that means that he deserves not merely defeat but utter annihilation. Such wars have no end, they continue even after victory — after all, the vanquished is not a human but a criminal who needs to be disciplined and reeducated.

Total war encompasses everything. This is the war waged by modern liberal civilisation when, on the one hand, they proclaim the necessity of establishing peace across the world, all the while as the American politicians (especially Democrats) declaring such stoke an immense number of wars in the Middle East, and not only there. This state of total war is characterised by the presence of terroristic components. An act of terror is what appears when there is no distinguished contour of enemy and friend, when everything is turned into the enemy. This phenomenon of change in scale testifies to the onset of total war. Jean Baudrillard also wrote about this phenomenon when he discussed the events of 9/11, which he described as a change in the scale of war and the arrival of a new paradigm.[13]

From Schmitt, de Benoist borrows the idea that there needs to exist the distinction of friend/enemy in politics and geopolitics. The figure of the enemy is a necessary category for defining the contours of a friend. The primordial map of geopolitics is built on positioning

---

13   Jean Baudrillard, *The Spirit of Terrorism and Other Essays*, trans. Chris Turner (London: Verso, 2012).

who is a friend and who is an enemy. Only afterwards can any further strategy be constructed. The European space, according to Schmitt, should be the space of Land, the civilisation of Land. De Benoist uses the traditional formulation "tellurocracy". Alain de Benoist's adoption of the view that Europe is the civilisation of Land explains, among other things, his orientation towards the East and his readiness for close cooperation with Russia.

Furthermore, Alain de Benoist's works pay much attention to the Third World. He even has a work entitled *Europe, Third World, One Struggle*. For the right, such an identification of Europe as a space in solidarity with the Third World is inconceivable. But for the New Right, to the contrary, this is the case because Europe, like the Third World, has been subjected to colonisation by the US and global liberal elites. Under the influence of Modernity and its materialist, progressivist dominance, Europeans have been deprived of the possibility to profess their own identity. Just like the people of Third World countries, they are downtrodden and oppressed. Hence the impossibility of any solidarity with the Atlanticist West, with the civilisation of Sea, with liberal, universalist hegemony. Therefore, Alain de Benoist takes up the position of solidarity with the countries of the Third World.

At the very outset I said that the "new right", such as the one in Russia described in Sobchak's film, has nothing to do with the real New Right. The film presents them as staunch anti-communists and anti-Soviet. But de Benoist himself would never agree with those whom the film calls "right" by virtue of their rejection of everything Soviet. De Benoist, to the contrary, has an interesting thought: the Soviet officer's cap is much closer to him than the American beret. He said back in the '80s: "I'd sooner put on a Soviet helmet than an American beret." This was a scandal for the European right of the time, who were very anti-communist. Therefore, those "new rightists" in Russia who have a pronounced anti-left position cannot be called "new right" in the sense of the New Right in the context of France and Europe. The people shown in the film could be called the "updated right". Sure, they might have some interesting ideas; they might be intellectuals who have a number of curious concepts and ideas. I even have good relations, am friends with, and talk with some of them, but they are not the New Right at all.

Also among those who had a big influence on Alain de Benoist and GRECE were figures like the anthropologist Arnold Gehlen and the zoologist Adolf Portmann. Arnold Gehlen believed that man is initially an "empty essence" (*Mangelwesen*), not filled with anything. Man gains all of his substance from culture, from society. Portmann, in turn, says that man is the only living creature that is born prematurely.[14] The gestation period of animals is proportional to the volume of their brain. Man's brain requires a longer period for maturation — it should spend 16–18 months in its mother's womb. When a human infant is born, it can't cope with what is unloaded on it. The only form for resolving this conflict, this inner tension, is culture. A newborn lands in a socio-cultural matrix where it goes through additional stages of gestation in order to be prepared for life. This has come to be called the theory of neoteny. Both Gehlen and Portmann explain the necessity of culture as the life environment of man on physical bases rather than metaphysical foundations. Culture is the possibility of the biological resolution of the human overload. This is a very interesting topic, and the New Right has many similar concepts. Biology, life, and its laws are of great interest to them.

For example, they in many ways follow Konrad Lorenz's concept that animals have social norms and that their behaviour is arranged in accordance with the principle of the behaviour of society. Portmann shares this idea.[15] If we talk about "animals" in the demeaning sense, then we are wrong. Animals also have collectives, societies, laws, norms, rules of the game, etc. Accordingly, the New Right has many different intersections which are extremely interesting to me and which I'm working through — anthropology, sociology, zoology, philosophy of

---

14   Adolf Portmann, *Biologie und Geist* (Zurich: Rhein-Verlag AG, 1956).

15   Adolf Portmann, *Animals as Social Beings*, trans. Oliver Coburn (New York: Viking Press, 1961).

life, ecology. Moreover, we find that they have a developed critique of capitalism and cities. Lorenz believed that cities destroy man, because they deprive him of the possibility of finding an ecosystem in space. The city tears man out of his own life context and wreaks destruction.

Voice from the audience: A city starts from how many thousand people?

Dugina: Well, Konrad Lorenz doesn't clarify this, but I think that he is talking about large cities with a population of several hundred thousand. He's mostly going after megalopolises.

Voice from the audience: A megalopolis can have a million or a hundred thousand — those are different cities.

Dugina: Well, sure, but in any case, what happens in cities is a loss of connection with earth. Man begins to be killed, to degrade, to be remoulded and transformed into a new entity: a pure consumer, a person torn from the living environment, who finds himself in a constant psychosis in many ways because he has no interaction with nature. In general, this is very clear to everyone who lives in cities and only rarely leaves for the countryside.

I myself, for example, was recently in the monastery at Safronieva pustyn', and after this trip to the monastery I was horrified by the city, by its scale. I need to say that I still haven't come around since. When a person lives through the cycles of nature and his own inner cycles align with it (Lorenz writes about this, and so does Guénon, another influence on the New right), then the exterior comes into harmony with the inner. The human life cycle is reflected in nature. This is very important. The New Right critiques this rift.

Gramscianism from the Right

Another important topic which Nikolai advised me to touch on today and which, if I'll finish writing in time, will be part of the Sun of the North's forthcoming almanac on counter-hegemony, is "Gramscianism from the right."[16] This is an extremely interesting topic.

---

16 Nikolai Arutyunov, the ideological inspiration of the Sun of the North intellectual club in Saint Petersburg and a friend of Daria's. The article in question,

It is for this "Gramscianism form the right" that the old right extremely dislike Alain de Benoist and all of his supporters, because they think that it is completely incorrect to equip oneself with a theory developed by a staunch communist.

If we look at things from Gramsci's point of view, then the old right to a certain extent turn out to be "Caesarists".[17] They proclaim the need to wage war in politics, but they reject the necessity of waging war in the sphere of culture. For the New Right, the foremost territory where revolutionary work should be conducted is the space of culture. Therefore, the term "Gramscianism from the right" becomes a key topic for them. De Benoist critiques the ideological and cultural hegemony of liberalism and declares the need to create an alternative doctrine. Here's what the New Right writes about Gramscianism from the right: "For us, being Gramscianists means acknowledging the importance of theory and the power of culture; the point is not to prepare power for one or another political party, but to transform the mentality so as to uphold a new system of values within which the political plane doesn't interest us."[18] This is what Prof. Michel Wayoff said at the opening of the colloquium on "Gramscianism from the right". What does Alain de Benoist himself have to say about this? He remarks that "political processes are now changing, but the ideological majority remains unchanged, and it is necessary to work on the front of ideas. Now we can speak more about consent than contradiction between the political, ideological, and sociological majority. This consent is the basic state of affairs."[19]

"The Phenomenon of 'Gramscianism from the Right': The Experience of the New Right", was published two months after Dugina's death and is reprinted below.

17 Antonio Gramsci, *Prison Notebooks*, vol. 1, trans. Joseph A. Buttigieg and Antonio Callari (New York: Columbia University Press, 1992).

18 *Pour un gramscisme de droite. Acte du XVIe colloque national du GRECE* (Paris: Le Labyrinthe, 1982), 7.

19 Ibid., 11.

Any consensus with capitalism, any recognition of the status quo, is an error. De Benoist argues that it is necessary to carry out a radical coup against the liberal system, against the status quo, and pass into the phase of working out an alternative agenda; that is counter-hegemony. He says: "We are at the point of midnight, we are at the prime meridian of active nihilism... Taking part in our undertaking does not mean choosing one clan against another. It means getting off the trolleybus that only runs between the two poles of one ideology, with or without stops."[20] This is to say that de Benoist argues that we need to change the universe of the ecumene, to re-impart the world with all of its colours, to restore the world's complexity. This complexity is the way out of the liberal universalist system of thinking.

For de Benoist, it is important to expose liberalism not only as a political phenomenon, but as a code, a cultural code, and to crush it, get rid of it, decode it, and create an alternative to it. He is not content with half-baked Caesarism; he is not satisfied with a system that is passively in solidarity with this hegemony and only opposes it on particular issues. The system tries to pretend that hegemony is a political action, while the cultural space is only an epiphenomenon. For the New Right, all of this is wrong. The New Right says that it is necessary to act from the standpoint of culture, to fight above all for the domain of ideas. Politics is only the leftovers, the crumbs of what we can achieve by acting effectively in the realm of metapolitics. Therefore, Gramscianism from the right and its synonym, "metapolitics", are the key and most important factor for the New Right. They perceive capitalism as a code. Capitalism is a kind of malaria, a viral infection, an epidemic. It is not first and foremost the economy and politics, but ideology and the dominant culture. It is this culture that needs to be fought above all. Here's what one figure of the New Right, Guillaume Faye, writes — I found this interesting quote on Gramscianism from the right in his speech at the GRECE colloquium: "Isolated intellectuals

20 Ibid., 21.

who are neutral and don't fight have never left their seal on history. GRECE by no means intends to give up ideology to the sciences, to liberals, to conservatives, or to the left."[21]

Look, there are immediately several interesting theses here. It turns out that there needs to be a Fourth Political Theory — yet not even a political one, but a fourth metapolitical theory. The New Right wants to bring the force of different ideas into society. Guillaume Faye continues:

> Effecting Gramscianism from the right means spreading a system of values that will work in the long term, that will bear competitive formulas and, in being carried out through a metapolitical strategy, will be positioned outside of the political institutions. GRECE is spreading a view of the world that can be expressed through actions in the sphere of culture or on the strictly intellectual plane by means of constructing a theoretical corpus, one that is never finished but always developing. Such a corpus presupposes incorporating numerous disciplines, from biology to philosophy.[22]

Guillaume Faye also says that the ideological corpus of GRECE, unlike all other intellectual movements, is radically open. This radical openness is what is amazing about GRECE. The authors they study can be put into incredible combinations to form any kind of hybrids. Indeed, Proudhon makes for a strange neighbour with Lorenz, and Gehlen is perhaps incompatible with Weber, Guénon, and Portmann — all of them are thinkers of a different order, of different levels. GRECE retains this radical openness. Accordingly, the movement always remains radically open and is in constant evolution. Overall, Gramscianism from the right is a phenomenon that deserves even more attention than what we've said about it.

Now I'd like to offer several porous definitions of who the allies of European identity are, and that means the allies of GRECE. These allies are:

---

21   Ibid., 72.

22   Ibid.

- The European ethnoi that preserve their cultures;

- The regions that continue folk traditions;

- Science and culture positing a metaphysical goal;

- On the geopolitical plane, Russia and the countries of the Third World that find themselves under colonial oppression from which they want liberation (by "colonial oppression" I mean above all the influence of liberal ideology and the deep penetration of Western culture).

Now, what are the goals of the New Right? They are:

- Establishing a multipolar world;

- Building a continentalist bloc of Europe from Dublin to Vladivostok, to use Thiriart's formula;

- Constructing a social economy;

- Ecological consciousness;

- Working out a new political model — or not even a political model but, I would say, an alternative to political models, i.e., an alternative theory to liberalism, fascism, and communism.

For de Benoist, what is important is that two ideologies (fascism and communism) have died, while the third (liberalism) has not died, but has been transformed, has passed into the sphere of culture, which means that it has claimed victory by means of infiltrating the super-structure. This is fundamental for him, and this is what he wants to oppose. Therefore, his works are constantly dedicated to critiquing liberalism. He also has works devoted to critiquing National Socialism as well as Marxism (though not as many, because he generally likes Marx). Those dedicated to critiquing liberalism number around 70% of his works.

Finally, I would like to say something about ecology. I really like this topic. In general, the New Right says that it is necessary to work in the sphere of deep ecology. The principles of deep ecology were formulated in the '70s in Norway by Arne Næss.[23] It posits that the ecologist should see man not as the centre of the cosmos, but as part of nature. Nature is a subject, not an object of exploitation. Since life, its energies, and its becoming are a primal value for the New Right, they also interpret culture, following Nietzsche, to be the highest tension of life forces. On this count, the New Right once again diverges from the old right, who more often than not are wholly skeptical towards ecology.

In any case, the phenomenon of the New Right is extraordinarily interesting and deserves close, constant attention.

Now let's move on to questions.

Questions and Answers

Question: In the West, as soon as people with alternative views to liberals, let's say, people on the right and their ideas, cross the border of pure theory into real political action — as soon as they become a real subject, they're completely crushed. They'll let the "folk news" genre pass, like talk shows or reenactment movements, but as soon as the right goes out into the streets and engages in real political acts, as happened with the torchlight march in the US in that one city...

Dugina: Charlottesville...

Question: Yes, they'll label you, destroy you, and the movement will be completely slandered and repressed. Doesn't it seem to be the case that this is a general Western trend? Or more broadly, a European-Western, or European-Atlanticist trend — to not let right-wing forces form a political movement?

Dugina: But the New Right is not right-wing. The New Right is in a certain sense anti-right.

---

23 Arne Næss, *Ecology, Community and Lifestyle: Outline of an Ecosophy*, trans. David Rothenberg (Cambridge: Cambridge University Press, 1989).

Question: Well, roughly speaking, in general…

Dugina: Yes, yes, wherever even a spark of a threat is posed to the liberal dictatorship, to liberal hegemony, the aggression of the system always manifests itself. Moreover, this aggression is even stronger towards the New Right. If the right in its manifest political movements — marches, torches, and even Trumpists or QAnon — is subject to persecution for politics, then the New Right is subject to persecution for its views, for its ideas. Hegemony's method of repression differs in this case: it is the method of hushing up, of keeping silent. I said that in 1979 Bernard-Henry Lévy argued that "the best way to talk about the New Right is to be silent about them". This is the worst form of repression…

Question: …I was just thinking about the question, and I don't think I can name any organised left force in the West. Even when young democrats are up and coming in the US, they are vigorously rolled back, as we are seeing now. The old party nomenclature takes power into its own hands. Even in the US. Does it not seem to you that there is a worldwide trend towards de-politicisation, the de-subjectisation of people as political actors? It's as if we're all supposed to be their fields from the matrix, that we won't ever see real power, and any political movement will be destroyed, whether left or right — it's just that it's easier to manage people by means of the left. How can we interpret this?

Dugina: This is the presence of the new hegemony. Contemporary liberal hegemony, liberalism in general, claims that it has left politics behind, that it has passed into an apolitical sphere, one which is in fact a form of cultural hegemony, domination, and inculcation of the very same liberal values. This is a very interesting and important question. It is tragic because I also can't think of any vivd left movements to mention. Every left movement has some kind of breakdown. Every right movement, in fact, does as well. Everything is bad! We need to turn on our eschatological optimism.[24]

Question: I wanted to thank you for the lecture. My question is connected to the previous questions: what kind of political influence does the New Right have? What is its strength? What is the mass scale of this phenomenon? You say that the priority for the human being is not the economy, but the sphere of culture and spirit. What ideology can be mass in scale? For example, I honestly don't know what influence the Traditionalists — Guénon and Evola — had on the New Right. Guénon had a fairly depressive view of things when it comes to politics. He believed that politics in the West and the modern world is no longer worth anything, that man should concentrate on himself and that's it. The same is the case with Jünger and his *Waldgang*, the forest passage. It seems to me that these thinkers clearly understood that the mass appeal of ideas is not their fate. I see a big problem with this and would like for you to comment on it.

Dugina: There is such a problem. It is a colossal problem, of course. The New Right advocates restoring the old hierarchy in which philosophy stood above the Kshatriyas and above the economy. For the New Right, this naturally means that the philosophical foundations will not be a mass domain, but rather the undertaking of the intellectual elite. The New Right believes that the right structure of the world is one in which the ideas of the world structure are dominant and rule at the top. This is like in Plato's *Republic*. There are few philosophers. There is a small community of Guardians. There are more of the Guardians' auxiliaries, that is warriors, and there are very many craftsmen (δημιουργός). The masses of society are the third, lower estate. This is a strict hierarchy, and the philosophers ensure justice for the whole state. This is the case despite the fact that their ideas are intelligible (and not even only their ideas, but ideas as such), even recognised, or able to be envisioned only by a small part of the

---

24 Daria Platonova Dugina, *Eschatological Optimism*, trans. Jafe Arnold, ed. John Stachelski (PRAV Publishing, 2023).

population of this ideal state. I think that, according to the New Right, it is this type of state — the Platonic — that should be restored. Now about the manifestation of Traditionalism: yes, they were influenced by Julius Evola and René Guénon. René Guénon influenced them with his reorientation of the West towards sacred Tradition, his critique of progress and the reign of quantity. Julius Evola influenced them above all on the question of the metaphysics of war and the metaphysics of order. Evola has a remarkable account of distinguishing the types of heroism in accordance with castes. De Benoist also mentions this, and he says that it is necessary to head towards the heroism of the higher type, when one engages in self-sacrifice for the sake of higher ideas instead of fame. To what extent can these ideas remain unknown to the masses, and should they even be mass in character? If they become mass in character, then they are distorted. In general, this is a very difficult and complex question.

Question: Greetings, I'm someone who is somewhat far away from all of this, but it was really interesting to come and listen to people who are more intelligent than myself...

Dugina: Are you sure about this? I have doubts...

Question: Over the course of the lecture, you repeatedly mentioned the creation of a Europe that will represent a different pole of power. What interests me is: how will the subject of this idea be brought together? After all, now, just like in the previous historical period, different parts of Europe, as well as parts of Asia, if we include Russia, have different historical memories, different cultural foundations, different religious foundations. If one nation were ever to become the bedrock for consolidating the smaller, different tribal elements, then how would this integration be accounted for? Is this not just another step towards globalism, only a somewhat different kind?

Dugina: You know, this is a difficult and complex question, because even in France there are many regional specificities, and although France itself is not exactly an artificial formation, it does have its contrasts between languages, which can even be seen in the modern

French language, where the name for an item in the south is one thing and in the north something completely different. There are even separatist tendencies in France, not only in Spain.

I'll respond to the question: on what principles will the unification of Europe come about? The first principle is the principle of hierarchy, that is the hierarchisation of the elements of life: the philosophical element, the intellect, which is the charioteer in Plato's triad of the soul; the inspirited (warrior) element; and the lustful (material) element, that is everything bound up with the economy, goods, the body, pleasure. In European historical memory, this hierarchy is something common, not individual to each nation. This is what needs to be appealed to. The man of the new Europe won't be an individual and won't be some kind of specific species of the abstract human, but will be a human being who has his own tradition.

Secondly, you correctly noted that there are many traditions and that disputes might arise. De Benoist would respond that the whole value lies in these disputes, in these differences, because there is a European pluriverse, not a European universe. He uses this notion when he describes the world. He says that the world should be arranged in accordance with the principle of the pluriverse, and it is in this diversity, in this plurality, in becoming a unity, that an empire will take shape. This will also be the constitutive principle for the incorporation of numerous traditions into the European space. They will not be denied in their multiplicity, and they won't be replaced by one or another tradition. De Benoist says that it would be incorrect if we were to say that there is only one tradition, for example the French tradition, or if we attempted to extrapolate it onto other countries. No, to the contrary, every region should retain its identity — not only countries, but regions. What is needed is a revival of the classical, pan-European tradition alongside preserving the entirety of local uniquenesses. In my last lecture, I said that GRECE has a centre near Marseille, *Domus*,[25]

---

25   Latin for "house" or "home".

where every room has the flag of a different region of France. One time you'll stay in Brittany, then in Occitania, then in Aquitaine, then somewhere else. This is an attentive and sensitive attitude towards the plurality of France's different regions. This manifests the principle of the pluriverse unified into an empire, which means that multiplicity is also very important. Every region of Europe and France (and equally Germany, Spain, Italy, etc.) should uphold and develop its own culture. This is necessary.

The third constitutive factor of Europe and the European Empire will be rejecting the primacy of the economy in human life and prioritising the spiritual over the economic. This should be the code for the construction of a new Europe, and for de Benoist this is the tradition of classical European culture.

It's always been difficult for me to answer how the fulfilment of these points would be possible in practice, because Europe is now disjointed, split into different camps and flanks. Even people who profess non-conformist ideas against liberal hegemony are on different sides of the barricades, like Mélenchon and Marine Le Pen, for example. They might have a similar agenda, such as France leaving NATO, but they're still in completely different camps and irreconcilable opponents towards each other. The way out of this is not evident to me now, but I believe that even the questions voiced today lead to a certain optimism. I won't dwell on the perspective of eschatological optimism now, but nevertheless, I believe that it is necessary to do everything in one's power in the sphere of influencing ideas, culture, society, and education, and maybe something will come out of it. And if not, then so be it — we did everything we could. It seems to me that we need to believe in the doctrines of the New Right, develop them, and maybe work through some practical parts. Unfortunately, French politicians are not going in this direction. Instead of studying and realising the New Right's theories and trying to adapt them to political life, they simply pick up one idea or another and speculate on it. What can we do — perhaps the way out is to pray that Europe can unify itself on the values that were primordially given to it.

Question: In connection with this, I realised that my question is more theoretical than practical. If the New Right abstracts away from the notion of politics as such, but they understand war, then is it necessary for the current politicians of some countries to adopt the ideas of the New Right and then force other countries in disagreement to join Europe? Is that right?

Dugina: I haven't thought in terms of this perspective. As for war, the New Right in no way presents any apologetics for violence. Moreover, any plans to violently seize countries and annex them to Europe are completely foreign to them. They call for waging, and they are waging, war against the liberal elements in their countries, the university elites who profess the American globalist doctrine. You've asked a very strange question.

Question: This is a cultural war?

Dugina: Yes, it is a cultural war.

Question: So targeted terrorism, like killing liberals, or what?

Dugina: What is this nonsense? No, we are talking about cultural war, about the war of ideas. This is a response to the cultural terrorism waged by liberals. The New Rights' strategy of intellectual war means entering the intellectual space of Europe and breaking the spell, getting rid of the hegemonic concepts of liberalism that have bewitched everyone, such as human rights, civil society, and so on. This is culture war. When Alain de Benoist appears on TV Libertés or RT France and says that human rights are something devised, that these are the rights of a completely abstract human entity, then this is the war that the New Right is engaged in.

Question: Daria, thank you again for your presentation. We've heard several questions about the direction of this movement, and I would like to develop and clarify this a bit more. In the end, the success of one or another political theory is based on two pillars: the philosophical and the political-technological. As far as I understand, everything is wonderful with the New Right's philosophers, but when it comes to political technologies, to put it mildly, not so much. I would like to understand: what is this movement's potential in the applied domain? I'm interested in the following questions: to what extent does the New Right, or its two thousand active participants, have any experience in governance and administration, or to what extent can they transform their ideas into legislative initiatives? This question stems from the examples that were mentioned of how, as soon as the right starts to be active, the system immediately represses them. Maybe the question here isn't about whether the opponent is so strong, but rather whether the right itself isn't cultivating effective, active fighters?

Dugina: Political technologies and transitioning to concrete forms of political struggle are not the task set by the New Right itself, but the task of their apprentices, so to speak. This is the task of the young guys, the next generations. In fact, the young guys from the Iliade Institute have developed the New Right's ideas, made their careers, occupied certain posts, and some work in the European Parliament. They've started applying these ideas in practice. Sure, this is a limited phenomenon for now, but the New Right didn't set itself up for tasks of a political character. They say that if we conquer culture, if we enter the cultural space, then politics itself will change.

Question: To develop this topic further, are there perhaps any other movements, besides the National Front, or any other "new" New Right that might take their ideas, insist on creative strategies, and insert themselves into the political plane? Are there any such trends?

Dugina: I haven't seen any yet. Indeed, the National Front came close to the position of the "new" New Right, or the New Right on the political plane, but it didn't live up to this challenge. It didn't hold out; Marine Le Pen lost and blamed her loss on Philippot, who put together her left-wing economic agenda. But the forces that appeared in the last minute, when Marine was almost winning, and compelled Fillon to call on his voters to vote for Macron, are themselves in Le Pen's party, of course. There are a number of people who are working against implementing the New Right's ideas and are helping liberal hegemony preserve itself.

Question: Can I ask another question? It's about the New Right's prospects of continuing to exist in the current realities of French society. How strong in French society are ideas like these which advocate a synthesis of different ideologies and movements and the erasure of the boundaries between the classical left and classical right? If I recall, there's one story about Macron, that when he was asked to define his political orientation, whether he's a liberal, socialist, communist, or something of the sort, he responded with a question: "How many variants can I choose?" How strong in society is the demand for a synthesis of ideas? Are there any paths now open to the New Right for accelerated development?

Dugina: Yes, it is incredibly strong. Moreover, it was manifest in the Yellow Vests movement in France in 2017, which launched an uprising against the so-called elites of the positional front, the bloc that is neither right nor left and which, in the face of Macron, unified the worst of the left-wing agenda and the worst of the right-wing agenda, capitalism, and values like human rights, which have nothing to do with the genuine French and which represent a pure abstraction that works only in the case of minority types, including the most exotic. These human rights aren't extended to the indigenous French. Accordingly, the Yellow Vests were a force that couldn't be called political. It was not a political force, but a force of a completely different character. Populism — that's the term for describing this phenomenon. In fact, in Europe, the theory of populism came together in many respects under the influence of the New Right's ideas. I worked in France in 2017 and I covered the Yellow Vest uprising. When I asked about their political identity, I heard in response: "We're neither left nor right; we're for common sense; we're for the people having the right to have their voice heard, the right to be represented, for their rights to be observed." The "rights of the people" is a thesis of the New Right. "The split into right and left is all nonsense" — this is what the Yellow Vests say. An

ordinary person who came from the French hinterlands to stand up
against Macron's politics couldn't have guessed that he was voicing
theses from GRECE's journal *Krisis* from 2009 — and this journal appeared back in 1987. In essence, the fact that the Yellow Vests are out
in the streets in France is an echo of the anti-liberal activities of the
New Right. Alain de Benoist so extolled this phenomenon because he
believed that it could be the people's revolution that the New Right had
foretold and substantiated. The moment will come when the people
will understand that they've been deceived, that left and right is an
artificial division. This is the new anti-liberal opposition, the erasure
of the borders between left and right, and the formation of new poles.
Even Marine Le Pen said in her speech, I think back in 2015, when
she suffered defeat in the regional elections, that there is no more left
and right, only globalists and patriots. The schism into globalism vs.
patriots and Macron vs. the Yellow Vests — this is the *clivage* that is
present. Marine Le Pen has started to position herself independently
of the ordinary political camps. She says that it is incorrect to count us
as a segment of the right, that we are simply representatives of common sense and the will of the people. So, yes, it is completely accurate
that this tendency is becoming manifest.

Question: Daria, could you name some movements from other
countries that are allied with the New Right? Who expresses ideas like
theirs, who do they talk with at conferences? Besides Eurasianists.

Dugina: This is a question that would require a separate post on
my Telegram channel. I'll devote my next post to this. There are too
many movements to count. There are the Identitarians, Casa Pound,
the Italian group around Maurizio Murelli, Rainaldo Graziani, Claudio
Mutti. This is a far-reaching chain. There are many of them. This is the
case with the New Right itself: I only mentioned their main publications, but if I were to list all of their circles and cultural associations,
then I think it would take 20 minutes. They have the Proudhon Circle
of intellectuals. Just as we have the Sun of the North cultural space,

they have the Proudhon Circle, the Circle Pol Vandromme, the Politea society. There is an uncountable amount of these circles.

Question: So they're not closed to themselves, but interact with people who are not entirely identical to them?

Dugina: Yes, and this is what I really like about the New Right: they are very open. As Guillaume Faye said at the congress, "GRECE is radical openness." You can feel this in them. It is very pleasant. Unlike liberalism, which proclaims radical openness while being completely, radically closed.

On the New Right, Dugin, and a Europe of a Thousand Flags[1]

Gleb Ervye: Hello, everyone, I'm Gleb Ervye and you're watching the channel Citadel. For the first time in a while, we're returning to the format of interviews with interesting people: today our guest is Daria Platonova, a graduate of Moscow State University's Faculty of Philosophy, a specialist in ancient and continental philosophy, and the daughter of [Alexander] Dugin.

Dugina: Well, that's everything, all the cards are revealed, so now there's no intrigue!

Ervye: Dasha, please tell us, does it not bother you at all when someone introduces you by saying "the daughter of Dugin", paying tribute to Dugin?

Daria Platonova Dugina: Well, it's actually a great honour to be the daughter of such a person. There are things that people strive for over the course of their whole life — they seek wisdom, ideas, whole bodies of knowledge. All of this was already given to me since my childhood. I remember — well, it's not about remembering as if to romanticise my biography, but the first episode of my political activism was when I was sitting in my mother's lap while she watched what was happening

1   Interview with Gleb Ervye for the Russian YouTube channel *Tsitadel'* in 2021.

at the White House.[2] It was 1993, when my dad was out defending the White House. In '91, he was for the State Committee on the State of Emergency[3] even though he adhered to anti-communist views. To be born into and live in such an environment where you meet Limonov,[4] Letov, Kuryokhin, great European thinkers like Alain de Benoist and Jean Parvulesco,[5] and many, many others, is a real honour for me.

2   The Russian White House, a government building in Moscow that serves as the primary office for the Russian Prime Minister, became a focal point of violent conflict in October 1993. During this period, a constitutional crisis erupted between President Boris Yeltsin and the Russian parliament, which culminated in Yeltsin ordering the military to suppress a parliamentary rebellion. The standoff resulted in intense fighting around the White House, including artillery shelling and tank assaults, which left parts of the building heavily damaged and resulted in numerous casualties among both protesters and military forces.

3   The State Committee on the State of Emergency (GKChP) was a self-declared governing body in the Soviet Union that attempted a coup in August 1991 to prevent the collapse of the USSR. Comprised of high-ranking Soviet officials opposed to President Mikhail Gorbachev's reforms and the shift towards a more decentralised and "democratic" Soviet structure, the committee declared a state of emergency, effectively sidelining Gorbachev. However, public resistance led by Boris Yeltsin and demonstrations against the coup thwarted the GKChP's efforts, and accelerated the dissolution of the Soviet Union.

4   Eduard Limonov (1943–2020) was a Russian writer, political dissident, and co-founder of the National Bolshevik Party (NBP), a radical political group that blended elements of nationalism and socialism. Known for his provocative persona and controversial views, Limonov formed the NBP together with Alexander Dugin, who shared his anti-liberal, anti-Western stance, However, they ultimately split due to ideological differences: Dugin increasingly embraced a traditionalist, Eurasianist vision focused on a multipolar world centred around a Russian-led alliance, while Limonov's focus remained on a revolutionary, nationalist approach that was less philosophically rooted in Eurasianism. Limonov preferred direct, oppositional activism within Russia, contrasting with Dugin's strategic alignment with Russian state structures and his emphasis on establishing a broader ideological framework beyond Russia.

5   Jean Parvulesco (1929–2010) was a Romanian-French novelist and esoteric philosopher known for exploring themes of mystical geopolitics and European destiny. His novel *Star of an Invisible Empire* depicts an apocalyptic struggle against Modernity's spiritual decay, centring on a secret order's efforts to thwart

Therefore, I'm proud to bear the standard of "being the daughter". I'm proud and I will do everything in dignity to bring glory to the name of my father and continue his ideas and struggle.

Ervye: A remarkable answer, which also anticipates my next question. I mentioned your family connection intentionally, since the main aim of our talk today is the philosophical school of the New Right, which is, I believe, unfortunately underestimated and generally too little covered in our country. Maybe this is due to the language barrier, or maybe because of something else — let's talk about this today. I think we should first go on an excursion into the history of your family: how did it happen that you ended up in France, that you got into contact with these people, penetrated the essence of their ideas, and why can you now be positioned as a kind of expert or specialist on the New Right? How, overall, did it come to this?

Dugina: I first learned of Alain de Benoist already at a conscious age, in 2007–2008, when he was in Moscow. My brother was in charge of organising his visit, and Benoist also went to Saint Petersburg, where he presented his book that had been published by Amfora. That was in 2008. There were presentations and conferences, which, by the way, already back then Soros structures tried to break up, infiltrating the room and trying to set up protests. For me, of course, back in 2008, all of this was something distant and unknown — there was France, sure; there was geopoltics, sure, but things like Carl Schmitt and *Großraum*[6]

---

demonic forces that manipulate global events through symbols like the "black pyramids" to herald the New World Order. Parvulesco's protagonist, Tony d'Antremont, embodies the mission to establish a Eurasian spiritual empire, combining the novel's metaphysical ambitions with a critique of Western materialism.

6   Carl Schmitt's concept of *Großraum* refers to a "greater spatial realm" or large geopolitical area under the influence of a dominant power that establishes a specific political and legal order. Schmitt argued that each *Großraum* should be organised by a central authority that rejects external interference, framing it as an alternative to Western universalism and emphasising the right of regional powers to shape political orders based on cultural and historical context.

were some kind of separate concepts. Alain de Benoist, the great ideologist, had come to visit. This was still something important for me even though I wasn't aware of the full importance of it until I went to France.

When it comes to France, I have a whole different story. I was studying at the philosophical faculty of Moscow State University, studying French, and reading Guénon (a book that my father advised me to read in order to master the French language), and at some point for distinguished students there appeared the opportunity to go for an internship. For some reason, I immediately wanted to go to France, to Paris. This was connected to the fact that in Paris, in France, there are still rather strong schools of scholarship on Neoplatonism — I wanted to go there to study philosophy under those who were engaged in studying Proclus, Simplicius, and Plotinus. Therefore, of course, I wanted to go to Paris. But Paris didn't figure in the distribution of internships, so they sent me to Bordeaux. When I got there, I immediately got started on my political and metapolitical activities.

I met representatives of the movement of the French sociologist Alain Soral.[7] He is a colourful personality who could be called the "French Limonov". He is the founder of the *Égalité et Réconciliation* movement, a kind of French "National Bolsheviks" — their "*Gauche du travail, Droite du valeurs*" can be translated as "the left of labour", that is left-wing economics, and "the right of values", that is right-wing politics or "right values". I started taking part in their conferences, organising meetings, and crossed paths with people from the National Front and from *Éléments*, and I started going to Paris regularly. There I personally met people like Alain de Benoist, Michel Thibault (the chairman of GRECE, *Groupement de recherche et d'études pour la*

7   Alain Soral (b. 1958) is a French writer and filmmaker known for his critiques of both liberalism and corporate globalism. While he champions traditional values and national sovereignty, he also incorporates social justice elements, addressing class inequality and opposing elite dominance in society, a mix that has resonated across ideological lines.

civilisation européenne, the Research and Study Group for European Civilisation, the centre of the New Right), and I immersed myself in this context. This was very difficult, because French thought is peculiar and evasive.

You mentioned that the New Right is underestimated in Russia. Well, French thinking very strongly differs from Russian thinking. It is very far ahead of Russian thought: where we are napping, the French mind has already woken up and is dwelling in a completely different phase. France is a country with an enormous intellectual and philosophical tradition, so to go to its soil and meet with the New Right is also a challenge for consciousness. I'm now working on part of the translation and introduction to the *Manifesto of the New Right*, and I thought that translating 10–15 pages would easily pass by for a person like me who knows French well. I studied French and I can even translate and interpret in real time (I did this with Alain de Benoist for an interview for Russian TV), but it took me four days, and I'm still not satisfied with the quality of the translation. They really have the ability to think, and we aren't entirely able to think. We think in a very "sporadic" way, or so to put it, in a "glyco-viscous"[8] manner, which means that our thought does not know clear-cut divisions, it "flows and mixes".

Ervye: Now that we've mentioned the *Manifesto*, which is a kind of brief exposition of ideas, let's try to complicate the matter and very succinctly expound these fifteen pages of text. Within a few minutes, could you explain to viewers what the New Right is? Where did this movement come from? How did it begin? What forms has it led into?

Dugina: Yes. The New Right are not conservatives, but Conservative Revolutionaries. The New Right is an ensemble of intellectuals, a community of intellectuals, which appeared in 1968–1969. It is an attempt to rethink the foundations of European culture and tradition, to reject capitalism, liberalism, and egalitarianism, and a call to restore the true,

---

8   *Glishroidno,* literally "sticky", is a term used in Gilbert Durand's sociology of the imagination, on which Dugina's father has authored several books.

deep Europe. For its part, the *Manifesto* I talked about, which is now being prepared for publication, is a text from 2000. It was written by Alain de Benoist, the founder of the New Right, along with his colleague, Charles Champetier. It is called the *Manifeste pour une renaissance européenne*, that is "Manifesto for a European Renaissance". It says that modern European civilisation finds itself in a most severe spiritual crisis, and that liberalism, capitalism, globalism ("mondialism" in French terminology) are demolishing European culture and atomising man, depriving him of his identity, tearing him away from Tradition, and thereby preparing the way for total robotisation and the complete extinction of the human being. Accordingly, it is necessary to rethink the foundations of European politics, culture, science, and social processes. In order to do so, it is necessary to stage an intellectual coup. The aim of the *Manifesto* is to show some of the points of support that exist in European culture and to which we might return: tradition, ecology, geopolitics, the Political (in Carl Schmitt's sense), the pluriverse, and classical culture — all of these things should be rethought from the point of view of anti-globalism and anti-liberalism. It is very important that the *Manifesto* calls liberalism the main enemy. This is not typical for the current political and intellectual elites in France. It is not typical because it is a rather avant-garde thought. In France, over the past few decades, a certain consensus on liberalism has taken shape: liberalism, they say, is the greatest good. Or, at the very least, it is the least evil, and everything else is certainly worse. This is what the main pool of intellectuals believes. The New Right say to this: "No, liberalism is the greatest threat to mankind, to the human being, to tradition."

Ervye: Then I have the following question: How does the New Right understand tradition? Those who follow our channel know that in several videos Evgeny Nechkasov[9] and I debated what tradition is. I

---

9   Published in English as Askr Svarte. Askr Svarte is a Russian Traditionalist philosopher, pagan activist, and the founding head of the Svarte Aske community. Descended from Bessarabian Germans exiled to Siberia in the early 20th century,

stand more on modernist positions, as I'm convinced that tradition is something handed down which does not exclude changes in cultural patterns. Evgeny Nechkasov shares Guénon's notion of the Golden Age and that everything only gets worse. What tradition is the New Right about?

Dugina: When we talk about tradition, we need to recall Traditionalism. Traditionalism is a phenomenon that appears whenever tradition is already dead. Let's recall that Evola has a book, *Men Among the Ruins*, where the main image is this "man among ruins".[10] The Traditionalist is a person who is already among the ruins of tradition. Tradition no longer exists except in some kind of excerpts or fragments, in estranged, written and fixed forms like legends, tales, myths. Both Traditionalism and the New Right's own "traditionalism" don't presume a full restoration of a tradition that once existed. What is important is preserving its spirit, its kernel, against the stream. Naturally, it adapts to the contemporary age. The New Right's traditionalism is manifest in the observance of certain holidays: they celebrate the solstices, the ancient European festivals of the Winter and Summer Solstice. The *Équinoxe de printemps* and *Équinoxe d'automne* are their holidays. They constantly appeal to regional folklore, to regionalism as such. The customs of different regions of France, local rites, and dialects (*patois*) mean a lot to them. For them, tradition is not a return and not a complete copy or blind reproduction of what was "back then" — it is an attempt to revive the "then" through us in the present moment.

Ervye: With what goal? What does the return to tradition solve? What political goal or, perhaps, global-existential goal does it set?

---

since 2009 he has been a practicing pagan in the Germanic-Scandinavian tradition and an active voice in the rebirth of paganism in Russia and Europe.

10   Julius Evola, *Men Among the Ruins: Postwar Reflections of a Radical Traditionalist*, trans. Guido Stucco (Vermont: Inner Traditions, 2002).

Dugina: It makes a person a human instead of some kind of piece or impersonal fragment of a big machine. It imparts man with soul and gives him breath.

Ervye: Do I understood correctly that this is some kind of attempt to solve the problem of alienation?

Dugina: Yes, this is one possible interpretation. Naturally, for the New Right what is fundamental is rejecting the economic grounds of Marxism. For them, it is impossible to ground human processes and human existence in the economy alone. For them, everything is to be seen in the philosophical layer, through the philosophical prism. For them, economics cannot explain the human being.

Ervye: I understand. They are people who don't accept materialism and fight against it. But there already exists an enormous layer of "critiques from the right". They [the New Right] are accused of a rapprochement with the left, with Marxism. What are they referring to when they have such things in mind?

Dugina: Yes, this is extremely interesting. I'll make a brief excursion into the history of the New Right. In '68-'69, in relation to other movements, they were essentially, de facto like a perpendicular line. They didn't intersect with the left wing, the new left wing, or the right wing. It was an absolutely new, unique movement. The right said that the New Right is going too far over to the left, that it might be some kind of special intelligence project or operation. Maybe purely tactical: to "hijack" the discourse, to steal and mislead it. The left said that they are "fascists" and simply a new rebranding of the ordinary right. That is, for everyone the New Right was some kind of Trojan horse entering their fiefdoms for unknown reasons. There were diverse conspiracy theories: it even reached the point that some wrote that the New Right was a Zionist project aimed at destroying the right-wing movement. I can tell you that the tension that existed between the right and the New Right was very large: the Poujadists, ordinary French chauvinists and conservatives, simply hated Alain de Benoist. Alain de Benoist, in turn, sharply criticised them in his works. This continued until around the '90s. Jean-Marie Le Pen and his National Front were not close comrades to him — more accurately, they were perhaps even an enemy. De Benoist was extremely negative about them.

There is a very important point here which it is worth taking note of: the New Right is not an updated right, not a rebranding. It is not a "right 2.0". In fact, in our Russian reality there is a big confusion: this term is applied to very different contemporary right-wing movements — to the right that has gone through a rebranding procedure, to a "right 2.0". This is not the New Right. The New Right, the *Nouvelle Droite*, is also not the "New Right" that we see, for example, in Thatcher in Britain or in Reagan and the Reaganists in the US. It is no mere "New Right" with the same economic liberalism, but something outright opposite. It has little in common with ordinary nationalists or conservatives. The New Right phenomenon is an intellectual movement that says that both left and right need to be overcome, that both left and right are a trap artificially created in order to divide the people into two warring clans, dividing the people in order to make them incapable of fighting against the elites who represent liberalism. Liberalism is the worst of ideologies. It destroys man, destroys identity, destroys everything human — it burns down everything.

Ervye: I completely agree. We even have a video about obsolete paradigms, about how the dichotomy between left and right no longer adequately works. And so, it looks like the New Right is a bifurcation point beyond which this history doesn't go any further. Let's concentrate on economics: what economic model does the New Right talk about?

Dugina: In economics, they are close to the "left" movement, but here I say "left" in scare quotes. They have some right-wing ideas, some left-wing ideas, but they don't adopt them as anything whole. The New Right themselves would even condemn me right now for saying "left" and "right".

Nevertheless, in economics they are first and foremost for social justice. For example, they really like Antonio Gramsci's ideas about the necessity of fighting capital. They essentially reinterpreted Gramsci and came to the conclusion that the "organic intellectual" needs to conclude a pact with Labour against Capital. The Italian communist Antonio Gramsci has an extremely interesting model. He says that today capitalism and its hegemony, which is bourgeois hegemony, needs to be fought in culture more so than in politics — and not so much in economics as in the space of ideology. For Gramsci, it is very important that intellectuals of his orientation (Neo-Marxist) are called to consciously conclude a pact with Labour. Gramsci believes that there are traditional intellectuals and organic intellectuals. Traditional ones are those engaged in apologetics for the powers that be, accepting the status quo, while the organic intellectual is the one who concludes a pact with Labour. The topic of Gramscianism, that is concluding a pact with Labour, is very important for the New Right. Sure, they understand Labour not entirely in the way that Gramsci does, but rather as a kind of existential self-manifestation, like Jünger's figure of the Worker. They even have a specific term: "Gramscianism from the right". Gramscianism is a left-wing theory: if you talk with European leftists, they'll take great pleasure in talking about Gramsci with you — Marxists and the new left are inspired by Gramsci. The New Right takes Gramscianism and says that we are developing a "Gramscianism from the right".

Ervye: So, roughly speaking, this means a redistribution of cultural capital — which is in some sense now happening in the United States, where ultra-left professors, often of a Trotskyist bent, have taken over entire universities.

Dugina: Of a left-liberal bent as well.

Ervye: Yes, yes. This is also a redistribution of cultural capital, only from different positions. Now I'll pose a more specific question: in whose hands should private ownership of the means of production be?

Dugina: I think that the New Right has different answers to this question, but first and foremost the workers. Their main figure is the Worker, the Labourer.

Ervye: How? Through what? Or in other words: since one can encounter a great amount of criticism which maintains that there is some kind of "reincarnation of fascism" underway in the New Right, is there private means of production? Is there some kind of counterpart financial sector? Or does everything belong to the state and the people?

Dugina: Honestly, I haven't found any complete concept of economics among the New Right. For them, subjecting the foundations of capitalism to philosophical critique is more important than singling out and presenting some kind of concrete economic model. If you read their works, there's no unambiguous answer here. This question is up in the air. The New Right simply doesn't represent a political movement or a specific political programme. They are metapoliticians; they work in the realm of ideas. There's no concretisation in the realm of ideas — it's parties that engage in concretisation afterwards. For example, the National Front shifted leftward in 2017 under the inspiration of the New Right. Marine Le Pen chose Florian Philippot as her advisor, and he began employing left-wing economic discourse. He speaks of the necessity of introducing and enlarging a progressive tax and many concrete economic details which are in favour of working people and go against big private capital. Here we find statist points in the direction of nationalising big private monopolies. There are also restrictions to be put on transnational corporations. But among the New Right itself, the topic of the economy is unfurled more from the point of view of philosophy, that is, they won't have a specific answer to the question of who should own the means of production.

Ervye: This is quite strange, properly speaking, because if the New Right is against bourgeoisness, then according to the logic of its idea, the economic contradiction that gives rise to bourgeoisness through the private ownership of the means of production should be overcome in a decent way. There are hints at this in the corpus of thinkers who are still unknown in Russia. In my own time, for example, I've discovered MacIntyre, whom de Benoist constantly refers to.[11] This is really a treasure trove which, for some reason unknown to me, no one in our country has even heard about. MacIntyre himself came out of Marxism and, as far as I understand, there is a more left-leaning wing within the New Right, is there not?

Dugina: Yes, but if in a dialogue with this so-called "left wing" you were to say, "So, you're from the left?", you'll immediately get an extremely negative reaction. This is the case with Charles Robin and David L'Épée — both of whom I know — who came out of radical left circles. One of them is from Switzerland and the other one is, I think, French. But, in actual fact, even if we're not talking to them or if we don't speak of this term, then we'll see that they have the left-leaning publication *Krisis*, which appeared in 1988 and was aimed at strengthening their influence on left audiences. It publishes left-wing intellectuals all the way up to Jean-Luc Mélenchon, who has published his speeches and even had a column there. Questions that are predominantly of interest to the left are discussed there: the question of Labour, the question of alienation, the question of Capital. At the same time, *Nouvelle École*, for instance, is dedicated more to the analysis of geopolitics and tradition: René Guénon, Carl Schmitt, Ernst Jünger, Oswald Spengler, Ernst Niekisch, etc. Each issue is devoted to different topics. They essentially have three main print publications. The first, *Nouvelle École*, appeared in 1968. The second, *Éléments*, which appeared in the '70s, is a journal that comes out twice a month and is devoted to current events: the Yellow Vests, populism, etc. In the latest issue we see an Italian dossier on the alliance between the right-wing politician Matteo Salvini and left populists from the Five Stars Movement; that is an alliance of left

11   Alasdair MacIntyre, *After Virtue: A Study in Moral Theory* (Notre Dame: University of Notre Dame Press, 1981). Alasdair MacIntyre (b. 1929) is a Scottish philosopher best known for his contributions to moral and political philosophy, particularly his revival of Aristotelian ethics in a modern context. He critiques contemporary moral relativism and argues for a return to virtue ethics grounded in tradition and communal life.

and right. This is something situational, sure, but here this alliance is reconceptualised through the prism of the New Right's philosophy. The third, *Krisis*, has been oriented towards left audiences since 1988.

Here's what's interesting: the New Right, when they were founded in 1968–1969, was in fact not called the "New Right". They began to be called this only in the '70s, specifically in 1979, when left politicians, right politicians, and representatives of the university milieux participated in one of the GRECE movement's colloquiums. This drew such strong ire from the system that within a few days the "New Right" became brand number one that everyone tried to demonise — *Libération*, *Le Parisien*, *Le Monde*;, I can go on listing all the publications for a long time. Everyone wrote about them. Even the Americans. For liberals, a disturbing picture was taking shape: a new threat arose, a *coup d'état* in the realm of culture had arisen in France. That's when the name "New Right" was born: when they started to pose a threat. And they started to present a threat because under their roof, under their patronage, under their influence, were both left and right and professors — everyone. Moreover, imagine — and now it's difficult to imagine something like this — that Alain de Benoist had his own column in *Le Figaro*. He was invited by Louis Pauwels, the chief editor of *Le Figaro* and an active supporter of the New Right. He was the author of the iconic book *Morning of the Magicians*, which treated different esoteric questions and a number of disturbing and dangerous topics. So, their influence was permeating everywhere.

Ervye: Let's get more specific. This is an anti-liberal, anti-bourgeois, anti-market school of thought that proposes to struggle against man's alienation from the proper meaning of his existence through developing various professional, creative, and national identities. Economics remains an unclear point. What about the organisation of state power? Is this a parliamentary story, a new republicanism, a party, an order?

Dugina: There's also no definite, clear-cut concept on this point. We encounter different opinions, but this is not something prescribed in the New Right's works. There is no clear-cut manifesto on what the state should look like. What's really interested me and what I really like is their interpretation of Carl Schmitt's ideas, particularly his concept of *Großraum*. They see Europe as a Europe of a thousand flags. Unlike the ordinary French right and French nationalists, they are for a united Europe. They essentially defend the EU, but as a European Union of healthy man, not what we have today, which is an anti-Europe subordinate to the US and founded on the total domination of liberal philosophy. The New Right is for the existence of plurality within a united Europe, so that all cultures have the possibility to present themselves. Therefore, for them it's important that France isn't a nation-state of the bourgeois, Enlightenment bent, but certain lands and regions. In GRECE's guest house in Aix-en-Provence near Marseille, each room has the flag of one of France's regions. They think of France as a confederation of communities and lands. De Benoist admires Russia, Eurasianism, the Eurasian Empire, because this Empire expresses a greater continental space, a *Großraum*. The mystery of empire is fulfilled here: the Platonic "One-Many" is created.[12] So, according to the New Right's theory, if we speak of their political vision, then the goal is a Europe of a thousand flags. We cannot give more precise clarifications, i.e. whether they're monarchists or not (they rather aren't) or supporters of one or another specific state structure. Their thinking is somewhat above this. They think and write about principles. The rest is to a greater extent the task of politicians, a matter of determining and deriving from these theories specific projects and programmes.

Ervye: I understand that this is a purely philosophical level that doesn't stoop down to the domain of concrete politics.

Dugina: They declare that they are metapoliticians.

---

12 The Platonic One-Many problem addresses the relationship between unity (the "One") and multiplicity (the "Many"), exploring how a singular, unchanging reality can underlie the diverse and changing world we experience. In Platonic thought, the "One" represents an ideal, unifying essence or Form, while the "Many" refers to the multiple, individual instances or manifestations of this essence in the physical world, which participate in but are distinct from the ideal unity.

Ervye: As far as I understand, there's simply been a blurring of discourse: some in one direction, others in another. In general, this is what always happens with such currents. Now let's return to Eurasianism, which you already mentioned, but first let's clarify one question: there are many criticisms and accusations of a "rehabilitation" or "reincarnation" of "fascism", as if the Fourth Political Theory were an attempt to bring back the "good old third theory". What can you say about this?

Dugina: Fascism categorically does not suit de Benoist. First and foremost, he is put off by the racial theory that is put forth by Nazism more so than Italian fascism. The very idea of a hierarchisation of peoples is inconceivable and unacceptable to him. As a follower of Carl Schmitt, he believes that what is needed is a political pluriverse, whereas hierarchisation is a step towards universalism, the domination of the modern West, and the crisis of mankind. De Benoist argues that the modern US and globalism are built on a racial basis. Above all in culture and the economy. The civilisation of Modernity built by modern white Europeans, with its technological development, market economy, and capitalist system, is taken to be the final word of "progress" and "development". All other civilisations, peoples, and races are prescribed to strictly follow this same path, to imitate the "white man", and specifically the Anglo-Saxons, in all respects. This is a mistake, a trap, an injustice. De Benoist is against racism. He says that racism is an extremely dangerous phenomenon that is erroneous in its foundations and depraved in its application. But he also doesn't support anti-racism. Because, he says, the anti-racists who stand opposed to racists also fall into the same trap and lead to a certain kind of hierarchisation. He says the following: if we stand for "black power", which is now BLM, then we should also stand for "white power", "yellow power", for all the "powers" there are. Then we simply have a different version of the very same racism. But the accusations against the New Right, which has nothing to do with racism, fascism, or nationalism, and which, to the contrary, has from the very outset sharply critiqued these phenomena in hundreds of works and thousands of articles, is a really

banal, stupid, and utterly false treatment. I think that it's intended
exclusively for liberals to spare them from thinking. The New Right is
fearless and isn't afraid of going against the system. If they really did
follow the Third Way, then they would say so. But Alain de Benoist
doesn't accept fascism; he rejects the Third Way and criticises it. Hence
the Fourth Political Theory. It is based on a developed and fundamental critique of all three of the main political ideologies of the modern
West: first and foremost liberalism, but also communism (especially
the dogmatic kind) and nationalism (fascism, Nazism, racism). These
three ideologies have collapsed. They have a common source which
is responsible for the rot of the whole body of these ideologies: the
modern West, European Modernity, the worldview of the modern age.
This is the main problem.

Ervye: Here, in fact, is where I would diverge with their position,
because the Third Way is not fascism as such. Fascism and National
Socialism were certain historical offshoots that came about as a consequence of how the Conservative Revolution was perceived. If we take
a non-Eurocentric view, then in the channel of the Third Way we'll
also find Tolstoy with his specific Christianity and draw towards social
justice as well as Gandhi and Gaddafi. If we look more broadly, beyond
the European experience, then it turns out that the Third Way is an
enormous river of currents that have tried to foster both traditional
culture and the draw towards social justice in socialist forms, often not
at all Marxist. I would say that movements that stand for a socialism
based on the principles of objective idealism, instead of a materialistic
socialism, would also be the Third Way. In my view, it would be very
incorrect to classify the Third Way under fascism.

Dugina: The accusations of fascism put forth against the New
Right are not about ideas; this is simply a strategy for discrediting the
movement, because the word "fascism" is now at the top of the list,
and if you pin this label on anyone, it's supposed to destroy them as
an opponent. In the case of the New Right, this is completely incorrect. In fact, here we can pay attention to the historical analogues

which the New Right itself says it is referring to: the Conservative Revolutionaries. The latter were in opposition to the Nazi regime. I think that our listeners and readers can see for themselves and figure out who it is that the New Right takes as their standard by getting acquainted with the biographies of people like Arthur Moeller van den Bruck, Oswald Spengler, or Ernst Niekisch. The lot of Niekisch, as well as the Jünger brothers, was a more difficult, complex relationship of opposition to the regime surrounding them. Both Moeller van den Bruck, whose idea of a "Third Empire"[13] has nothing in common with Hitler's Third Reich, and Oswald Spengler died before the Nazis came to power and had nothing to do with them.

Ervye: Put briefly, in order to understand the New Right, we need to think in a more complex manner rather than on the level of habitual dichotomies and constructs. Another question before we finally come to the link with Eurasianism: If we try to describe the picture of the future that the New Right proposes, perhaps without political specifics, then what would it be? For example, against the backdrop of the conflict with Guillaume Faye, we can say what it wouldn't be. The Archeofuturist project of Eurosiberia that Faye put forth[14], as far as I understand, was entirely rejected by de Benoist.[15] And so, what would

---

13   Arthur Moeller van den Bruck, *Germany's Third Empire*, trans. E. O. Lorimer (London: Arktos, 2012). Arthur Moeller van den Bruck (1876–1925) was a German cultural historian and philosopher best known for his influential book *Das Dritte Reich* (The Third Reich), published in 1923. In this work, he outlined his vision for a "Third Empire" that would unify Germany beyond both monarchy and parliamentary democracy, seeking a conservative, spiritual revival distinct from Western liberalism and Soviet communism. Although his ideas influenced later German nationalist thought, Moeller van den Bruck himself opposed the Nazi Party, criticising its crude populism and lack of intellectual and cultural depth.

14   Guillaume Faye, *Archeofuturism: European Visions of the Post-Catastrophic Age*, trans. Sergio Knipe (London: Arktos, 2010).

15   Alain de Benoist rejected Guillaume Faye's concept of Archeofuturism because he saw it as overly radical and inconsistent with the principles of the New Right. Faye's ideas emphasised an apocalyptic, survivalist future where advanced

the future Europe be in a general outline from the point of view of de Benoist himself as one of the leaders of the New Right?

Dugina: This is a complex question. I'll respond in broad strokes. It is a Europe in which man is something connected to his culture and tradition. It is a Europe in which every point is not a "hotel room", as Jacques Attali said, not something faceless. Jacques Attali is an ultra-globalist thinker, a philosopher who inspired Bernard-Henri Lévy and Macron.[16] For the New Right, the right Europe is a Europe in which every region manifests something unique. It is a Europe of small towns. The New Right is against megalopolises — they say that big cities, what we [in Russian] call "anthills" and "cells", destroy and level everything that is human. Technology shouldn't beat man down and subordinate him. Technology should assist him, adapt him to the world, but in no way destroy him.

It is a Europe in which, no matter how strange this might sound, there will be equality of the sexes, but a special equality: not so much equality as harmony and dialogue between woman and man. It is a Europe in which the completely unprecedented forms of the Cybelean element that are manifest in modern liberal feminism won't dominate.[17] It will be a Europe in which woman and man will coexist in

---

technology and traditional values would merge to confront civilisational collapse, which conflicted with de Benoist's more conservative, community-focused perspective on cultural renewal. De Benoist favoured a gradual revival of traditional European values within a stable society, while Faye's visions involved dramatic upheavals, which de Benoist criticised as lacking practical, sustainable solutions for Europe's future.

16 Jacques Attali (b. 1943) is a French economist and writer known for his influence on economic and social policy and his advocacy for globalisation and European integration. He served as an advisor to President François Mitterrand, playing a significant role during his presidency and promoting policies focused on economic modernisation and European unity.

17 The "Cybelean element" refers to a symbolic concept rooted in the worship of the goddess Cybele, also known as the *Magna Mater* or Great Mother, associated with nature, fertility, and the raw, untamed aspects of the earth. In philosophical and cultural studies, particularly in the Eurasianist context, the

harmony. This is a very important part of Alain de Benoist's teaching — rethinking the role of woman. GRECE supporters even have a women's movement called Antigone. Its members speak of the need to return to traditional woman. She can be a warrior or a mother — she has her own mission. This traditional woman won't be completely subordinated to man, nor, to the contrary, will she dominate over man as is the case now, when feminists try to be above men. This will be a completely different world. Such is standpoint feminism: when woman and man are different worlds and live in harmony. Although, of course, there is the "great war of the sexes" between them, this is something incredibly beautiful: it is a dance, it's what can be seen in our traditional *rucheyok*[18] game. In fact, this is a marriage ritual where competition, opposition, and even struggle reach culmination in love and marriage. It is a Europe in which there will be this harmony.

It is a Europe in which nature will be respected and venerated — nature in the sense that the New Right stand for deep ecology. For them, it is very important that nature is no longer treated as a resource. They stand for an animated Europe, a Europe full of soul. Here the element of their pagan attitude makes itself felt. This is magical Europe. I can't go into specifics and say that "you'll get off the train at Gare Montparnasse and you'll see there..." What we'll see in such

---

"Cybelean Logos" symbolises a chthonic, or earth-bound, principle representing primordial forces, the chaotic, and the maternal essence of life that stands in contrast to the rational or celestial elements (e.g. the Apollonian). This term can also denote the instinctual, wild aspects that coexist with civilisation but remain largely outside of structured, rational norms.

18   The Russian game *Rucheyok* (meaning "little stream") is a traditional children's game similar to a lighthearted matchmaking activity. In this game, children form two rows facing each other, raising their hands to create a tunnel, or "stream." One child, who is left without a partner, walks through the tunnel with eyes closed, choosing a new partner by tapping someone in the line. The selected partner then joins the child at the end of the line, and the player left without a partner continues the game by passing through the tunnel to select someone else, keeping the cycle going.

a sacred Europe, re-renchanted after long eras of disenchantment by capitalism, is a mystery.

It will be a flourishing Europe, the likes of which we probably can't see now. When were you in Europe last?

Ervye: The 2019–2020 New Year.

Dugina: Before Coronavirus?

Ervye: Yes, I was in Rome. It was beautiful, of course.

Dugina: Surely, it was beautiful, but with the migration crisis it was probably already a bit dark, no?

Ervye: I haven't lived in Europe, but I was there every month for a period of three years. At some point I learned how to filter what my eyes saw.

Dugina: Well, I remember this Europe — before the outbreak of the migration crisis, before Covid. In fact, the New Right is the real Europe. I remember when we celebrated the 50th anniversary of GRECE in 2019, when the Yellow Vest uprising was ongoing. I went to a restaurant with Stanislas, Jean Parvulesco's grandson, to celebrate the 50th anniversary of GRECE. I remember how incredible it was: here were the Yellow Vests, and here was GRECE. Rallies were raging on the streets, crowds of anti-liberals were clashing with the police, while the ones who formulated the ideas of right-left populism, who foretold it, who told of it before it became reality, who had always known that sooner or later the people would begin to rise up against the elites, were sitting in a comfortable restaurant and observing confirmation of their correctness out of the window. It was incredible.

I remember this Europe when I was in *Domus*, the New Right's house in Aix-en-Provence, the small headquarters of GRECE, where they organise camps and sing songs in different French dialects. Back then I didn't understand much, but I knew that this is the real Europe, eternal Europe. I feel it, I accept it. Unfortunately, I'm not a person who grew up in it. But, nevertheless, I really feel it. I remember how distinct your perception of reality becomes when you're in GRECE, when you talk with representatives of GRECE, including those who joined Alain de Benoist when they were young, when they were 20 in 1969, and now they're over 60. You look at them, talk with them, and then you go outside on the street and see a completely different, liberal France that is falling apart. I don't know how to describe this feeling.

Ervye: You said that it's unfortunate that you didn't grow up in the European environment. I understand that there is a certain resonance with Eurasianism here. Do you not consider Russia to be part of European civilisation?

Dugina: I think that we are on the semantic axes of two civilisations, Europe and Asia, and this is indeed what Eurasianism is about. "Yes, we are Scythians, yes we are Asians!"[19] I wasn't entirely correct when I said that it's unfortunate that I didn't grow up there. I would like to live two lives: one childhood here, one childhood there — and even a third somewhere else in order to capture the totality of cultures. But Eurasianism says that we represent both Europe and Asia. On the one hand, we have a strict idea of hierarchy that comes to a greater extent from Asia; on the other hand, we have some European traits.

Ervye: What is the bridge running from the New Right to your father and to the theory of Eurasianism in general? How did these two currents of thought befriend each other and merge into the Fourth Political Theory?

Dugina: There are a number of common traits here which unite Alexander Gelyevich [Dugin] and Alain de Benoist. Alexander Gelyevich considers himself to be a student of Alain de Benoist to a certain extent. He went to France to visit him in the '80s. He went there with a point, already knowing him and having studied his works. What brings them together? First, anti-liberalism. This is the first point of

---

19   A reference to Alexander Blok's most famous poem from 1918: "Scythians". The poem is a powerful work that portrays Russia as a bridge between Europe and Asia, embodying both the fierce, untamed spirit of the East and the cultural depth of the West. Written during the turbulent period of World War One, the poem serves as both a warning and an appeal to Europe, suggesting that if Russia's dual nature is misunderstood or mistreated, it could unleash a force as unpredictable and formidable as the Scythians of old.

interaction. The second is Traditionalism. There is also the fascination with Jünger, Heidegger, and the Conservative Revolutionaries. Thirdly, there is the common geopolitical worldview. This is the division of the world into the civilisation of Land and civilisation of Sea. This means posing and perceiving the civilisation of Sea as the enemy and, along with it, the whole philosophy of the civilisation of Sea, the philosophy of individualism and liberalism. This is an understanding of one's own country, one's own space, as a "great space". Eurasianism borrows Carl Schmitt's concept of *Großraum* and applies it to the space of Eurasia. This is identical to the French understanding of continental Europe. I think there are similarities here in philosophical, geopolitical, and even political features.

Ervye: So the next question: What influence does the New Right actually exert on current politics? Are they not just some marginals from philosophy? To what extent are they actually represented in the discourse — to which, unfortunately, Russia has a a rather indirect relationship?

Dugina: Back in the '70s, when this phenomenon, the New Right, just appeared, Bernard-Henri Lévy said that the best option for fighting them is to silence any mention of them. It's better not to talk about the New Right at all — nothing and never. In essence, the New Right really did become a victim of this silence on the part of the central French media. Alain de Benoist, unfortunately, can't be found on the central TV channels, only on Arte or TV Libertés. The latter is a very interesting French channel, a re-information agency. In Europe today, re-information is a new current of anti-globalist media. Their common slogan is the following: "We want to re-inform you — you've been deceived by the official channels, now let's tell you the truth." This is not media as a means of information, but as a means of re-information. Whenever you encounter a re-information agency, whether in France, Italy, or in Spain, you're dealing with an anti-globalist initiative.

And so they decided to silence the New Right and they did. At the same time, however, the events that we're seeing in France, for example the Yellow Vests or the ideology of the National Front, where in 2017 left economic ideas were united with right political ideas, when Marine Le Pen ran in the elections with her advisor Florian Philippot and formed a completely avant-garde and to a certain extent National Bolshevik model —- all of this is the influence of the New Right. The influence of the New Right is not necessarily direct. We don't need to cite a mass of evidence as to where and when Alain de Benoist crossed paths with Marine Le Pen or how many issues of *Éléments* Marine Le Pen has read. This is not a case where something needs to be proven in terms of the fact of personalities crossing paths or having an online correspondence. Here, the question is one of complex, multifaceted influence. What has happened in Italy, I believe, is also the influence of the New Right: Lega Nord's unification, albeit not long-term, with the Five Stars Movement— this coalition, which really came about, was foretold and substantially argued for by Alain de Benoist. It is a coalition of the anti-liberal left and anti-liberal right. It is a coalition that erases the artificial division into two groups and speaks to a new *clivage*, a new schism, this time between the people and the elites. All the anti-elite uprisings that were taking place in Europe before the Coronavirus, and the populist movement itself, are the influence of the New Right's ideas. This is what I think.

Ervye: I understand, sure, that there really is a bridge, and that's interesting. I recently drew for myself the following schema of how culture works in general, if we break it down from the standpoint of the Hegelian dialectic. In culture we have two vectors in different directions: one is directed towards the survival of the community that professes and accepts this culture, the other is directed towards the hope that it's possible to live in other ways. This hope is expendable in relation to survival. It's often irrational. But, nevertheless, this tendency exists and there is constantly someone, some pole of revolution, against the pole of reaction that represents the tendency towards survival. The revolutionary pole requires the development of cultural patterns, the development of ideas, changing the structure of society, and this often ends with the death of this community. But it also often doesn't, and then there's a definite leap. Accordingly, one of the strategies taking into account these two tendencies might be what we call the Conservative Revolution, that is, an attempt to observe a certain boundary and moderation with respect to these two different directions of movement. The New Right looks to me as though it were something in this vein. In connection with this, my question is: What is the place of progress for the New Right?

Dugina: First I'll comment on the idea of survival and the revolutionary. This idea reminds me of Lev Gumilyov[20] and his idea that there exist two types: the passionary and the harmonic. The harmonic invests as much effort in his life as is needed to survive; the passionary, to the contrary, has so much excessive energy that his passionarity is much higher than his survival instinct. This Gumilyovian formula can be appropriately applied here.

Ervye: Yes, this is simply the Hegelian interpretation of the figures of the Conservative and the Revolutionary.

Dugina: Yes, that's completely right. And your question was about the idea of progress. The idea of progress is an idea of liberal philosophy. It is completely unacceptable to the New Right. The idea of progress lies in that everything that is happening now is better than what was yesterday. For de Benoist, the idea of progress is a myth that liberalism imposes so as to destroy everything human. And, of course, progress for them is a curse. In this respect, they are also following Guénon, who saw world history as a history of total regress. Therefore,

---

20 Lev Gumilyov (1912–1992) was a Russian historian, ethnologist, and philosopher known for his theory of passionarity, a concept describing the energetic drive within certain individuals in an ethnic group that fuels the group's collective rise, influence, and expansion through historical cycles. Son of poets Anna Akhmatova and Nikolay Gumilyov, he focused on Eurasian history and argued that Russia's identity is deeply rooted in a synthesis of Slavic and Turkic-Mongolian cultures, challenging Western-centric historical narratives. Gumilyov's ideas, particularly his theories on ethnogenesis and cultural vitality, have remained influential in post-Soviet Eurasianist thought.

what is important for them is a conservative revolution at the point of the absolute night that is setting in now, the point of existential darkness. In fact, when I'm now talking about this existential darkness, this is not a metaphor. In the anthology *Gramscianism from the Right*, Guillaume Faye permitted himself to express such formulas. The New Right are generally very academic, but sometimes they allow themselves to express things in very Heideggerian ways. At this point of absolute night, it is necessary to carry out a coup. This should be a coup of conservative revolution against progress, against progressist ideology.

Ervye: This is very interesting. I'm constantly frustrated by the fact that there are no adequate translations. As far as I know, in Russian translation we have *Against Liberalism: Towards the Fourth Political Theory*, and the *Manifesto* is currently in the final editing stage. Is there anything else? What can we recommend to those watching?

Dugina: I can also refer you to the journal *Elementy*, which my father published. There are several issues in Russian. It is the Russian version of *Éléments*. There are translations from the French *Éléments* as well as a number of works written by Russian scholars. There's Vasily Molodyakov's article "The Moscow-Berlin-Tokyo Axis", which delved into the idea of a possible congenital alliance between Germany, Russia, and Japan.[21] There is much that is interesting there. I've also seen that Alain de Benoist's books *Beyond Human Rights* and *Carl Schmitt Today* have been translated. These translations aren't very much to my liking, but I'm very picky when it comes to translations because I can read French and, naturally, a person who deals with the New Right will criticise everything. We are indeed translating the *Manifesto*. Big thanks are owed to Ross Marsov, because he motivated me to think through the *Manifesto* and translate a small introduction, and the rest he translated with his colleagues. This, I think, will mark

---

21   Later developed into a book: V. E. Molodyakov, *Nesostoyavshaiasia os': Berlin-Moskva-Tokio* [The Axis that Didn't Happen: Berlin-Moscow-Tokyo] (Moscow: Veche, 2004).

the appearance of the most important programmatic document of the New Right in the Russian intellectual space, because everything, the whole agenda of the New Right, takes shape in this *Manifesto*.

Ervye: Wonderful, we're really waiting! I promise that I'll make a separate video and talk about it as soon as it appears. I'll immediately say that I'm not an outright adept of the New Right. It just seems to me that this is a very interesting current of thought. For me, it really lacks the economic perspective. But, nevertheless, it is a current that deserves all kinds of attention.

The Phenomenon of "Gramscianism from the Right": The Experience of the New Right[1]

THE "NEW RIGHT" is an ensemble of intellectual movements that appeared in France in 1968 as a reaction to ideological crisis and the strengthening of liberal hegemony in Europe. By 1968, the classical "right-wing" movements had become riddled with liberal ideological motifs, such as the acceptance of capitalism, pro-American sentiments, and statism. In turn, the "left-wing" agenda, the core of which is constituted by opposition to capitalism, was also affected by liberal influences. According to the New Right, moreover, "left-wing" doctrine did not go beyond the "consensus" of Modernity and capitalism. By taking the economy to be the main axis of human existence, the left remained within the liberal paradigm even while taking the side of the "oppressed". Egalitarianism, individualism, the negation of differences between cultures, and universalism turned "left-wing" movements into allies and partners of liberal doctrine.

The New Right ensemble of intellectuals engaged in studying European identity and was originally distinct from its contemporaries

---

1   A previous version of this text, translated by a team headed by P. A. Kiselev, appeared in the *Sun of the North* almanac, *The Theory of Hegemony and Counter-Hegemony*, ed. N. V. Arutyunov and A. G. Dugin (Saint Petersburg: Sun of the North Publishing House, 2022). It has been re-edited for this volume.

in that it did not consider itself to belong to any of the "left" or "right" movements. The movement's main ideologists spoke about the necessity of overcoming the artificial political schism and transitioning to a new doctrine, one which would be a mix of the best ideas from both the "left-wing" and "right-wing" intellectual spaces. As Guillaume Faye remarked in 1981 at a conference of the Research and Study Group for European Civilisation (GRECE): "Our society is no longer inspired by the renewal of its ideology. This ideology today has reached its 'apogee'; accordingly, at the onset of decline, dead ideas have become moral canon, systems of habits, and ideological taboos which no longer draw any enthusiasm."[2]

The very name "New Right" dates back to 1979, when it was impossible not to notice the influence of GRECE on the political culture and intellectual life of France. Such a "label" appeared in the summer of 1979, first in French and later in European and even American media. More than 500 publications were published in just one summer, whose main goal was quite obvious: to diminish the influence of Alain de Benoist and his supporters' ideas. Such a media campaign only strengthened the positions of the movement — it started to emerge in a number of European countries. The New Right accomplished the colossal work of compiling a unified set (encyclopaedia) of the best European thinkers (from Plato to Nietzsche, Lorenz to Jünger). They opened up France to the ideas of the Conservative Revolutionaries, the National Bolsheviks, the philosophers of the "New Beginning", and other phenomenologists, sociologists, social anthropologists, and ethnologists who greatly contributed to the development of European culture. Among their inspirations were Ernst Niekisch, Ernst Jünger, Arthur Moeller van den Bruck, Oswald Spengler, Friedrich Nietzsche, Martin Heidegger, Claude Lévi-Strauss, Arnold Gehlen, Jean Thiriart, Louis Dumont, and Pierre-Joseph Proudhon.

---

2   *Pour un gramscisme de droite. Acte du XVIe colloque national du GRECE*, 72.

A complex rethinking of European civilisation and creating a front of "counter-hegemony" that would confront the universalism, globalism, egalitarianism carried out under the liberal agenda through an alternative and somewhat symmetric ideology, as well as by reconstructing European culture in all of its diversity, came to be the main tasks of the New Right. The movement initially took shape around GRECE and the journal *Nouvelle École*.

In 1973, the New Right launched the iconic magazine *Éléments*, which became a new platform for the meeting of intellectuals who set before themselves the task of reviving European culture along the principles of holism, anti-liberalism, tradition, and anti-capitalism. In 1988, the New Right launched the publication *Krisis*, a magazine for "ideas and debates". Unlike many other political publications coming out of France at the time, the New Right's print editions proclaimed themselves to be platforms where the opposition between "left and right" was being overcome. As de Benoist wrote in the book *Les Idées à l'endroit*, the New Right practically "flipped the table of ideas" existing at the time and left the field of the classic confrontation between "left" and "right".

One important aspect of the New Right's work was developing a theory of "Gramscianism from the right". Building on the works of Antonio Gramsci, Alain de Benoist critiqued the ideological and cultural hegemony of liberalism and declared the need for creating an alternative that would be founded on the values of European civilisation — holism, tradition, a pluriversal perception of the world, Europe's continental identity, and replacing abstract "human rights" with "rights of peoples". De Benoist remarked: "In a certain sense, and if we stick exclusively to the methodological aspects of the theory of cultural power, then some of Gramsci's views are virtually prophetic."[3]

"Gramscianism from the right" was the subject of one of GRECE's conferences (the 16th *colloque national*) which took place on 29

---

3   Alain de Benoist, *Les Idées à l'endroit*, 258.

November 1981 in the *Palais des Congrès* in Versailles. At the opening of the conference, Professor Michel Wayoff of Nancy University
emphasised: "For us, being 'Gramscianists' means acknowledging
the importance of the theory of cultural power [*pouvoir culturel*]; the
point is not to prepare power for one or another political party, but to
transform the mentality so as to uphold a new system of values within
which a political translation (the political plane) doesn't interest us."[4]
Alain de Benoist, the historian of ideas and chief ideologist of GRECE,
also remarked that political processes change all the time, but the "ideological majority" remains the same: "Now we can speak more about
consent than contradiction between the political, ideological, and
sociological majority. This consent is the basic state of affairs."[5] From
de Benoist's point of view, "left-wing" ideology, riddled with liberal
tendencies (individualism, the primacy of the economic sphere over
all others), has created a climate in which no political development
can take place. For de Benoist, it is important to highlight the fact that
behind the façade of "left-wing" ideas in recent decades hides the very
same liberalism (liberal ideology and culture) and "consumer society".
The goal of right-wing Gramscianism is to get out of the system of
liberal hegemony through the development of alternative culture and
metapolitical codes. De Benoist describes such a way out of the "universalist" culture in existential categories: "We are at the point of midnight; we are at the prime meridian of active nihilism… Taking part in
our undertaking does not mean choosing one clan against another. It
means getting off the trolleybus that only runs between the two poles
of one ideology, with or without stops."[6] De Benoist notes that we are
talking about "changing the ecumene of the universe", "re-imparting

---

4   *Pour un gramscisme de droite*, 7.

5   Ibid., 11.

6   Ibid., 21.

the world with its colours, giving memory back its dimensions, and giving peoples back their historical possibility and destiny of being".[7]

For the New Right, ideas become weapons: As Guillaume Faye remarked:

> Isolated intellectuals who are neutral and don't fight have never left their seal on history… GRECE and all of our movement by no means intend to give up ideology to the sciences, to liberals, to conservatives, or to the left, but rather wants to bring the force of different ideas to society in all of its complexity. Effecting Gramscianism from the right means spreading a system of values that will work in the long term, that will bear competitive formulas and, in being carried out through a metapolitical strategy, will be positioned outside of the political institutions. GRECE is spreading a view of the world that can be expressed through actions in the sphere of culture or on the strictly intellectual plane by means of constructing a theoretical corpus, one that is never finished but always developing. Such a corpus presupposes incorporating numerous disciplines, from biology to philosophy.[8]

Also in his speech at the GRECE conference on Gramscianism from the right, he emphasised that "the ideological corpus [of GRECE] is radically open, is in constant evolution, unites new disciplines, accepts new ideas, is in constant interaction with reality".[9]

"Gramscianism from the right" thus exposes the dominance of liberalism in the field of culture and advocates the construction of a counter-hegemony. For the New Right, the positions of "right-wingers" in relation to liberal hegemony in culture are not suitable, as the "right" refrains from engaging in the war for ideas. De Benoist considers this to be a fatal mistake (Caesarism), insofar as losing and leaving culture to liberalism leads to any politics inevitably turning into liberal politics. But de Benoist also views the "left-wing" opposition to liberal culture as ineffective. Capitalism in both the "right-wing" and

---

7   Ibid.

8   Ibid., 72.

9   Ibid.

"left-wing" intellectual space becomes a kind of code which can only be resisted by an alternative code.

In positioning and describing such a "Gramscianism from the right", "independence from ideologies" is also important. Representatives of the New Right have formulated the idea that the ideologies of Modernity that have been in strict opposition and a state of struggle are a phenomenon exclusive to Western culture. The position of Gramscianism from the right is based on the idea of building a "territory free of ideologies". This territory would reject individualism, egalitarianism, and the concept of abstract human rights (which are interpreted by the New Right to be a forgery of liberal doctrine).

Gramscianism from the right is therefore conceived as a territory of metapolitics beyond the influence of hegemony, that is, outside of the authority of liberal culture with its algorithms, practices, and institutions. Gramsci himself viewed communism as an alternative to hegemony or counter-hegemony, primarily in its active Leninist version, where politics is ahead of economics and culture is ahead of politics. GRECE, however, attributes contemporary communism to hegemony, i.e. they interpret it to be an extreme "left-wing" version of liberalism itself.

And then the thesis of Gramscianism from the right acquires all its meaning: it is an invitation to create a new version of counter-hegemony that would challenge the entire political theology of modern times. From Gramsci, the New Right took, first of all, the thesis that the source of power should be sought precisely in culture, in the historical pact that the intellectual freely concludes with this or that historical dominant.

De Benoist chooses the side of Labour against Capital (in this he is a consistent Gramscianist), but he interprets the principle of Labour (*Arbeit*) rather in the spirit of Ernst Jünger and his Worker (*der Arbeiter*). Again, here we are not talking about nationalism as another version of the same capitalist culture (and, therefore, about another version of the same hegemony), but about going beyond the boundaries of Modernity as a whole, into yet unknown territory — beyond "right" and "left".

Therefore, "Gramscianism from the right" is only a conventional term. It is not so much "right-wing" as it is "non-left-wing", i.e., it does not recognise communism to be an adequate counter-hegemony. But it is also not "right-wing" in the conventional sense, since it rejects capitalism and nationalism. The French sociologist Alain Soral, who continued this line, would later call this counter-hegemonic synthesis "left-wing Labour + right-wing Values".

This is most fully reflected in the Fourth Political Theory, to which A. de Benoist came in the 2000s. Here, as in Gramsci, an antithesis to hegemony (including its interpretation by Gramsci himself as international — imperialist — capitalism) is posed and the primacy of culture is recognised. But Marxism — at least in its dogmatic version — is discarded and a free search begins for philosophical, sociological, and anthropological studies which do not fall under the classical criteria and which can come to form the basis of a new metapolitical topology.

Over the course of 40 years, the New Right has traversed a long path in developing their metapolitical theory and related strategies. To this day, the conceptual apparatus and theoretical algorithms developed by them are the most adequate for the interpretation of such phenomena as European populism, the crisis of globalism, and the emergence of multipolarity. This is increasingly recognised not only by the "right", but also by the "left", such as by the Italian communist Massimo Cacciari, the French sociologists Serge Latouche and Jean-Claude Michéa, and the left-wing intellectual Chantal Mouffe.

The Fourth Political Theory in the French Political Space[1]

THREE IDEOLOGIES COEXISTED and fought amongst themselves in the 20th century: liberalism, communism, and fascism. Liberalism, both right and left, was worked out in the 18th century and was a certain disclosure of the philosophical foundations of the Enlightenment. The subject of liberal doctrine is the individual. This individual proclaims "freedom from". It says that it is free from God, from the state, from the homeland. Then, in the 20th century, communism became one of the leading ideologies, having been worked out in the 19th century and its subject being class. The third ideology is fascism, or National Socialism, the scope of which also included a failed attempt to return to the traditional society of Hyperborean myth. The subject of fascism is the state; of National Socialism — the nation or race.

It is important to say that today we no longer find ourselves in a situation in which there are three ideologies, nor are we even in a situation in which liberalism reigns. I will now explain my thesis. The fact of the matter is that we find ourselves in the space of post-liberalism. The liberalism that existed in the 20th century has ceased to exist. It has been transformed, mutated like a virus. In the contemporary space,

---

1   Presentation at the Centre for Ontological Studies conference, "The Fourth Political Theory: Horizons of a New Worldview", on 31 October 2015.

we see an inverted structure of values, the society of the spectacle,[2] the proclamation of the end of ideologies, and simulacra of the Political. If in classical liberalism there was a clearly expressed subject, the individual, whose slogan of being was "freedom from", then in post-liberalism, in the contemporary situation, in postmodernism, we are dealing with an absence of a subject, with a void. Deleuze[3] wrote that postmodernism has the duty of overcoming any ideology, any vertical, hierarchy, philosophy, or "culture tree", as he called Modernity. Deleuze advocated a new type of thinking and proposed that we think in terms of the rhizome[4] and simulacrum. Thus, we are confronted with a very difficult and complex situation. On the one hand, it would be easy to say that we live in the liberal epoch, that liberalism has prevailed, but this is not entirely the case. The point is that liberalism has mutated and turned into dangerous post-liberalism, where the contours of sub-jectivity are erased. The contemporary political subject lacks thinking and political will. This is much more dangerous than strictly classical liberalism. In order to overcome this, we should turn to the Fourth Political Theory.

---

2   *The Society of the Spectacle*, written by French theorist Guy Debord in 1967, criticises modern capitalist society, arguing that authentic social life has been replaced by representations and images, which he calls the "spectacle". Debord describes the spectacle as a collection of media and consumerist images that dominate public consciousness, leading individuals to passively consume rather than actively experience life. He contends that this immersion in spectacle alienates people from genuine social connections, making human interactions increasingly mediated by the commercialised, image-driven forces of capitalism.

3   Gilles Deleuze (1925–1995) was a French philosopher known for his work in metaphysics, epistemology, and political theory, often associated with post-structuralism and postmodern thought.

4   Deleuze's concept of the rhizome, developed with Félix Guattari, represents a non-hierarchical, decentralised model of knowledge and social organisation that contrasts with traditional "tree-like" structures. In a rhizome, elements connect in multiple, unpredictable ways, allowing for fluid, interconnected net-works without a singular point of origin or endpoint, embodying adaptability and resistance to rigid structures.

The Fourth Political Theory overcomes the situation of post-politics and post-liberalism *from above*. It is a critique of the very roots of liberalism and post-liberalism. It is of interest that Alain de Benoit critiques not only contemporary liberalism, but also the roots of liberalism, the metaphysical prerequisites of liberal doctrine. He also critiques the post-liberal political space of French politics.

In turn, I would like to shift our research in the direction of the French political space by looking at the case of the division between left and right in France and clarifying what the post-liberal epoch is.

And so, we are dealing with a simulacrum of the Political. The main parties in France are the following:

1. The Socialists, represented by Hollande;

2. The Union for a Popular Movement (UMP), now called the Republicans, which is Nicolas Sarkozy's movement, over the presidency of which he is now fighting with Alain Juppé;

3. The third political party is the National Front, represented by Marine Le Pen, which is now actively gaining in votes. At the recent preliminary elections in France's regions, the National Front was rather clearly successful.

If we examine the Socialist Party and UMP, then we won't see any substantive difference. Why? Because both left and right in the contemporary French political space are infected by the virus of liberalism. Hollande, a socialist, is for LGBT interests, for legalising light narcotics, for migration policies which entail accepting waves of refugees, for atheism, for multiculturalism, for replacing "sex" with the the concept of "gender" as something that a person can choose, and he totally supports Brussels' hegemony.

Let's go to the UMP, now the Republicans, and Sarkozy. Sarkozy promotes privatisation and private property, he is right-wing in economics. At the same time, however, he by all means avoids matters of preserving tradition and remains silent when faced with direct questions about gender and gay marriage. Thus, he is a representative of the classic right-wing political structure in the same way that Hollande is the classic left.

We are now dealing only with liberalism, no matter whether left or right. The only party that is excluded from the common chain of this political system, from the common liberal space, is the National Front. It is of interest that when Florian Philippot became Marine Le Pen's main advisor, the party adopted a course towards socialism in economics and conservatism in politics. Thus, the National Front is potentially the party that might, given certain circumstances, come close to the Fourth Political Theory and unite left and right.

Moving on, I would like to take the case of the Greek crisis[5] so as to tell of how French society perceives people who represent the National Front. When the Greek crisis broke out and a referendum was held on 5 July, an article came out in *Le Point* which was centred around a photo of Marine Le Pen, Alexis Tsipras, and Jean-Luc Mélenchon, the last of whom represented the ultra-left *Front de gauche* (Left Front). As soon as the first Eurosceptic tendencies and signs of a rapprochement between the National Front and the left bloc appeared, *Le Point*, seemingly a publication that fought for right-wing interests, began to discredit (in the most vile manner of slander) the ideas and people who were moving towards overcoming the *clivage*, the schism between left and right.

Whoever tries to go beyond the logic of left and right ends up being marginalised and is promptly placed in the periphery of society. Yet, the Fourth Political Theory is gradually becoming rather well-known and popular in France. It is more popular there than in Russia. Alexander Gelyevich Dugin has mentioned that his book has been translated into various languages, and that includes French. It was translated in 2013, and we organised a presentation in Bordeaux. Then, in 2015, a conference was held on the Fourth Political Theory and the principles of the Eurasian path in Paris, which 400 people attended.

---

5   Dugina covered the Greek economic crisis in her capacity as a journalist for Tsargrad TV.

Some of them couldn't even fit into the hall. In Russia, of course, not as many people come to conferences on the Fourth Political Theory, but let us look at Europe, where more attention is being shown towards it.

With respect to the development of the Fourth Political Theory in the French political space, we should first and foremost mention Alain de Benoist. He is the founder of GRECE, an organisation constituted in 1968. In French society, he is seen as ultra-right, but this is not at all the case. The fact of the matter is that whenever liberal society encounters something it doesn't clearly understand, it tries either to throw it out, not to notice it, or to accuse it of whatever extreme form of totalitarianism, "fascism", and slander it in any possible way. This has happened with Alain de Benoist, who advocates overcoming the division between left and right, which he considers to be a simulacrum of the Political, all the while as they accuse him of ultra-right views. Alain de Benoist's main ideas boil down to overcoming the division between left and right and to critiquing the European Union as a space organised by global financial capital against Tradition and against Europe, as an entity founded on purely material values.

Furthermore, I'd like to mention that there is one more important movement in French politics, an alternative movement that advocates the Fourth Political Theory. This is Alain Soral's movement, *Égalité & Réconciliation*, whose main slogan proclaims "left in economics, right in politics". In his book *Understanding the Empire*, where Soral takes "empire" to mean the global network of world government by finance capital, he examines the origins of the idea of the EU as a ploy of the global financial elites, and he shines light on the role of Goldman Sachs and banks in the political life of Europe.[6]

A final note. *Égalité & Réconciliation*'s participants include such a person as Dieudonné M'bala M'bala. He is half French, half

---

6   Alain Soral, *Comprendre l'Empire: Demain la gouvernance globale ou la révolte des Nations?* (Paris: Editions Blanche, 2011); Russian edition: *Poniat' Imperiiu. Griadushchee globalnoe upravlenie ili vosstanie natsii?* (Moscow: Academic Project, 2017).

Cameroonian. For 30 years he was a popular comedian among the people, but 10 years ago, when he started expressing criticism of banks, global financial capital, and Zionism, he became an enemy of the French liberal establishment. Thousands of criminal cases have been opened against him. He constantly has to deal with court cases and was recently imprisoned for a month, after which they let him out. Thus, in tolerant European society, even a Cameroonian (or at least half Cameroonian) who begins criticising global financial capital is thrown out and ends up in prison.

Today, as Europe is living out its final days, we need to think about a new political strategy. This new political strategy is the Fourth Political Theory. Only the development of this doctrine can help us get out of the totalitarian, post-liberal society that currently dominates the world.

The Decline of the West and the Resistance of the New Europe[1]

D EAR FRIENDS, thank you very much for inviting me to and organising this truly brilliant conference. What we heard yesterday was already impressive, but today we are getting to work on a very important mission. I think this is important because today the spiritual-metaphysical aspect, which Monk Isidor called us to pay attention to[2], entails the necessity of an apologetics for politics, and this is obvious. I am preparing my candidate dissertation on this topic at the philosophical faculty in Moscow. The false impression sometimes arises that politics is not necessary, that metaphysics is the goal and politics is only a rung, but no, this is not at all the case.

If you look at the seventh book of Plato's *Republic* as a source, then you'll see a description of the philosophical process of getting out of the cave, but immediately afterwards Plato, through Socrates, says that what is extremely necessary is in fact to return to the cave, to begin to rule. Because the philosopher is not simply a person who has got out of the cave (the cave of shadows, false opinions, and nihilism), but the

---

1   Presentation at the Chisinau Forum's conference "From the Atlantic to the Pacific: For the Common Destiny of Eurasian Peoples", 26–27 May 2017.

2   Monk Isidor of Athos gave a presentation on political hesychasm at the conference.

one who returns in order to begin passing along his understanding of the Idea of the Good to others.

And so, today is an extremely important day for us, because we are gathering to begin to discuss politics in the spiritual paradigm. My presentation is called "The Decline of the West and the Resistance of the New Europe".

First of all, we should briefly present the situation today in its eschatological meaning. Let us look at the apostolic prophets, who were already mentioned by Monk Isidor, that is the eschatological prophets who were like those from before the First Coming of Christ, who said that before the End of the World there will be a war between God and the devil that will last a thousand years. We are now living in a phase of war, and in political reality we see many signs of the End Times. I think everyone agrees with me that today we are living in the eschatological sphere that has been most precisely described by religious figures and prophets. But a very similar picture also emerges in the accounts of insightful people working in the sphere of culture, cultural studies, political science, and sociology.

I would like to speak about the outstanding philosopher Oswald Spengler, who ingeniously foretold the end of European civilisation in his renowned work *The Decline of the West*.[3] It is extremely important that this work's Italian translation was done by Julius Evola.[4] I think this is symbolic. Of course, I know that you are familiar with these ideas, but I nevertheless want to say a few words about this concept. Spengler argued that Europe has passed from the phase of culture into a new period which he called a period of decline, that is the period of civilisation. In Spengler's opinion, the death of European civilisation would come in the early 2000s. Now we understand that we really are at this end.

---

3   Oswald Spengler, *The Decline of the West*, 2 vols. (London: Arktos, 2021).

4   Oswald Spengler, *Il tramonto dell'occidente*, a cura di Julius Evola (Milano: Longanesi, 1957).

It is also interesting, as some have noticed, that in this case we are talking about the End of the World as a process. It is not a moment, but a process, an "ending end". The End of the World is a process. This is how it is. In fact, Heidegger said the same of the End of the World and the end of the paradigm of Modernity when he said that the end won't just arrive, but remains "*noch nicht*", that is "not yet" in German. The end is coming, but it doesn't just come and happen.

In Spengler's opinion, the advent of totalitarianism in the political sphere is a symbol of the reform of civilisation. He used the term "tyranny". I would like to say a bit about totalitarianism, because at the present moment we don't yet have any real tyranny. I would also like to talk about the migration of peoples. This is what we are now observing amidst the decline of European civilisation. Two phenomena are taking place: the migration of peoples and totalitarianism — digital totalitarianism, or the coming of a third, liberal totalitarianism in the sphere of politics.

Today, without a doubt, we live in a world of a new totalitarianism, especially in Europe. This is not at all communist or fascist totalitarianism, but liberal totalitarianism. It is extremely important to point out that liberalism in its essence is just as totalitarian as other totalitarian regimes under communism and fascism. If we return to the eschatological and religious perspective, then we of course see the prospect of liberal totalitarianism sooner or later coming into one pair of hands, to a tyrant. Today, the West is ruled by one man, but he is not sovereign: Trump. Rather, he is a kind of postmodern caricature of a tyrant. A caricature, because he is not a tyrant in the likes of which Plato saw, but rather a simulacrum of a Platonic tyrant.

I've worked a lot on covering and analysing the presidential elections in France, and I know well the details of this new totalitarianism. We know that another Satanic figure, one close to the figure of the Antichrist as described by some religious philosophers, Emmanuel Macron, has come to power in a rather strange way, like an algorithm. These were not elections in the direct sense, but really something strange. An invisible force simply appointed Macron to this post without paying any attention to ideology or programme. The bizarre Macron phenomenon is a vivid model of the "third totalitarianism". I would like to emphasise one wholly noteworthy trait of this personality — the level of development of his theory from the point of view of a philosophical paradigm. If we look at Macron, then we can see that he is really well educated. Despite appearing to have eclectic views, he has his own developed theory and he represents a closed system. He combines right-wing economics and left-wing politics, i.e. an integral right-left liberalism with a big dose of populism. But there is no life in him. If we look closely, we find something technical in all of this, something that is lethally boring.

At the same time, if we look at the philosophy of Marine Le Pen, we discover a fantastic contrast. It may be difficult to recognize a theory, a paradigm, behind her rhetoric and polemics and her contradictory populism which combines right-wing politics and left-wing economics. But if we look more attentively, we'll catch sight of a fully structured philosophy and clear system standing behind her. On the outside, it seems as though behind Marine Le Pen stands a very vague paradigm, whereas the paradigm behind Macron is really rather differentiated. But we believe that the intellectual weakness that is characteristic of Marine Le Pen, her populism, which at times looks altogether naive, potentially harbours the roots of a new, alternative political philosophy. Why? Because she represents life.

If we use Bergson's terminology, then we could say that that it is the *élan vital* (the "vital impulse", the "energy of life") that lies at the core of historical and political development.[5] But this impulse doesn't wield the clearest view of one's self and surroundings. The vital impulse

---

5   Henri Bergson (1859–1941) was a French philosopher renowned for his theories on time, consciousness, and creativity. His concept of *élan vital*, or "vital impulse", proposed that life is driven by a dynamic, creative force, which he argued could not be fully understood through scientific or rational analysis alone, influencing existentialist and process philosophy.

precedes reflection. The energy of life is blind in its movement, and this is clearly visible in the case of Marine Le Pen. Meanwhile, Macron overall completely represents death, the end of the vital impulse, due to his nihilism, which is a nihilism not from the point of view of Nietzsche, but of Spengler, in the sense of negating all traditional values and hierarchies. Of course, he is against the hierarchy of arms, the order of arms in the state and in metaphysics. He completely rejects the Platonic verticality, the Apollonian axis. In fact, moreover, I think he is even perfectly capable of reinterpreting it in the opposite sense. After all, he not only rejects it, but at times inverts it, brings the matter to an anti-hierarchy, anti-aristocracy, anti-Europe, and anti-France.

Marine Le Pen does not reject traditional values and traditional hierarchies, but she can't bring herself to unite with them, because if she were to return to them, it would be written off as reactionary or conservative. This wouldn't be conservatism in the best sense of the word, like the Conservative Revolution, but, to use the terminology of the political scientist René Rémond, would be a kind of "right legitimism".[6] I'm not certain, but if I have correctly understood Rémond, then I think that this would be a kind of "reactionarity". Marine Le Pen is defending a new ideology which she doesn't understand. Her rigidity exists because she doesn't understand where to go. In fact, she lost, but she lost to the same extent that the people did — she doesn't understand, but to the same extent that the people doesn't. So, we can observe a naivety and even intellectual impotence on Marine Le Pen's part in the face of the well-conceived doctrine that stands behind Macron.

However, if we view this interesting distinction through the prism of Leo Frobenius' cultural morphology, then we can see an extremely interesting and importance circumstance.[7] Frobenius, a friend of

6   René Rémond, *Les Droites aujourd'hui* (Paris: Louis Audiber, 2005).

7   Leo Frobenius, *Paideuma: Umrisse einer Kultur- und Seelenlehre* (Munich: C. H. Beck, 1921). Leo Frobenius (1873–1938) was a German ethnologist and archaeologist known for his studies on African cultures, challenging Eurocentric views by emphasising the complexity and depth of African civilisations. His work in

Spengler's, worked out the doctrine of "captivation" (*Ergriffenheit*). He said that the personality, culture, and the state are irreproachable in all societies, especially the personality and culture. There are three phases: (1) *Ergriffenheit*, that is "captivation", "emotional engagement", or even "obsession", (2) "expression" (*Ausdruck*), and (3) "application" (*Anwendung*). When we are captivated by something, we are enchanted by it. This is life, the energy of life, the principal of the vital impulse, the principle of creation. This is the first phase of culture, including political culture, and resembles the ideal Platonic position in which the philosopher is "engaged" or "captivated" by the idea, the Idea of the Good, and is enchanted in this state. The second phase, according to Frobenius, is expression. When the "captivation" is given a name, like when ideas of reform are formulated into theories and programmes, this is "expression". In psychology, this is the cure, i.e. when we have understood our obsession and try to express it, which means that, once we succeed in doing so, the spiritual sickness is overcome. The third phase is the employment (*Anwendung*) of the vital impulse as expressed in concrete reality, its application. In this third phase of development, culture is completely de-sacralized and is overloaded with technology.

What Yvan Blot once told me in a private conversation is important: Macron is the *Gestell*, a Heideggerian term which is applied to the civilisation of Modernity, the civilisation of technology. Heidegger uses the term *Gestell* to designate the "process of the death of the world". This is a very important notion in Heidegger's later philosophy. Macron himself, liberal globalism, the paradigm that stands behind Macron is death. This is the third phase of culture according to Frobenius, the phase of application (*Anwendung*) and technology. It could also be called the "hegemony of the cave", the cave that has been hermetically sealed off. This is in comparison to the open doctrine of Marine Le Pen, which has no final philosophical shape and is merely

cultural morphology sought to understand the symbolic patterns and shared cultural elements across societies.

a rather approximate contour of a doctrine, one that is blind to its own vitality and its "captivation". This is very, very important. As we know, Alain de Benoist has called Macron an "algorithm", that is, a tiny technical detail, a cog in the system, a tiny rock in the cave — after all, Macron's system is closed shut.

And so the time has come to draw out the comparison with Plato's cave as described in the seventh book of the *Republic*. We have two orders, two models. The first model is the closed cave, where the prisoners remain ignorant of the Idea of the Good. This model represents liberal hegemony and the nihilistic dictatorship which Europe lives under today. The second model is the cave with the open possibility of leaving it — this is populism. This is an alternative to the closed system.

The people who are representing Europe today at our colloquium have before themselves the goal of getting out of the cave of nihilism. You are exiting the cave like the philosopher-king who makes it out of the cave of illusion and begins to see the Idea of the Good. Of course, after the darkness of the cave it is always difficult to catch sight of the Idea of the Good; after all, your eyes haven't got used to the light and are still closed. But this step is extremely important.

Today, we live in a division into two Europes. The first Europe is the closed-off Europe of the cave of nihilism, the dictatorship of nihilism in Plato's Cave, where all the people are prisoners. The second system, which all of you here today represent, is the system of intellectuals who are getting out of the cave in order to see the Light of the Good, and who return to the people so as to tell them what it is.

Today, the alternative to the cave with no way out, the cave that has a way out to contemplate the Good, is, without a doubt, populism. Populism in our days is a new form of anti-totalitarianism, a struggle to get out of the nihilistic dictatorship of the cave. It is the alternative to liberal hegemony.

It is interesting that today the political division is no longer horizontal, as it was before, as the schism between left and right has ended, but is vertical, so now the actual, relevant schism is above all between the elites and those below, the people. It is important that the representatives of this cave hegemony, the nihilistic cave, necessarily want the people to stay as prisoners at the bottom. After all, they themselves are not philosophers who have made their way out of the cave to govern. They themselves are prisoners of the very same cave, the liberal religion, only on the second floor. To recall, Plato's cave has three levels, among which the lowest level is the masses subjected to harsh dictatorship, chained by their hands and legs and incapable of turning their heads away from the endless projections on the screen.

We have no ideology in the current conditions. We need to establish, affirm, and develop one. This conference is an invitation to create and develop a new ideology for Europe. We can't say that we are populists. Populism is only a stage in life, the stage of "captivation". It is part of the sickness. We are more like psychoanalysts. We are the psychologists of the birth process of a new populism, and we must give a schema, a philosophical paradigm, an explanation, an expression (*Ausdruck*) to this captivation.

The people are captivated and engaged in the fight against the elites — this is the main idea of populism according to Ernesto Laclau and Chantal Mouffe, the idea of how to direct and wage war against the liberal elites ruling over the people in these new conditions. In line with Frobenius, our role is to give expression to the *élan vital*, to the blind captivation of the masses, and to interpret the vital impulse of the people. I believe that conferences like this one are opportunities for carrying this out. However, we have a great labour ahead of us — in Europe, in Russia, everywhere. Therefore, I hope that today's conference will prove to be an invitation to create and affirm a new ideology. Thank you for your attention.

Interview with
Alain de Benoist[1]

Daria Dugina: What are the sources and reasons for the European crisis?

Alain de Benoist: I think we are talking about a crisis that has a universal character. It is universal because it is manifest in all spheres: political, social, financial — it is a civilisational crisis overall. It goes far beyond France. It is connected to the general development of events that led us out of Modernity and into Postmodernity. The old systems of reference that allowed people to orient themselves in life have been blurred, deleted, and destroyed, and so we've found ourselves in a so-called crisis. Crisis is a bit of a vague word which indicates that nothing is happening normally anymore, as it used to be, and that we no longer know where to look. This might seem rather abstract, but there are quite obvious, concrete consequences on the social level, in particular the decline and stagnation of wages. Economic growth has stopped and people's purchasing power is falling. The harsh economic measures adopted by various governments after the financial crisis of 2008 have turned into enormous national debt. We learned how to carry out harsh economic policies, but the consequences turned out to be catastrophic. Besides the material aspects that we ourselves are creating and which people have been very sensitive to, there's also a general civilisational crisis. There is a depletion of doctrines and narratives, an exhaustion of everything that gave meaning. In the final

---

1   Interview conducted in 2017, published on *geopolitika.ru* and *paideuma.tv*.

analysis, the best definition that we could give to the present crisis is that it is a loss of meaning. Meaning which people simply need in order to live.

Dugina: Do you think that this loss of meaning was orchestrated by postmodernist doctrine, like the doctrine of Foucault and Bourdieu?

de Benoist: It plays a certain role, but we can't say that the crisis was created by Foucault or Derrida. They contributed to the deconstruction of a definite quantity of things, and then, afterwards, there arose a certain dynamic which is not always a directed dynamic that is manageable by people. It is like a cybernetic phenomenon, resembling science or technoscience, which develops of its own accord, with no one managing it, but the result is the same. Approximately the same thing is happening in the financial world.

Dugina: And if we look at politics…

de Benoist: Indeed, on the political level, inasmuch as we should return to the political level, we are observing a depletion of the old political class represented by the big government parties, who over the years have been gathering increasingly fewer votes. I would say that we've left a certain type of society behind — you know, there is a theory which says that we had a two-thirds society, which meant that we lived in a society where approximately two-thirds of people were more or less satisfied with the world they were living in, while there was always a third who were discontent. Today everything has been turned on its head. In other words, now two-thirds are discontent and only a third of people are satisfied with their situation. This is a huge change. It is expressed in particular in the distrust that public opinion polls have measured and which has grown over the past 20 years — distrust of the financial, political, and media elites, all the upper strata, who are perceived as an oligarchy that only aspires to defend its own interests. A chasm has therefore opened up between the ruling class and the people. The rift between the left-wing parties and the people is especially noticeable, because it was conventionally maintained that the left parties defend the people. Today this is no longer the case. This is very visible on the theoretical level above all. The left-wing parties have united with the capitalist system, returned to the market system. On the other hand, today people are more likely to vote for the right, such as the National Front, or to abstain. Thus, the crisis of distrust has reached the point of shifting votes on the one hand, and on the other towards an increase in the number of those who abstain from voting. The number of people who are disappointed by the fact that they will never find what satisfies them is growing. Another important factor at play is the reorientation of programmes: parties that call themselves right or left are, in the final analysis, pursuing the same policies. Although people understand that they are voting for one or the other, in the final analysis they understand that this changes little. People also see that they are never consulted on the issues that have influenced their daily lives the most, such as migration, globalisation, and the evolution of the European Union, and when they were consulted, their desires weren't taken into account, as was the case in 2005, when the French said "no" to the European Constitutional Treaty but, in the end, everyone acted as if they had said "yes". Was this not the case?

And so, at the core of the crisis on the political levels lies distrust, a rift between the people and new parties, and the growth of atypical movements. Yesterday's marginal movements are taking on more and more significance, and they are contemptuously or derogatorily called populist parties, but they are steadily growing to the detriment of the main political parties. There have been many such examples. For example, the rise of Syriza in Greece led to the disappearance of the old Socialist Party. Approximately the same thing is now happening in Spain with the rise of Podemos. The presidential elections in Austria saw a clash between an environmentalist and a populist — the two main Austrian parties were absent from the ballots. There's the Brexit phenomenon and there's the phenomenon of Donald Trump's election. Therefore, we can see well that a general destabilisation is happening. In France as well, where everything has developed much more rapidly than I thought it would, we are observing approximately the same phenomenon. We have a few weeks left until the presidential elections, very important ones, I would say historic ones, because they are the first to happen in such a strange way with twists and turns, surprises, and all sorts of other curious things. These are the first elections in which, for both the left and the right, their favourites have been pushed aside, that is Sarkozy and Juppé on the one side and Valls and Montebourg on the other, in favour of Fillon and Hamon, at the same time as two tendencies, two currents, have risen which we have discussed most of all: Marine Le Pen's National Front and a new movement created by the former minister of the economy, Emmanuel Macron, which represents yesterday's political-financial elites. Thus, we are observing a new type of polarisation. Before, the classical polarisation consisted in that the right was always against the left and the left was always against the right. There was a kind of horizontal line, and the cursor moved along either in one direction or the other. Today we find ourselves in a vertical schema, not a horizontal one. There are those who are at the bottom, the people, and those at the top, the elites, who are today discredited as an oligarchy which has been rather harmful to the people's interests, the interests of the popular classes, as well as the middle classes, who are now threatened with being downgraded. The completely extraordinary, completely new result is that, for the first time ever since the first presidential elections, since the president of the Republic was elected by a universal vote, there is the rather big likelihood that Emmanuel Macron and Marine Le Pen will meet in the second round — that is, the representatives of the upper and lower strata. This means that for the first time the two government parties that have governed France for 30 or 40 years, those who are now called the Republicans and the left party which has for a long time been called the Socialist Party, will not be present in the second round. This has never happened before. Everything depends on these circumstances, and in the few weeks before the elections you never know what will happen, because something is always changing, but, in any case, the possibility of such a scenario shows that we are, to a certain extent, leaving the Fifth Republic as we know it behind, and we are facing a completely new schema and a complete reconstruction of the political landscape.

Dugina: From your point of view, can we consider Jean-Luc Mélenchon a populist?

de Benoist: Yes and no. Because there is no longer the former working class. Today, the former working class has sunk into a broader bloc which we call the popular classes and which includes workers as well as service employees, and which represents a multiplicity of different people — that is, it is impossible to win the majority without these classes. Jean-Luc Mélenchon is trying to create what is called left populism. His model is somewhat similar to Podemos in Spain or Syriza in Greece. Of course, he has many difficulties to face because in France there is always the very difficult issue of immigration and the social pathologies generated by too rapid, too large, poorly conducted and poorly organised immigration. The negative consequences of immigration are especially acutely felt by the popular classes. The working classes live in close contact with the population of immigrant origin, not the elites, who live in beautiful quarters where there are no immigrants. Insofar as Mélenchon can't take a very tough position on immigration due to his political position, people prefer to vote for Marine Le Pen. But, at the same time, there is a certain similarity between Marine Le Pen and Jean-Luc Mélenchon, firstly because they have an analogous style. Both are also hostile to the old political class. It is for this reason that Mélenchon hasn't withdrawn his candidacy in favour of Benoît Hamon, for which he has been criticised by many. If Mélenchon adhered to the old schema of "left and right", he would say: "Well, that's it, we'll add up my votes and Hamon's; if we unite, we'll have the chance to make it into the second round." But no, he has refrained from doing so. It is obvious that because of his refusal the left won't make it into the second round, so he has taken a very great responsibility upon himself. But this corresponds to his populist character, his popular style.

Dugina: Do you think that populism will become an ideology instead of only a style?

de Benoist: I don't think so. When it comes to populism, I think that it would be incorrect to speak of a populist ideology. When we look at the populist movements, we see an extraordinary diversity. This is why, for the sake of convenient language, we speak of "right populists" and "left populists". Some populist movements are very liberal on the economic or social plane while others are completely anti-liberal. So, the truth is that populism can be combined with any ideology. In itself, it is not an ideology. It is a style. It is a means for reworking politics from scratch, addressing the people, or speaking in the name of the people and in accordance with the schema that I've just presented.

We, the people, don't want this corrupt, egotistical ruling class that doesn't listen to citizens. Appealing to the people is at the core of the populist style. So now, when we historians and political scientists study the history of populism, we discover in the past what to a significant extent led to the emergence of populism at the same time in Russia and the United States. The *Narodniki* movement emerged in Russia — they were socialists who "went to the people" and campaigned for literacy, for developing the people's political consciousness, and they hedged their bets on the peasant community, which they believed to be the best means for opposing the expansion of Western capitalism. Then, in the United States, at around the same time in 1860–1870, a movement emerged to defend farmers and small landowners. This movement came to be called the "Grange" and led to the creation of the first political party that became a "popular party" and was very active until the early 20th century. Then appeared other cases which one could cite. It bears recalling that populism always manifests itself in crisis situations. It appears in the moment when liberal democracy shows its limits. Liberal democracy is parliamentarian and representative democracy, and it reaches its limits when a representative no longer represents anything.

The critique of representative democracy that Carl Schmitt expressed in the 20th century had already been made in the 18th century by Jean-Jacques Rousseau. Rousseau was completely right when he remarked that in liberal democracy the people is sovereign on the day of elections and only on that day. Because already the next day after elections, the people gives up its sovereignty in favour of its representatives who use it as they wish, which is not always what their electors want. There is a great deal of truth in this critique. This is why populism wants to bring back more consistent, more real democracy, with procedures like the imperative mandate that allows for deputies to be controlled after their election, to check whether they are doing what was expected of them. Jean-Luc Mélenchon has proposes measures of this type that would allow for controlling the elected, including the head of state, to ensure that they match what they were granted authority for. Forms of more direct democracy and democratic participation are also to be used. One can always contrast participatory democracy to representative democracy. There are also referendums, or plebiscitary democracy, or civil initiatives on referendums, such as what Marine Le Pen proposes, for example, which somewhat resembles the referendum model in Switzerland. This means that the initiator of a referendum is not only the central government when it wishes to organise a referendum, but can be the people itself. When 300,000 or 500,000 or millions of people demand that a question be raised, then a referendum is held.

Therefore, I consider it important to note that populism itself is not an ideology, but a style. Will this be the case in the future? I don't know whether this is possible or impossible. We lack a sufficient range of coverage of this phenomenon. This is also taking into consideration the fact that populism is very diverse, and it is becoming clear that when the time comes to take stock of the results, they will necessarily be ambiguous. Some populists will be successful while others, without a doubt, will fail. And then we'll see what will happen with populism. But I think that at this moment, populism should be interpreted as a transitory phenomenon. There is the old world with the old parties and the old ruling elites, and the growth of populism has led to their disappearance, to their increasing displacement. So, we are talking about a transition. To what? Where is everything going? To what type of institutionalisation, to what kind of political movement? It is too early to tell.

Dugina: Perhaps, as Russians say, everything is heading towards the end of the world?

de Benoist: The end of the old times, but not the end of the world. The end of the old times should not be confused with the end of the world. But an end of a cycle, a kind of historical pivot, is observable now practically everywhere.

Dugina: Is there any philosophy behind populism?

de Benoist: No, I don't think so, because it is not at all an intellectual movement. In fact, it is a movement oriented towards the popular masses, who usually don't read philosophers. Of course, there are exceptions. But, nevertheless, there are authors who have tried to theorize populism, like Ernesto Laclau. An important author from the United States also comes to mind, Christopher Lasch, who was in many respects inspired by George Orwell. In France, essays about Orwell have been written by Jean-Claude Michéa. These are political philosophers. There's also Chantal Mouffe, Laclau's wife, who is still active even though Laclau himself died several years ago. From the point of view of political philosophy, there are authors who theorize and even try to give some indications or advice to the populist movement. But we can't say that the populist movements as such possess many intellectual references. If we take Marine Le Pen, for example, then I believe that Marine Le Pen has other dignified qualities, but she does not wield any significant philosophical or theoretical knowledge. Then again, people don't expect this from her.

The anti-populists adhere to the ruling ideology. What is this ruling ideology? It is not the old left; we no longer live in the time of the dominance of old Marxism. Other times have come: liberalism is taken as the foundation. Thus arises a certain mix of liberalism, individualism, and the ideology of individual rights. This is the ideology of human rights expanded into infinity, so to say, spreading rights which, in order to be satisfied, would require increasing institutionalisation to recognize any desire or any fantasy as something justified and represented as a completely natural and essential need. It is obvious that all of this boils down to economism, that is, to the idea that the economy is above politics. Thus, the primacy of politics is negated. The individualist concept, which rejects holism and denies the idea that the people is something greater than a sum of individuals, is the phenomenon of consumption, or what Karl Marx called commodity fetishism. In other words, the idea is formed that man is here on Earth in order to maximise his personal material interests. Therefore, everything that would give meaning to human existence and man's presence in the world should be discarded as something of no great importance, or in any case should be derived from the private sphere. This clumsy ideology finds its natural continuation in globalism and cosmopolitanism. I would say that this ideology is directed towards eliminating all restrictions, that is, it wants to crush all limits, differences, and borders, anything that allows for standing out and being different.

Capitalism is a system of world government, a system that is driven by limitlessness, infinitude, and always needs more — more profit, more markets, more goods. The slogan of this tendency is: more is always needed. This means that in order to turn the planet into a gigantic market, it is necessary to eliminate all political, social, and cultural barriers, which means eliminating all differences. This is why universalism leads to the thought or judgement that differences between peoples, languages, cultures, and histories should be erased, because it is necessary to make everything homogeneous, to make everything uniform, and to turn the planet into a smooth space inhabited by homogenous people. Every person would be from here and nowhere, de facto some kind of abstract person with no soil under his feet. Borders are also limits. The "no borders" movement that we see today is in fact anti-populism, since at the core of populist aspirations is the hope of every people to remain itself, to continue existing with its own values, its own history, its own culture, its own way of life, its own way of existence — and this, so it seems, is threatened today. In the populist protest there is present, I would say, not only the populism of the populist parties, but also what Vincent Coussedière calls "people's populism", that is, the desire to pass something down from generation to generation, to preserve oneself, to continue to exist and, to this end, to be sovereign over the conditions of one's own social and historical reproduction. Here lies the essence of the question of the ideology of populism's opponents. Populism wants the local; anti-populists want the global. The first want to be re-rooted; the others want to uproot themselves. The first want the long run; the others want the short run. As a result, there is a fundamental schism that goes beyond the familiar past confrontation between right and left.

Dugina: Can we say that the opposition between populism and anti-populism is a kind of religion?

de Benoist: In Western Europe the problem isn't so acute. Take a country like France where, as you know, the majority are atheists. Such is the state of affairs. We could consider this to be very good or very bad, but it is the reality. Populist movements are rarely confessional. Yet, they uphold some kind of original spirituality. Many of their adherents, of course, might individually belong to the Catholic, Protestant, or Orthodox churches, but the movements themselves do not call themselves confessional. Not too long ago in France there was a lot of noise over what was called "*La Manif pour tous*" ("Manifesto for all"). The name in fact represented a broad protest movement against laws allowing same-sex marriage and similar things, and as a result there once again appeared on the scene many people who were majority Catholic. But this movement did not position itself as Christian. On the other hand, they upheld the Christian dimension of France's history, insisted on what is commonly called the Christian roots of Europe, or something of the sort. However, here we shouldn't draw a parallel with Russia or America. America is a highly materialistic country, yet for many Americans, mainly Protestants, religion is very significant. Russia is another special case. The Orthodox religion plays an extremely important and significant role. The relationship that has taken shape between Orthodoxy and politics throughout Russian history is completely different than in the case of Catholicism. It is very difficult to draw any parallel here. In France, indeed especially in France, there is the concept of secularism, but this word can in no way be translated into other languages. The English say "secular" and "secularism", but this is not what is meant in France. French ideology proposes neutrality, the principle of separating the state from the church and the neutrality of the state on matters of religion. Theoretically, this is the essence of secularism. In recent time, this concept has taken on a somewhat different shade due to polemics over the rise of Islam in France, which has given rise to problems that didn't exist before when there were only Catholics, Protestants, and Jews.

Dugina: Public opinion polls — do they show reality?

de Benoist: You know, the polemic over polling is as old as polls themselves. Public opinion polls have improved their method and are not as bad as they once were, but the problem is that they have no prognostic value. When today some candidate is attributed 10%, 15%, or 25%, people think "that's how much he'll get in the presidential elections". This is not true. If presidential elections were to be held today, these would be accurate results. But everything is constantly changing, intensifying, and many people have not decided or don't know what to say when they're asked, and the further we are from the final deadline of elections, the more such people there are. It bears taking into account the fact that people who say, "I'll vote for Marine Le Pen", "I'll vote for Macron", or "I'll vote for Mélenchon", have different degrees of certainty. When they're asked, "Is your choice absolutely final or might you still change it?", their answers differ strongly. When it comes to Marine Le Pen, few people want to change their initial choice. Eighty percent say, "I'll vote for Marine Le Pen regardless." On the other hand, when it comes to Macron, for example, 60% of those who say, "Yes, I'll vote for Macron", when asked whether they might change their mind, respond, "Well, maybe." This is the problem. This is the error of polling. We can never achieve a result that would precisely figure within a one or two percent margin. When we say that Macron has 25%, this means that he has around 25%, maybe 26%, maybe 24% or 23%. The same is the case with other candidates. So, polls are always disputed and regularly criticised. After the publication of polls, the candidates with the best results get an advantage, because people think, *This one will win, so I'll vote for him*. However, it is clear that some people go on to act the opposite way after the publication of polls: *Well, well! Someone I don't like might win, so I'll vote for the others*. This is called a "distortion" of polling results. This is no simple matter. It bears remembering that polls are not elections, above all because a poll is conduced at the time it is and because there exists a fundamental difference between the public and private. Polls are intended for private individuals who are called at their homes and asked whom they'll vote for. But voting is a public act, an expression of a civic position. In order to vote, a person has to go out somewhere. These are two completely different approaches. The paradox of polls and their main limitation is that they claim to reconstruct public opinion by way of summating private opinions.

Dugina: Last question. What do you think — what values should the future Europe be based on?

de Benoist: This is a trick question, because there is no simple answer. Europe's distinctive trait is its incredible diversity. It's as if you were to ask me what the European way of organising society is, but we've been through all sorts of ways. We've had cities, we've had nations, we've had empires, we've had dictatorships, we've had monarchies, we've had totalitarian systems, we've had democracies — we've experienced everything. If we nevertheless need to speak of values, I would propose a concept of man that is more balanced and less reductive than the one that is presently put forth. A concept that sees man from the point of view of his material and spiritual needs, the life of his soul, mind, and body — man who forms a coherent whole only when you look at him closely. There are values like history, memory, and the *longue durée*.[2] We are the owners of an extraordinarily rich heritage. This heritage cannot be treated in reactionary and restorationist terms, such as when they say, "It was better before." That things were better before does not mean that everything will go back to normal. Traditions are established in order to be renewed and transformed. Identity is not something that never changes, but something that allows us to remain ourselves while constantly changing. The history of Europe represents a series of metamorphoses. Today's Europe is not the Europe of the Industrial Revolution, the Renaissance, the Middle Ages, or antiquity, but it is undoubtedly still Europe. In a word, there are constants which allow us to go through different times while constantly renewing ourselves. There are also crisis periods. We are now in a crisis period. We no longer understand how to reconstruct Europe, nations, and peoples on the basis of new values. There are no prescriptions. If there was a simple answer to Lenin's old question, "What is to be done?", it would have been found long ago. Before we give a prognosis, we need to give a diagnosis. Consequently, we need to discern what is wrong, and as soon as we determine what is wrong, we'll begin to eliminate what's wrong and what is destroying us. Then we'll create the space in which something different, something new, something more positive might manifest itself.

---

2   *Longue durée* is a concept from French historian Fernand Braudel (1902–1985), referring to the long-term perspective in historical analysis, focusing on underlying structures and enduring patterns that shape societies over centuries, rather than short-term events.

Interview with François Bousquet[1]

Daria Dugina: What are the causes of the ideological, political, and philosophical crisis in Europe today?

François Bousquet: This crisis has ancient roots, and it is very difficult to analyse them and give a Nietzschean or Spenglerian reading of the crisis. According to Nietzsche, this crisis is the opening of a new chapter of nihilism, especially in Western Europe. This is my reading. Or there is the Spenglerian reading, which to me seems to be too catastrophic and crepuscular: the West, and in this case Europe, Western Europe, is too rotten to survive, as though Europe has outlived itself. I prefer the Nietzschean reading.

We are going through a new chapter of nihilism. Active nihilism in Europe. Western Europe has left history and politics — in a word, it has exited reality. Today, Nietzsche's last man is celebrating in Brussels and in all the capitals of Western Europe. This last man declares that he is committed to charity. He is in the famous "empire of the good" as Philippe Murer has described it. This is the empire that is killing us, and now it's the politics of human rights, which is no politics at all. As the French intellectual Marcel Gauchet once said, "Human rights is non-politics, a political dead-end." We've left politics, and this is killing us. It is a very deep evil. So, we need to hedge our bets

1   Interview conducted on 18 March 2017 at the Iliade Institute conference *"Européens: transmettre ou disparaître"* (Europeans: Preserve Your Heritage or Face Extinction), published on *geopolitika.ru*.

like Dominique Venner did, who brought us here today at the Iliade Institute. Venner's bet is that Europe must go through an eclipse, a historical eclipse, and then it won't even be an eclipse — it will be what he called an "assumption".

Europe has been plunged into slumber, but it is possible that it will wake up. This is the bet we should make. The path runs through cultural battle. Hence our presence here, which can infuse us with hope and foreshadow the return of political power in the future. But this crisis — the migration crisis, the economic crisis — is only a chapter, a variation of the crisis of nihilism.

Dugina: If we look at France, where are the roots of this nihilism? Sometimes people say that they are hidden back in the era of the Enlightenment, and sometimes experts and philosophers draw a connection with the ideology of 1968, as you pointed out today. What do you think: where are the roots of this new kind of nihilism?

Bousquet: Like Nietzsche did, I trace them back to the end of the 19th century, to what is called the waves of accursed poets. I am an unconditional supporter of Arthur Rimbaud,[2] whom I consider to be the greatest French poet, and whom the French so poorly live up to. He is as great as Nietzsche, or as great as your Sergei Yesenin.[3] The evil of Postmodernity influenced Rimbaud. In his famous "Letters of the Seer", which he wrote when he was 16, he outlines the programme of postmodernism. In fact, I see the roots of this evil in the late 19th

---

2   Arthur Rimbaud (1854–1891) was a French symbolist poet known for his revolutionary impact on modern literature. He wrote his most influential works, including *A Season in Hell* and *Illuminations*, as a teenager, experimenting with language and themes that challenged traditional forms and explored surreal imagery. Despite his early literary success, Rimbaud abruptly abandoned poetry at age 20, spending his remaining years as a traveller and trader in Africa.

3   Sergey Yesenin (1895–1925) was a Russian poet known for his lyrical and romantic verse that celebrated rural life and the beauty of the Russian countryside. His works, marked by a blend of nostalgia and melancholy, gained him fame during the early Soviet era, but his chaotic personal life and disillusionment with the new regime led to his tragic death by suicide.

century. Rimbaud says the following, and all the avantgardists identify with this idea: "I am the Other." This means I am not I, which means that I've lost my identity, my identifying signs, and the first identifying sign is sexual identity. If I am the Other, then I am a woman, I am a man, I am a cyborg, I am trans. Out of the beautiful ignorance of his unconscious, out of his poetic premonition, Rimbaud documented the big bold line of the postmodern programme.

This is like being tired of being human. This is the morality of the West since the Greeks. We have disenchanted the world, and this disenchantment of the world has led us to disappointing disillusionment. According to Nietzsche, this is the final stage of nihilism, the final stage of disenchanted man. We no longer take responsibility for our human condition. What is our human condition? It is the assignment of a specific identity, finitude, death, sickness, as Buddha said. It is a sickness, death, and old age which we don't want. We want to overcome this finitude, because it is unpleasant, and postmodernism joins up with transhumanism through this great exhaustion from being ourselves that is gong on across the whole European continent.

These are all the masters we've given ourselves since 1968 — and 1968 was nothing more than transmitting to the masses the revolution that had already been initiated by the avant-garde through pop culture, through what is called the '68 subculture that carried everyone with it. This revolution, which came to fruition over the course of virtually an entire century, is a revolution of desire, of regression, since desire is a regression to childhood, and this corresponds to our historical phase.

We have stopped being producers. Today the producers are in Russia and China. There is what we could a paleo-bourgeoisie. This paleo-bourgeoisie has many shortcomings, but it has a quality that we need to acknowledge: the capacity for gain, which entails labour, work. This is the bourgeoisie described by Max Weber. We have become neo-bourgeoisie, hence the term "*bobo*", "bohemian bourgeoisie", to describe who we are. We are merely consumers. The first thing that a consumer needs is for his desires to be liberated, and this is what was done in 1968.

Dugina: What can you say about Macron?

Bousquet: Macron… I think we can interpret the Macron phenomenon in France in the following way… It can't be ruled out that neither of the two candidates from the central parties that have dominated the French political scene for 50 years, the Socialists and the Republicans, will make it into the second round of the presidential elections in 2017. Macron slipped into the gap left by the absence of the two central parties. I think that Macron is the system's reaction along the German model of centrist coalitions: left-centrist, right-centrist, soft-centrist. This is a reaction to the growth of populism.

The whole dilemma, the whole drama of populism, and in France it is even more striking than among our European neighbours, is that France has both a left-wing populism in the face of Mélenchon, who is in the minority, constituting around 10%, and a right-wing populism, that of Marine Le Pen, who represents around 25%, perhaps even more. There is no agreement between these two populisms. In any scenario, Mélenchon would refuse to ally with Marine Le Pen, even if Marine Le Pen herself called for such an alliance. So, the coalition of the centre, that is, the system's response and the response of nihilism, is taking the risk of the Macron phenomenon in order to win in 2017. He is the candidate for power who is nothing more than a personification of John F. Kennedy. In France in the '60s, we had personages like Giscard, a symbolic figure of liberal and libertarian youth. Unfortunately, this type is on the way to triumph.

Dugina: Can you comment more on the phenomenon of populism in France?

Bousquet: France's problem in the current circumstances is that France is on the forefront when it comes to populism, without a doubt thanks to the first Le Pen-ism, the Le Pen-ism of Jean-Marie Le Pen, the father of Marine Le Pen. There is no question that we have been the pioneering country in Europe in this respect: after all, populism started to unfold in France in the 1980s. Unfortunately, it hit a ceiling in 2002. In 2002, Jean-Marie Le Pen made it to the second round of presidential elections; the system mobilised against him on a broad and mass scale, and we in our circles ignored this. In Russia you have less that catches one's eye, but in Western Europe the power of the system is really striking. The system has many resources and is capable of deceit. We saw this in Austria. Recall the first presidential elections. It is obvious that with electronic voting there was mass fraud that let foreigners vote. Without a doubt, the populist candidate suffered defeat. I believe that the system is ready to do anything to hinder and block the trio of populists in France. We should understand that in all possible and conceivable scenarios, Marine Le Pen will not come to power in France. The system is deceitful. We don't know what could let her come to power. Some would say terrorist attacks. Sure, let's assume so, such as when there were the Bataclan attacks. Immediately afterwards, France held regional elections in which Marine Le Pen gained a decent amount of votes, but she didn't win a single region. It seems as though in France the system has all the means to ensure its own preservation and survival.

Dugina: If we look at the philosophical foundation of the resistance to nihilism and the resistance to the unipolar world, which out of its agony is trying to extend its lifespan by artificial means, then what is the ideology of resistance? What are its philosophical grounds? What do you think?

Bousquet: We are laying down these philosophical foundations today. We have been lagging behind, especially on the right, since we have been neglecting the battle of ideas and we thought that intellectualism is something along the likes of what in French is called "brain juice", that is, a struggle that is useless, superficial, and unnecessary, and so we've been behind. There has been a long, dark eclipse of conservative thought in France. All the significant thinkers in France over the last half a century, with the exception of Alain de Benoist (who nowadays talks well with both right and left), have come from the left.

Now our time has come, and for the Iliade Institute this means returning to the fold of the cultural Gramscianism theorised by Alain de Benoist in the late 1970s, returning to fight for hegemony in culture. When it comes to hegemony in culture in France, we on the right, or in any case conservatives, whether right or left, are taking it back. There is a lot of work ahead of us because we have been so far behind. I'm used to saying that in France the system is completely blocked by cultural leftism, in this case by libertarians and liberals, who profess one and the same doctrine. What is this doctrine? It is convenient anti-racism, socially conditioned human rights, and it is a shameful commitment, often forced, but a commitment nonetheless, to the ideology of the market. This ideology has triumphed in France and has a monopoly. This cultural leftism has a complete monopoly in the universities, in the sphere of education, in the sphere of culture, and in the mainstream media. In short, it holds absolutely everything. The system wields all of them, and they control the system. This control over the system is what we need to push back. But how can it be forced to retreat? I think it is about winning the battle of discourse, pushing aside the field of what is banned, because it seems to me that the real and only power is the possession of totems and taboos.

There are no other forces. When writing his political theology, Carl Schmitt believed that the political comes from the religious. I think that the political really does come from the religious. What is the religious? It is the ability to distinguish the pure from the impure, the forbidden from the permitted, and politics symbolically stems from this difference, from this segregation, which governs the religious and what is banned. The field of what is forbidden is the privilege, the monopoly of the left in culture.

Dugina: Could you say something about the strategy of "re-information"?

Bousquet: Re-information has turned out to be a matter of necessity for us, just as it turned out to be a necessity for Americans half a century ago, when the Americans laid the groundwork for Trump and for a conservative revolution. In France we've understood — and this is really astonishing — that all the central media are really blocked by the system. We have no access to the central media. We can't utter the word that we want to address our competitors with. In the outskirts, in the periphery of the media system, a hazy galaxy has taken shape — it is much more than a galaxy, more of an abundance, a flowerbed — of so-called re-information sites. The system calls them the "fascosphere", but it is none other than a re-infosphere that allows for bypassing the blockade of the media system.

This is very encouraging, because if we take the websites of the so-called re-infosphere, for example the two loudest ones, Alain Soral's "Equality and Reconciliation" or "Pureblood F", founded by someone else, then it is obvious that these two sites are almost the most visited sites by French people today. They view these sites more often than the websites of the big newspapers or audiovisual media.

Thanks to re-information, thanks to this re-infosphere, we have some breathing room, we can get out of the crowded corner in which they wanted to shut us off. We have laid this groundwork, because we want to have a configuration like the Americans have. After the defeat of the Republican candidate in the '60s — I think it was Barry Goldwater — the Americans recognised their ideological defeat. I'm talking about the American Republicans, or more accurately those whom we call paleoconservatives (people who fear a clash of civilisations and don't want to export or import civilisation, and this is a rather interesting conservative right wing). All the central mainstream media, the whole university system, and editorial production was in the hands of the left, who in the US are called Democrats or liberals. So it came to laying the groundwork for a system of re-information. How? By publishing books, creating think tanks, establishing foundations, creating radio stations, creating audiovisual media and, consequently, in the long run, over a period of 30–40 years, they planted the seeds that grew into the Trump phenomenon — which, even though I think it has disappointed us, is still happening. This is even more eye-catching for you Russians, because he has almost, if not finally, crossed the t's and dotted the i's for a rapprochement with Russia.

Despite everything, these sites came to exist in the periphery of the system, and this achievement of the conservative revolution led to Trump's success in the US presidential elections. We want this to happen in France.

Post-Politics vs. Existential Politics[1]

THE 20TH CENTURY was the century of rivalry between three ideologies. One of them managed to reign for several centuries (liberalism), the others only for a few decades or a few years (communism
and National Socialism). But their death appears to be self-evident
to us. All three ideologies, born out of the philosophy of Modernity,
have left the space of the Political. The era of Modernity has come to
a conclusion.

The End of the Era of Modernity

The death of liberalism is not as obvious as the death of communism
or National Socialism. When Francis Fukuyama proclaimed the End
of History, he meant the end of the competition between the three ideologies and the final victory of the liberal doctrine. But liberalism did
not win. We can see this if we pay attention to the subject of politics
today. If in classical liberalism the subject of politics was the individual
(whose main virtue was declared to be freedom in the negative understanding, as was precisely described by Helvétius: "A man at liberty is
a person neither in chains, under confinement, nor intimidated like
a slave by the fear of punishment"[2]), then today this individual is no

---

1   Originally published as an article on *geopolitika.ru* on 15 December 2015 (coin-
    cidentally, Dugina's 23rd birthday).

2   C. A. Helvétius, *De l'esprit, or Essays on the Mind and Its Several Faculties*
    (London: Albion Press, 1810).

more. The subject of classical liberalism has been eliminated from all spheres; its integrity has been called into doubt, and even its identity, even negatively defined, is characterised as a kind of malfunction in the global virtual system. The world has passed into the sphere of post-politics and post-liberalism.

Rhizomatic Politics

The individual has turned into the rhizome; the contours of the subject have melted away along with faith in Modernity ("We were never modern", proclaims Bruno Latour, who saw in Modernity a lot of contradictions and a lack of observance of its own proper rules of functioning and constitution).[3] "We are tired of the tree!" — the *logos* of Modernity is mocked by the streaming liquid society of Postmodernity. A new actor of politics appears: the post-subject. It thinks chaotically — the slides in its head change at lightning-fast pace, interfering with the classical, logical strategies of thinking. The new thinking is chaosmosis, glitch-thinking.[4] The Political is turned into the "wonderland" in which the actor-event-Alice grows and shrinks in the psychedelic pattern of the new post-rationality.

The contemporary left and right are an example of this pattern. The recent left-right coalition against the National Front following the first round of regional elections showed the end of the political model of Modernity. Left and right values are mixed together, unified by a new type of liberal virus. The contemporary left starts to play with capital, actively defending right-wing political values (ecology), and the right takes on the comic character of zealous nationalists.

The peculiarity of post-politics is the blurring of the contours of the scale of the "event". The scales change abruptly back and forth

3   Gilles Deleuze, *The Logic of Sense*, trans. Mark Lester and Charles Stivale (New York: Columbia University Press, 1990); Bruno Latour, *We Have Never Been Modern*, trans. Catherine Porter (Cambridge: Harvard University Press, 1993).

4   Félix Guattari, *Chaosmosis: An Ethico-Aesthetic Paradigm*, trans. Julian Pefanis (Bloomington: Indiana University Press, 1995).

("Alice grows, Alice shrinks"). Wars take on new shapes. Baudrillard called the system's current confrontation with terrorism the "Fourth World War". This is distinct from the previous wars that have been waged: the first two world wars, which were of world-scale, and the third war, the Cold War, which was a confrontation between two key geopolitical poles (the US and the USSR). The fourth war is a war of soft power, a quasi-media war, which is ready at any moment to become a war using new kinds of weapons. The "Fourth World War" is a war of postmodernist bent, where both friend and enemies are in a cunning fusion (terrorism becomes part of the political system).[5] The "Fourth World War" plays and flirts with different scales: its main characteristic is its non-systematic, chaotic, and arbitrary character when it comes to defining the scale of events (a micro-narrative becomes an event while macro-narratives are ignored). A terrorist attack occupies a small square: one building, one hall, several rooms, or a balcony (micro-narrative). In classical wars, there were points of orientation, on the basis of whose correlation we could tell the significance of events. In the contemporary political world, such points are absent — like Alice in Wonderland, who shrinks and grows, but there's no way to distinguish her "normal, ideal" growth (this is the chaosmos described by Deleuze in *The Logic of Sense*). The logic of the Political has been cancelled.

Acts of terror (130 people were killed in Paris on Friday the 13th) shock the Political more than large-scale wars (Syria). This testifies to the fact that the world is entering a new phase: the phase of rhizomatic politics. To understand contemporary politics, we need to learn to think in terms of the rhizome, to incorporate the chaosmos. Post-politics is a world of political spin technologies, a five-second-left-socialist and five-second-right-republican one. Identity changes with the click of a TV remote control, with technology. Only then does the question arise: Who is managing the remote control; who decides to change the

---

5   Baudrillard, *The Spirit of Terrorism.*

slide? In Martin Heidegger's terms, the main force of contemporary post-politics is *Machenschaft* and τεχνή.[6]

The Alternative to Rhizomatic Politics in the Situation of the Death of Ideologies

Martin Heidegger's works propose a special view of the organisation of the Political. In liberal Western society, Heidegger's works, and especially his political philosophy (which is not presented explicitly), are insufficiently studied. The study of Heidegger's political philosophy is, as a general rule, reduced to trying to find the philosopher engaged in apologetics for fascism and anti-Semitism (one such case is the philosophical community's reaction to the recently published *Black Notebooks*[7], and especially telling is the French historian Emmanuel Faye's reaction[8]). Such an interpretation ignores the metaphysical

---

6 Heidegger's concept of *Machenschaft*, often translated as "machination" or "calculative domination", refers to the pervasive drive within Modernity to control, manipulate, and exploit beings, reducing the world to mere resources. This stands in contrast to τέχνη (*technē*), an ancient Greek term denoting a form of craftsmanship or art that brings forth truth and reveals the essence of things, rather than dominating them. Heidegger saw *Machenschaft* as a distortion of τέχνη, transforming it from a means of revealing truth into a tool for manipulation and instrumentalisation, ultimately obscuring authentic human and existential relationships with the world.

7 Martin Heidegger, *Ponderings II-VI: Black Notebooks 1931–1938*, trans. Richard Rojcewicz (Bloomington: Indiana University Press, 2016); idem, *Ponderings VII-XI: Black Notebooks 1938–1939*, trans. Richard Rojcewicz (Bloomington: Indiana University Press, 2017); idem, *Ponderings XII-XV: Black Notebooks 1939–1941*, trans. Richard Rojcewicz (Bloomington: Indiana University Press, 2017). The long-awaited and controversial *Black Notebooks* from 1942–1948 are forthcoming from Indiana University Press in 2025 (they have been available in Russian since 2022).

8 Emmanuel Faye, *Heidegger, le sol, la communauté, la race* (Paris: Beauchesne, 2014). Faye is a little-known French writer who collaborates with the Soros Foundation and specialises in custom-ordered philosophical denunciations. He argues that the *Black Notebooks* reveal Heidegger's deep-seated anti-Semitism

dimension of Heidegger's philosophy and seems to us to be superfluous, superficial, and distorting of Heidegger's teaching.

Martin Heidegger cannot be interpreted in the context of any single political theory in the 20th century. His critique of *Machenschaft* ("machination") is applied not only to the Jews (in terms of metaphysical principle, not biological) but, to an even greater extent, to National Socialism. In this sense, we can say that Martin Heidegger puts forth a fundamental critique of National Socialism, in which he sees clear manifestations of *Machenschaft* (unlike the hypothetical "spiritual" and authentic German movement which, according to Heidegger, was not realised within the framework of Hitler's rule).

Heidegger recognises the deep crisis of all political systems. Applying the history of Being to the history of the Political, politics appears as the process of the gradual oblivion of Being in the direction of the domain of mere present beings. The modern Political has no existential dimension; it is inauthentic. Politics and ontology are inseparable, as Plato pointed out in the *Republic* when he introduced a homology between the political and the ontological (justice in the soul is the same as justice in the state).

Applying fundamental ontology to the sphere of the Political, we can suppose that the Political can exist authentically and inauthentically.[9] The authentic existence of politics lies in its allegiance to Being; the inauthentic existence of politics means excessive investment in present beings and the oblivion of Being. The state in which the Political exists authentically is hierarchical. The ontological stands above the ontic, the authentic above the inauthentic. The types of lordship stand in a strict vertical: from *Machenschaft* to *Herrschaft*.[10]

---

and his alignment with Nazi ideology, challenging the separation between Heidegger's philosophical work and his political beliefs.

9   Alexander Dugin, *Martin Heidegger: The Philosophy of Another Beginning*, trans. Nina Kouprianova (Arlington: Radix / Washington Summit Publishers, 2014).

10   German for "rule".

In the situation of the contemporary crisis of the Political, existential politics deserves special attention and seems to us to be a genuine alternative to rhizomatic politics. We need deep study and further deliberation.

PART II

DECONSTRUCTING
FRENCH POLITICS

American Ideology in Modern French Politics[1]

S TARTING IN 1968, French society began to gradually pass over to American ideology, which meant rejecting the right-wing politics of conservatism, traditions, and hierarchies in favour of left-wing liberalism. Since 2007, France's political elites have been fully under the influence of American ideology (in 2009, France fully rejoined NATO). How does American ideology manifest itself in the French political space? The main traits of American ideology are:

- Confidence in universal progress, the peak of which is Western capitalist civilisation (with the US as the unconditional leader);

- Extreme individualism, the rejection of collective identities (religious, national, ethnic), and the destruction of traditional values, including the rejection of sex (gender politics) and the traditional family;

- Taking technology and technological development to be the main goal, leaving the moral aspect aside as unessential and secondary;

- The US and the West have the full moral right to dictate to all other peoples which path they should follow and how they should live (American hegemony on a global scale).

---

1   Analytical report published by the Katehon think tank and the Russian Institute for Strategic Studies in March 2016.

Right and Left (in Politics and Economics)

In order to see how American ideology is implemented in the European space, it is necessary to examine the schema of the political structure of Western European societies: this is the division into right and left (in politics and economics). This model of dividing political parties into right and left was born at the National Constituent Assembly (1789), where the supporters of the monarchy, "royalists", and conservatives were seated on the right side of the room, while the revolutionaries, anti-monarchists, and radical democrats were on the left.

The main traits of the right in politics are: defending traditional values, conservatism, upholding continuity with the past in terms of national, religious, and state identity. In the economic sphere, right-wing parties defend private property (the primacy of private property and private ownership over collective property, whether state, national, or communal) and the construction of a free, planetary market without national and state borders.

The main traits of left forces in politics are: negating identity (national, religious, ethnic), rejecting traditional values, anti-conservatism, and universalism. In the economic sphere, the left advocates the primacy of various forms of collective property over private ownership (such as the nationalisation of private property).

France before 1968

Before 1968, the influence of American ideology in France was weak. This was in many respects thanks to the efforts of President de Gaulle, who consistently pursued anti-American policies aimed at building a sovereign continental Europe "from the Atlantic to the Urals" (Rimland):

- De Gaulle opposed England's entry into the European Economic Community and aspired to build a European Union without the Anglo-Saxons' involvement;

- De Gaulle removed American military bases from France's national territory;

- De Gaulle freed France from defense commitments to NATO (in 1966 France left the alliance's military organisations) and left the Defence Planning Committee and the Nuclear Planning Group (although France continued to participate in the alliance's political structures, the North Atlantic Council);

- In 1965, de Gaulle declared that France would not use the dollar in international transactions and would transition to a unified gold standard;

- De Gaulle turned France into a leader of the Non-Aligned Movement between the two blocs of the Cold War; France thus chose a "third way" (Rimland as an independent zone);

- France refused to submit to the American Empire, condemning the US' actions against the countries of Indochina and supporting Palestine in 1967 (condemning Israel's actions in the Six-Day War of 1967).

What Happened in May 1968?

American ideology penetrated France in May 1968. Radical left-wing student actions, demonstrations, and mass unrest saw millions of students take to the streets. Paradoxically, in this time France was experiencing unprecedented economic growth (the so-called "Glorious Thirty").

Several tendencies can be highlighted within the structure of "Red May":

1. The anarchists, whose slogans were "*Il est interdit d'interdire*" ("It is forbidden to forbid") and "*Ni Dieu ni maître!*" ("No God, no Master!");

2. The left-Gaucheists, whose slogan was "*Travailleur: Tu as 25 ans mais ton syndicat est de l'autre siècle*" ("Worker, you're 25, but your union is from the past century");

3. The left-liberals, whose aim was to destabilise the de Gaulle regime and remove de Gaulle from power.

If the first tendency had practically no positive programme, then the second and especially the third fronts of Red May had a clear-cut idea of a future France in which there should not be a de Gaulle figure. De Gaulle's right-wing, anti-American regime was overthrown by left-wing, anti-American sentiments (the left-wing protestors criticised the American intervention in Vietnam with the slogan "*Imagine: c'est la guerre et personne n'y va!*" — "Imagine: there's a war and nobody's going!"). The youth protested against the war in Vietnam and the US' war policies while at the same time being under the influence of Anglo-Saxon culture. American ideology appeared in the French political space through these anti-American protests.

France after "Red May"

After May 1968, American ideology gradually penetrated the French political space, giving rise to a new society in which the main ideology was liberal-libertarianism, the main aim of which was to destroy (1) the left-wing social model (defended by the Communist Party of France) and (2) the right-wing legal model (created by de Gaulle).

The contours of left and right in politics and economics gradually became blurred. The right started to stand only for bourgeois liberalism and capitalism, ignoring conservatism, while the left advocated globalisation and progress, ignoring the economic sphere (neglecting demands to protect workers' rights and the primacy of collective property over private).

France under the *Diktat* of American Ideology

France today is ruled by a real ideological dictatorship, the hegemony of the *pensée unique*[2] that is American ideology. Whoever has something against left-wing liberalism (even without acting in the name of right-wing liberalism) ends up on the list of "untouchables" and marginals, becomes an enemy of the system, even a "terrorist" (especially telling are the system's heightened attention to the National Front and the recent raid searches at the National Front's main office that lasted more than 24 hours). The ruling ideology in France — American ideology — is based on bringing together right-wing market liberalism and left-wing globalism.

Under Sarkozy's presidency, France fully passed to being under the roof of American ideology:

- In March 2009, France joined NATO, which was a betrayal of the Gaullist legacy and meant France's official subordination to American command;

- Unification with left-wing liberals;

- Assisting the US in overthrowing anti-American regimes in the Middle East (Libya in 2011).

Since 2012, Hollande has consistently:

- Continued the policies of his predecessor (despite the fact that he represented left-wing forces, Hollande ignores the left-wing parties' values in economics; the unemployment rate has risen to 10% under him);

- Supported sanctions against Russia and broken the Mistrals contract[3];

---

2   French for "one-track thinking".

3   The Mistral contract was a 2011 agreement in which France, under President Nicolas Sarkozy, committed to selling two Mistral-class amphibious assault

- Legalised same-sex marriages.

The Alternative to American Ideology in France

Is there any realistic alternative to the ruling American ideology in the French political space today? There is not, but there is an intensive search for such. The National Front party is one political force that opposes the system of American ideology in France and is engaged in developing an alternative. Their critique of the EU's migration policy, their Euroscepticism, their orientation towards conservatism and pre-serving traditions (family, marriage, religion), and their criticism of the Atlanticist orientation of the French ruling elite represent the will of the French people in the political space and are an alternative to the government's left-liberal course. The ruling political forces see the National Front as a threat to the system, as an anti-system party whose programme unites left-wing anti-liberal values (social equality, justice, anti-capitalism) as well as right-wing, non-liberal values (conservatism, a strong state, anti-migration policy).

Following the 2015 regional elections, it became obvious that the National Front is not only a legitimate political force, but now one with a legal mandate. This greatly worried the liberal left (Socialists) and right (Republicans) parties and provoked the creation of a new left-right coalition to eliminate the National Front from the arena of political struggle.

---

ships to Russia. President François Hollande's decision to break the contract in 2014, influenced by American pressure and anti-Russian sanctions after the Crimea annexation, was an act of political submission that undermined fair commerce and strategic trust between France and Russia.

The Battle of Europe: Globalists vs. Patriots[1]

Andrei Kovalenko: Greetings, dear friends! Today at the Ordynka Club we're joined by Daria Platonova, an analyst for *Geopolitika. ru*, and Manuel Ochsenreiter, the head representative of the German Centre for Eurasian Studies. Hello!

Manuel Ochsenreiter: Hello!

Kovalenko: Our main question is about the recent first round of the elections in France and the rapidly incoming second round. Daria, knowing the situation and having dealt with it personally, how do you assess the results of the first round and what prospects are there ahead of the second round? Is what is happening there a general trend or something local?

Daria Platonova Dugina: I would highlight several peculiarities of these elections. First and foremost is that none of the representatives of the classic French parties have made it into the second round — neither the Republicans nor the Socialists. Neither Fillon nor Hamon will be in the second round. This means the end of the political division into "left" and "right" — interestingly enough, a legal and legitimate end — and the beginning of a new division into "populist" and "anti-populist" forces.

The essence of the matter is that today's France is in the vanguard of this political battle, because if in Germany we see some kind of

---

opposition between the old forces, then here both of the actors of the political process are new forces. An absolutely new political space has emerged. If Le Pen, for instance, were opposed by the classic Socialists or Republicans, as was the case in the 2015 regional elections, then this would be the well-known, classic schema. Both the left-wing system and the right-wing system are against Marine Le Pen. But here we see something completely different: as if out of a laboratory, a demon has come out of a test tube. Emmanuel Macron has appeared—a representative of the Rothschilds, an agent of the globalists, a 39-year-old banker, who suddenly…

Kovalenko: Almost as if he's been grown in a test tube…

Dugina: Like an embryo! And now he suddenly starts asserting very strange things, namely that there's no "right" or "left", that he himself isn't "right" or "left", that he's for progress, and that, so to speak, there are progressives and there are conservatives. What's interesting in these elections is that the candidate who won in the first round, Macron, is deliberately thinking a step ahead of the "left" and "right" political spin technologists. He says that there is no left and right; there is progress and there is regress. Marine Le Pen has the same position, but opposite of Macron. Everything else in the political space—the political scientists and so on—is simply behind. This new, lab-grown candidate of globalism is an enormous danger to all the peoples of Europe. In every country today, this mind of a liberal anti-populist is appearing, is being spawned, and the problem is that…

Kovalenko: In some places, these forces are still in embryonic form, while in others they're already mature, but they can be highlighted in any European state. France here is in the vanguard, just as their revolution happened before everyone else.

Dugina: This is a very interesting moment: on the one hand, there really is a political war going on, while on the other, there is a renunciation of the past, which is really reminiscent of the philosophy of the Enlightenment. Once again, there is a division between the elites, who are more enlightened than the people, and the people itself, which is "backwards" and is "in a phase of slumber and ignorance of the truth". This Masonic Enlightenment ideology today is represented by Macron; it hasn't gone away. On the one hand, a new political space has emerged or is being imitated, as Macron presents himself as neither "left" nor "right". But this is an absolute lie: being a liberal, he embodies the worst of right-wing economics (the domination of big finance capital) and the lowest of the left spectrum, which is to say that he incorporates left-wing politics in the likes of globalism, LGBT propaganda, other forms of perversions, unregulated immigration, and Euro integration, itself also a perversion of its own sort, at least in the form which Macron upholds. Thus, a revolutionary situation is taking shape.

Kovalenko: Understood. Daria, perhaps you could ask our German guest, Manuel, the same question, and you can translate what he says?

Dugina: Manuel, we are talking about the division between populists and anti-populists. I just said a few words about the National Front and Macron, who is a new, neither right nor left politician on the scene. I want to ask you: What do you think about Germany? Is there such a split, and do you think that there will be some similar personality in the parliamentary elections like Macron who will appear to be somebody new from the political avant-garde of globalism in the parliamentary elections and become the new avant-garde of globalism?

Ochsenreiter: In Germany they will for sure not present someone new now, because we have two perfect candidates of the globalist system: Angela Merkel and Martin Scholz. Both of their parties are in a coalition right now, so they are even governing together: the Social Democrats and Christian Democratic Union. But we have from the other side for the first time a real oppositional force with the Alternative for Germany [AfD], where we see the beginnings of a similar development like in France with the National Front or Austria with the FPÖ.[2]

---

2   The FPÖ (Freedom Party of Austria) is a political party that champions national sovereignty, traditional values, and the interests of Austrian citizens, emphasizing a commitment to preserving cultural identity and economic stability.

As an example, in East Germany a lot of the electorate of the AfD party used to vote for Die Linke.[3] But right now the party is not ready to be what the National Front or the Freedom Party became. The party right now doesn't represent this mix of traditional left and traditional right topics like patriotism and social justice. But just one point I would like to add when it comes to the so-called left or far-left movements: today we connect this whole open border and mass migration topic with the left; it came from them; they were lobbying for that. But we shouldn't forget that this has nothing to do with Marxist points of view or something with socialist theory. It is something artificial. In Germany, we have Sahra Wagenknecht,[4] who knows exactly that if you want to have a social state with a social network, you need borders. There is no social system possible without borders. But for liberal capitalism, of course, borders are the worst thing ever. We see in this example how the left has become the useful idiot of the liberal capitalists.

Kovalenko: As far as I understood what you said, in France society as a whole is increasingly beginning to understand that "left" and "right" in the classic parties is a certain swindle. In France more people understand this, but it seems that in Germany this isn't yet fully recognised: people and society are still under the pressure of the propaganda. They really believe in "left" and "right" because they went through the so-called "de-Nazification" processes and even overall

3   Die Linke (The Left) is a far-left political party in Germany that promotes so-cialist and Marxist principles, calling for extensive state intervention and wealth redistribution. Its progressive, woke agenda — emphasising identity politics, open borders, and radical social policies — undermines economic freedom, national cohesion, and traditional European values.

4   Sahra Wagenknecht (b. 1969) is a prominent German politician and former leading figure of Die Linke who, due to internal party conflicts, founded her own party, the Sahra Wagenknecht Alliance (BSW), in 2024. Known for advocating a left-wing populist platform that challenges neoliberalism and calls for strong social cohesion, she has become a distinctive voice opposing mass immigration and woke policies, positioning herself as a champion of pragmatic and socially conservative leftism. Some even call her a National Bolshevik.

brainwashing, not only concerning fascism and Nazism but the past as such. Everything has been chased away to somewhere deep in the unconscious, and people need a long time and, perhaps, real empirical experience in order to become aware of what has been happening and to figure out the characteristics of political forces.

Dugina: You mean that France is in the vanguard of awareness of the end of the division into "right" and "left"?

Kovalenko: If we compare it to Germany, then in France more people understand this, but in Germany this consciousness is still foggy. People hardly see the picture as we're discussing it now.

Dugina: This is also an interesting point. I'll say a few words on France before we ask Manuel. I'm afraid that people in France also don't understand that the "left-right" division has come to an end. There is some unconscious disappointment with these forces, not to mention that they are considered dangerous…

Kovaenko: It's not yet formulated…

Dugina: Yes, not yet formulated. That's why Alain de Benoist calls populism a "style", not an "ideology". The people still aren't aware of what the leading intellectuals of Europe are aware of—like Alain de Benoist and the left-wing intellectuals Chantal Mouffe and Ernesto Laclau, an Argentinian political scientist. The point is that the people don't understand this, don't think in such categories, and they still haven't really understood what "left" and "right" are. These are the excesses of everyday, banal consciousness that is not capable of distinguishing between concepts and the dialectic of concepts.

Kovalenko: There is a certain social inertia in the consciousness of those who come out to vote. So this is more of a general tendency.

Ochsenreiter: I think what we had in Greece, for example, with the government built on the one side by Syriza and on the other side by right-wing populists, and what we had in Slovakia as well, where a left-wing populist party went into government with a right-wing populist party—I personally believe that this might be the future for the whole of Europe. But again, Germany might be an exception. Because as long as people from the right support Merkel instead of some forces from the left, and as long as people from the left support Merkel rather than people who think likewise on the right, then Merkel will always win.

Kovalenko: And the last question for you: very briefly, maybe even in figures or percentages, what is your forecast for the second round of the presidential elections in France? And Manuel, I want to ask you about the lineup for September in Germany.

Dugina: I think that Macron will win this battle. The only thing that could happen is if Mélenchon refrains from calling for voting for Macron, then Marine could have a good percentage: she could have up to 40% in the second round and Macron could have plus-minus 60 percent.[5] In fact, these are the forecasts now being given by the leading survey centres — although I've never trusted them because it seems to me that when they ask only around 1,500 people, then the data is…

Kovalenko: Not representative…

Dugina: Yes, not representative. However, when we look at the results of the first round, the figures that came in at 9 pm Moscow time, they really resembled what the French liberals have been doing for a long time: uniting against Le Pen. Therefore, I'm afraid that Marine Le Pen doesn't have big chances at victory in the second round. Everyone is blocking her and trying to thwart her from winning. But, nevertheless, there is the feeling that colossal success awaits her in the first round of the parliamentary elections, and then in the second round they'll skilfully block her again. Some political scientists say that France is not yet ready for Marine Le Pen, which means that France needs another five years of left-liberal terror and dictatorship before it matures.

Manuel, what do you think about Alternative for Germany's chances at victory in the parliamentary elections and the prospects of the other parties?

Ochsenreiter: I'm convinced they will enter the parliament, and that they will, of course, have more than 5%, which is what you need

---

5   Dugina's forecast proved correct: Macron won with 58.5% of the vote against Le Pen's 41.5%.

in Germany in order to make it into parliament. I believe at the same time that they will stay very much below the real possibilities — they will for sure not be in the next government, and also very surely not in the government after that. But they will hopefully use the parliament seats they gain to do real oppositional politics. Because that is precisely the big chance of these elections — it's not about getting into the government, but using parliament seats for oppositional politics.

Kovalenko: Thank you, this was a very interesting meeting. We would be happy to see you again after the second round of elections in France and closer to the elections in Germany.

Macron Loses France[1]

Igor Shatrov: You're watching the programme "Geopolitical Kitchen" on the channel Pravda.ru, and I'm its author and host, Igor Shatrov. Greetings, friends! In our studio we talk with respected experts about the foreign policy interests that, although they can change over time, always remain the main basis for decision-making in the international arena. The meeting between Emmanuel Macron and Vladimir Putin has become one in a whole chain of what would seem to be similar discussions that the Russian president is now holding with world leaders. However, Russian-French relations have their own history, their own agenda, and the French president has his own plans. While speaking in the name of the European Union, which France is now chairing, Macron is first and foremost saying what he wanted to, so it seemed to me. We're going to break this down with Daria Platonova, a political observer of the International Eurasian Movement. Greetings, Dasha.

Daria Dugina: Greetings, I'm very happy to be here with you again.

Shatrov: Thank you, the feeling's mutual, I was glad to invite you. And so, what's so special about Russian-French relations? I've just said this, but maybe I'm really exaggerating some kind of special style in our relations?

Dugina: Without a doubt, we have common ties, we have common political traditions — for example, de Gaulle's view that Russia is one of the most important poles of continental Europe alongside France and Germany. De Gaulle's theses on "Europe from the Atlantic to the

---

1 A discussion with the political analyst Igor Shatrov aired on the show *Geopolitical Kitchen* before the 2022 French elections.

Urals" presupposed that Russia would be in this continental bloc, in an alliance with Europe. We have examples of quite productive geopolitical collaboration along the Moscow-Berlin-Paris axis — directly with Chirac.

In other words, in the recent history of France, we can find a wholly fruitful French-Russian friendship. But today, relations between France and Russia are quite weak. Macron doesn't represent the Gaullist flank. He's tried to act and position himself at various meetings and conferences as a peacemaker, as the person who can solve all conflict and open dialogue that no one before him could, and solve questions that no one else could solve. Macron is a "glitch" in the system of Franco-Russian friendship — such a serious one that all of his opponents, who will oppose him in the coming presidential elections (I'll remind you that they'll be held on April 10th, very soon; there's de facto "nothing" left, or *rien*, as the French like to say), are for normalising relations between Russia and France and are discontent with how Macron has kept up this line and how he's managed to solve the crises that have arisen between the EU, which is under the control of the Anglo-Saxon agenda, and Russia, which is the proponent of multipolarity, of a continental bloc, of the civilisation of Land against the civilisation of Sea, if we think in geopolitical terms.

Shatrov: Yes, but in Russian-French relations we always end up relying on the past. Dasha, it seems to me that in mentioning Chirac and de Gaulle, you're passing over the next presidents, who weren't very distinguished in terms of greatness and whom it's difficult to compare with the personages you've named. They have been personages similar to Macron. This crisis in the political system of France didn't start with Macron.

Dugina: The crisis, yes, but on the other hand, if we look at the whole line of presidents since de Gaulle (like Mitterrand and Valéry Giscard d'Éstaing), then we'll see one important point: they all belong to either the "left" or the "right" political bloc and can be politically identified as either "left" or "right". Of course, the right-liberal politicians will have strategic claims and comments addressed against Russia, because they are oriented towards cooperating with American politicians and don't have a "dual orientation" or course towards dual-polarity. The French "left" had its pretences against the USSR which, so they say, discredited them with its radicalism and its thesis on the dictatorship of the proletariat.

If we look at Macron, then the situation here is unique: from the point of view of the classical "left" and "right" flanks, he doesn't represent either of the poles. In 2017, when he came to power, he said: "I'm more left in values and more right in economics." This is the classic globalist agenda. Right-wing economics means big private monopolies, pure liberalism, capitalism in the stage of imperialism. Left-wing values means individualism, maximum freedom of the individual, rejecting any societal determinations, freedom from ethnos, from the state, from place of residence, from language, from gender, etc. In essence, Macron is the first president who doesn't belong to the classic parties. He's not a Socialist and he's not a Republican. He is a president who is blowing up the constant tension between the two blocs that the French are used to and understand. In so doing, he is demonstrating a completely new political agenda.

In general, Macron and his appearance on the political scene symbolise a new era in political analysis and in the French political space. If before France could be fixated within the opposition between left and right (some of them more globalist-oriented, some of them less so), then now we see globalism as a mix of left-wing politics (LGBT, open doors migration, "refugees welcome") and right-wing economics (capitalism), which totally imposes itself as the globalist "centre", and we see the opposing "anti-centre" today represented by Marine Le Pen.

As for the other candidates when it comes to the French elections, there's an interesting struggle underway for the "right bloc", a struggle to preserve it in its traditional right variant (right-wing economics and right-wing values). But these are non-classical parties with non-classical, new personages. Among them is Mr. Eric Zemmour, a rather strong and interesting right-wing publicist who openly positions himself as a Gaullist, has released campaign videos in the spirit of de Gaulle, and generally asserts that France needs to leave NATO, or leave the NATO command, as was the case back in 1966.

In other words, Macron is incomparable to the presidents who came before him because he is a completely new type of figure, just like Marine Le Pen, who opposes him and brings together the idea of left-wing economics and right-wing politics (values). This is a very interesting hybrid in the spirit of National Bolshevism, if you will.

At the same time, the parties and confrontations observed at the previous stage are gradually being removed from the agenda. What's left is a kind of new fury: Macron against his people, the fury of the anti-popular, globalist elite that has been compelled to partially compromise with the people. Because of this, Macron is still surrounded by the classical left and right; he is de facto locked between them; they have him by the throat. The left-wing Mélenchon calls for friendship with Russia and Marine Le Pen is against globalism, harshly hitting at Macron for being an artificial candidate, while the right is inclined to really return to Gaullism. In this situation, Macron is simply compelled in negotiations and debates to demonstrate softness, evasiveness, cunning, and not to be as harsh as he would like to be.

Shatrov: About the negotiations. We'll come to the global agenda beyond France a bit later. You already started talking about the coming elections, so let's continue with this topic. Many experts have concluded that after Macron's visit to Russia, he will somehow use the results of this visit for his election campaign. But I don't know — I haven't seen any such powerful breakthroughs. In whose interest — not on the plane of personal views (Le Pen, for example, and so on), but on the plane of selling to the domestic French market — are these results, and what results from his visit to Russia and dialogue with Putin would his political opponents like to gain?

Dugina: Why did Macron come to Russia? For legitimisation back in his country. Why? Because the protest movement is discontent with his economics and with his politics: trade unions, representatives of the left front, as well as those who are against migration (the "right") are all coming out against him. In fact, as a general rule, "right-wing" rallies against migration are repressed and not even mentioned, while rallies from the "left" still get coverage.

Macron has a rather unstable situation inside the country. He absolutely needs to legitimise himself — his approval rating is 33%. This is too little for a president. His rating in the first round, if he goes to the elections now, is 23%, and in the second, if he clashes with Pécresse or Le Pen, the votes could be divided up to 50/50. He needs to do something. Therefore, he's taking over his opponents' agenda.

How is his visit to Moscow being used in the press? All the mainstream media controlled by the media magnate Patrick Drahi — a big representative of globalist structures in the spirit of Jacques Attali and Bernard-Henri Lévy in the media field — have presented Macron's meeting with Putin as Macron's triumph, as if Macron were acting as a peacemaker and convinced Putin of the need to deescalate the conflict in Ukraine. They repeat the statement Macron made in Kiev that he convinced Putin to start the deescalation process.

Shatrov: I'll read one such "replica" now: "He convinced Putin to take troops out of Belarus after exercises are done." Does anyone seriously read this and think, *Yes, that's Macron's success*?

Dugina: In fact, I took a look at the right-conservative magazine *Le Figaro*, and there was a survey of approximately 80,000 respondents, *Figaro* readers, who were asked: "Did this visit lead to any concrete results?" Around 70% of *Figaro* readers said that it didn't. This means that the audience no longer believes in such, even when the aggressive media campaigns waged by Mr. Patrick Drahi and his press insist that Macron is a peacemaker. On another note, when I watched Macron's press conference, a journalist from the French pool asked: "Could you please tell us what's going on with Mali?"

Shatrov: In general, that press conference ended up being about Mali, as if he had flown to Putin to solve this issue. I understand that the situation in French, former Francophone Africa is his biggest problem on the internal agenda.

Dugina: It's like out of a fiction novel: he was asked about Mali by journalists from his own pool. Can you imagine that these people, who're supposed to in one way or another agree on questions, are asking: "Mr. President, you've been talking with Mr. President Putin while Russian mercenaries are in Mali." To the question, "Why are there Russian mercenaries in Mali?", our president gave a wonderful answer: "It's not the Russian state, but private Russian companies, so excuse me, but it's their relations with Mali, so why are you asking us?" Macron, if we analyse his posture, closed up after this question. It was his failure, because just before this the media were saying that Russia had gone into Mali, that Russia had taken over French Africa, that Russia had entered the Sahel, and so on. In fact, this was a collapse for him, a defeat he suffered. Of course, they tried not to pay too much attention to this in the Western press and directly in the French press, but I would like to draw attention to this, because his model of *Françafrique* was based on a very incorrect analysis of the situation in these territories and particularly, directly in Mali.

The Malians' main pretence towards France now, and this was confirmed by Mali's minister of culture and minister of state reconstruction at a recent conference, is that the French have unleashed their economic ambitions in the region, and profit has blinded them: they don't understand or take into consideration the factor of ethno-diversity, of ethnic pluralism. The French ignore the country's historical, cultural, ethnographic, and sociological problems: they don't even know who they're fighting in what is essentially yet another neo-colonial bootsetting foot on this continent. In Mali, there are the Tuaregs who are for establishing Azawad, an independent Tuareg state, and there are completely different terrorist groups connected with Al-Qaeda and Ansar ad-Din. This is an enormous space whose problems globalism can't solve. Ethnosociology is very needed and important here. Macron's failure in Africa is similar to the failure in Afghanistan, and this is in fact what French intelligence is saying, such as in the book by the former director of the DGSE.[2] This is the analogue of the Russian SVR,[3] and its former director emphasises in his book that "Macron practically led us into a second Afghanistan".

Shatrov: Yes, Afghanistan — only in Africa. I've been watching what they're saying about where Russian private military companies are, in which countries, and almost 80% of the list is former Francophone Africa: Libya, Sudan, Central African Republic, Zimbabwe, Botswana, Congo, Angola, Algeria, Mali, Mauritania, Mozambique, and then there's also Syria, Venezuela, and Madagascar. Many of these countries are part of Francophone Africa. It turns out that we have yet another point of intersection and conflicts with France: Africa. Or is this not the case? We understand Vladimir Vladimirovich's [Putin] words, and we also perfectly understand when representatives of any Russian company (I've also talked with representatives of some of these countries in this studio) say, "How can we not work in the interests of Russia? How can one work in African countries against Russia? Of course, we're working in Russia's interests. But we don't ask for permission from the Russian state. We reach agreements with the leaders here, and these leaders perceive us simply as people from Russia — we represent the brand 'Russia'." Now it turns out that this topic is present on the internal French agenda. In this situation, does Russia, in your opinion, have the possibility to somehow propose to reconsider Russo-French relations under this angle? As if they could say: we have common interests in some places and different interests elsewhere, where you,

2   DGSE stands for Direction Générale de la Sécurité Extérieure, which is the French external intelligence agency. It operates under the Ministry of Armed Forces and is responsible for gathering intelligence, conducting covert operations, and ensuring France's national security abroad.

3   The Russian SVR (*Sluzhba Vneshnei Razvedki*) is the Foreign Intelligence Service of the Russian Federation. It is responsible for conducting intelligence and espionage activities outside of Russia, focusing on foreign policy, national security, and counterintelligence, and serves as a successor to the First Chief Directorate of the KGB after the Soviet Union's dissolution.

esteemed Paris, the EU, and NATO, shouldn't cross paths! Can Russia do so, is it worth it, and how could we operate better in general?

Dugina: If we're talking about Africa, then this question is very complex. Of course, cooperating with the French, who have been there for a long time, starting with Operation Barkhane, is necessary. The issue is only that this won't happen with Macron, because he has paralysed all of Africa with economic poison. In essence, *Françafrique* is a concept that arose after their emancipation from the oppression of French colonialism; it is a model of governance through economic resources. Of course, Macron won't share anything until the French people get rid of him. The French people are unhappy that the money that flows from there doesn't make it to the people; the contracts that are concluded stay somewhere at the top, settling in the so-called "dark space of the Élysée Palace", because *Françafrique* isn't coordinated through the Ministry of Foreign Affairs, but through none other than the Élysée Palace. Jacques Foccart, who is considered "Mr. *Françafrique*", has coordinated this strategy from the Élysée Palace.

You know, it's very difficult to answer whether Franco-Russian dialogue on Africa is possible. For example, I've looked at the candidates from this point of view: when it comes to Le Pen, I think it'd be possible, because she doesn't have a strong strategy for Africa, and in principle she doesn't particularly want to get drawn into this region…

Shatrov: She also uses this region to frighten the French, because of potential migrants from there…

Dugina: Yes, her position is to close the borders and control the migration influx. But a gentleman like Eric Zemmour, for example, who is a friend of Mr. Vensan Bolloré, a big media oligarch who owns a number of TV channels and is the owner of Bolloré Logistics (an enormous group that permeates all of *Françafrique*) — with Zemmour there would be a very difficult but interesting conversation if he were to become president. Because France really can't just abandon its influence. If it abandons its influence, this would be a betrayal of national interests.

On the other hand, France needs — and Zemmour and Bolloré lean towards this — to work with the region more delicately, not to practise the direct, expansionist, globalist agenda, but instead seek a different, more subtle and more thorough one. You know, one French scholar of Africa, Bernard Lugan, has said: "We need to enlighten Africa, but we should understand who they are; we should study their culture, study their ethnic diversity, and if we approach Africa in this way, not like the Anglo-Saxons who simply push everything around with money, then we can build dialogue with African countries as well as" — Bernard Lugan makes a point to emphasize this — "with Russia."

Shatrov: It seems to me that it's not for nothing that the Mali topic has come up against the backdrop of talks, and in general that these events are happening now. This seems to me to be a signal that we still have a common topic with France that we don't have with Germany, for example (there we have other topics, like Nord Stream). There's not only the signal that these events are happening, but these events were caught on to by French journalists from the pool who should have been silent about them, as it would have been better for them to ask Macron elsewhere, but they themselves brought this up on the agenda at this press conference. By and large, it turns out that there is an instrument — the only thing is whether Russia will use it. Well, anyway, it turns out that Macron, in accordance with French tradition, claims the role of the main diplomat of Europe — even Biden has openly called him de Gaulle and claimed that he is trying to be the new de Gaulle, which means that credit can even be given where it's due...

Dugina: Flattering...

Shatrov: Yes, credit can be given to Biden for saying something "original". And so, Macron personally can't be the main meditator and main diplomat of Europe by virtue of his own personal qualities. And in general, will France, as a subject of international law, continue to claim this role, and does it have the prospects of becoming the main diplomat of Europe?

Dugina: All of Macron's opponents, of course, are for France gaining or regaining its mission, including its diplomatic, mediating mission when it comes to solving issues between the Anglo-Saxon bloc and the bloc of the civilisation of Land. Do you remember how Nicholas Spykman put it? This famous English geopolitician said that whoever controls the Rimland (the coastal zone) controls the whole world. Now the Rimland is no longer controlled by the Anglo-Saxons, and a fermentation process is underway — this can be seen in Italy; it's partially visible in Germany, and it is really visible in France. Le Pen, Zemmour, Mélenchon, and now Macron are trying to restore the balance of forces and get out from under the influence of the civilisation of Sea. France could play an important role in resolving conflicts and in international mediation in general. The only problem is that Macron is a hostage of globalism; he can't get out of this paradigm, whereas Zemmour, for instance, proposes the following: he says that we need to leave the NATO military command but remain in NATO in order to veto, for instance, accepting Ukraine, Georgia, Moldova, or other countries, that is, in order to resolve and regulate conflicts within the framework of the old bloc.

I'm confident that France could play a great role, but this won't be Macron's France — it'll be the France of the next elites. Even if Pécresse, a Republican who is sometimes called "Macron in a dress", wins, then I'm still sure that there will be dialogue with Russia in a completely different tone and on a more real plane. Macron, who is generally called a "political chameleon", is too elastic: his words depend on where he's going. If he's visiting the left, then he immediately orients himself towards the left agenda. For example, he's criticised colonialism, but on the other hand he himself is a colonialist and he supports the idea of *Françafrique* like no other. Where did he spend Christmas? Remember the photos of him on Twitter spending each Christmas visiting soldiers: in Mali, in other countries — this is the classic imperialist "sir". And if he is paying a visit to the "right", then he expounds the right-wing agenda and says "no migrants".

In the meanwhile, his presidential term has seen an enormous amount of terrorist attacks. He boasts that migration fell under him, but, sorry, this was only during the few months of quarantine and closed borders. He's an utterly absurd person, a political chameleon, his words can't be trusted. He came to Moscow and said that we agreed to go step by step towards peace. Then he comes to Kiev and says: "I convinced Putin to deescalate." These are completely different expressions; one does not follow the other, and these are incompatible meetings. This person acts like a litmus test: he comes to some territory, takes a whiff, and says: "Aha, here there's an anti-Putin agenda; here there's a pro-Russian agenda," and he issues statements accordingly.

Shatrov: With regards to the African vector, we've seen that there some points can be found where our interests might converge, or that there exist points which are now inactive. It's clear that we have very pragmatic relations with Germany, and I don't know whether such pragmatic relations could take shape with France. Where are these points, and if the matter is not pragmatic but rather about some kind of ideology or idea, then where?

Dugina: I think that there are some converging pragmatic points: firstly, cooperation, even the most banal and on the simplest level, with French farmers, who were very upset when sanctions were imposed. In Europe in general…

Shatrov: They've already got used to it, I think…

Dugina: They've got used to it, of course, but still, the French actually love Russia. Russia is something dear for them. Dostoevsky, Pushkin, all of Russian literature — whenever you say you're Russian, they'll immediately mention some kind of Russian verses, quotes, or metaphors which not even you remember. In this sense, they are deeply turned towards us and pay great attention to our culture. But it seems to me that the main opposition is in ideology. Russia has the ideology of continentalism, the ideology of sovereignty, of opposition to modern Western values, the ideology of Tradition, which is now being artificially displaced out of French society by figures like Macron.

Shatrov: So on this point we're closer to them than we could be or even will be able to be in the future if the globalists purge France.

Dugina: Yes, we're closer to them than to Germany. For example, imagine that Eric Zemmour, at one of his last rallies in Vendée, spoke out in defence of a monument to the Archangel Michael. It is so surprising even for us that a politician would visit a place like Vendée where some people want to remove a monument to the Archangel Michael and build some building, and that they would proceed to speak out for the real traditional France. It seems to me that our politicians could borrow something from Zemmour and Le Pen's election campaign slogans, because such attention to one's history, one's culture, one's identity, is very correct, and perhaps France could enrich us in this way.

I often follow Zemmour's speeches, and it needs to be said that every time I listen to them, I get goosebumps: "We are a great country, we are a great people, we should break the yoke of Anglo-Saxon hegemony, we are Rome, we are the heirs!" These are completely prophetic leaps, maybe even in the apostolic style. He speaks like a pastor, like when in America at various religious assemblies the preachers galvanise the whole crowd. Zemmour has this potential; I really believe in him; I really like him as a candidate. He is very investing; he has a clearly Gaullist agenda, and, in fact, he has made the very right move: he's started telling things as they are. He hasn't gone down the path of political correctness that Marine Le Pen tried to take by hiding her rather harsh theses on French identity and trying to adapt to the newspapers. Zemmour has immediately gone full steam ahead, and in doing so he's enriched the entire space of political life in France, even affecting Macron, who came to Russia and, in the end, didn't present any ultimatums.

Shatrov: On the matter of their love for Russia and their serious treatment of political speeches, each of which can even be considered a literary-philosophical work, for sure, I sometimes listen to French politicians and compare them to American ones—it's like heaven and earth. They speak the language that our politicians try to, that Vladimir Vladimirovich [Putin] does, even though he might use more down-to-earth epithets that are understood by the people…

Dugina: Citing Leontiev, Ilyin…

Shatrov: Yes, but on the other hand, what an enormous amount of ideas, images, and historical analogies! I've even observed this in Macron. I think his speechwriters sometimes write serious speeches, when he speaks in the name of France, and this, of course, surprises me, and it brings our peoples closer together. This is probably why we accept French culture and French art "without a translator", so to speak. We don't need to be explained what they wanted to say in cinema; we can easily watch and understand French cinema, which shares the same traditions with Russian cinema.

Dugina: It is *the* cinema!

Shatrov: *The* cinema, yes! Whereas American cinema, for example, is already different. We have some kind of historical closeness to France. The point I'm getting at is: what does France need us for? Besides the fact that we are close, how can we, Russia, help France?

Dugina: We are a guarantor of their sovereignty to a certain extent.

Shatrov: How?

Dugina: We allow for their traditions not to be destroyed, because if we were gone, if there wouldn't be this influence from us, then the influence would come from only one side, the Anglo-Saxon world, and this would be simply the ice rink of hegemony that is incinerating all of French identity. We, as it were, shift the Overton window in the world. Russia acts as a bulwark, as a guarantor of traditional values. Remember when you and I recently discussed the decree on traditional values[4] as the primacy of the spiritual over the material? For the French, this is in principle also something dear, because they are very spiritual people. Sure, maybe they don't pray, but they have

---

4   Executive Order of the President of the Russian Federation, No. 809, "On Approving the Fundamentals of State Policy to Preserve and Strengthen Traditional Russian Spiritual and Moral Values", signed on 9 November 2022.

a very developed culture of emotions and feelings. They pay a lot of attention to feeling, to everything that doesn't show up on an X-ray. By virtue of our Russian spirit, as it were, I think that we allow them to manifest their spirit, because if there was no us, they would also die…

Shatrov: In other words, they're not alone. Despite the fact that Russia is, in the opinion of the rest of the West, something strange, they're not alone and Russia is as they are.

Dugina: We speak European languages; we speak a language that is close to theirs—I have in mind culture and philosophy. We understand them; they understand us; we have rather close cultures, unlike, for example, China, which also represents traditional values but…

Shatrov: Other values.

Dugina: Completely right. They have a rather negative attitude towards China—all the French candidates do. They say in the spirit of Trump that China is a threat, that some attack might come from China. Zemmour's agenda has gone through some restructuring, so now he has a neutral analysis of China. China isn't intelligible to them, but Russia is.

Shatrov: Does France not dream of taking over leadership from Germany? Is France not ready for such a turn of events?

Dugina: Of course it is ready; this is what it's trying to do now. When the Merkel period came to a close and the German flourishing came to an end, the French immediately tried to take advantage of this. Macron is trying to take advantage of this disarray.

Shatrov: Even Macron?

Dugina: Yes, of course. Overall, he dreams of being the leader of the whole world. His idea is that this world should be globalist, that there should be no borders, that the world should be united under the slogans of human rights and liberal democracy, and he's tried to seize the initiative. His trip to Moscow was an attempt to seize the initiative of EU leadership as a counterweight to Germany. As long as the partners are arguing, as long as there is no consensus between Scholz and Baerbock, he is trying to become the new leader of this space.

Shatrov: I think, and I'm certain, that all of these topics, such as the "Chancellor Act", are being discussed on the highest political levels. I think that the German chancellor went to the US because that's what's prescribed, because he simply needs to go to the US after an election. Jokes and conspiracy theories aside, but I think that these conspiracy jokes are also discussed on the highest political level. When Scholz went to report to Biden, Macron busied himself with real affairs, like going to calm Putin down — this is more important, right? And what are the prospects? Besides ambitions, Germany still keeps all of Europe together with its economy. How is France actually faring on the economic plane now? After all, these Yellow Vests that practically immediately greeted Macron — aren't they a sign of an economic crisis in France?

Dugina: Yes, without a doubt, there is an economic crisis. What is it that the Yellow Vests are actually complaining about? First and foremost, it's liberal economics. This is connected with the fact that Macron launched a procedure that allows people to be fired without receiving any social payouts. It's also connected with high inflation and with raising the retirement age from 62 to 64. This is to say that, in general, the economic situation in France now is not the best. Nevertheless, for Macron, this still doesn't mean the complete end of France's economy; it is simply a reaction, a sign that some things are incorrectly distributed within the country, but this does not mean that France is now in a severe financial situation. The matter at hand is more about the distribution of funds that France possesses: France's resources are distributed in the interests of the elites, not in the interests of the people — this is the main grievance of the Yellow Vests.

Shatrov: Why am I trying to delve into what's going on inside France? In order to understand whether dialogue is important and needed or if it's pointless. Why should Putin go to the Munich Security Conference if he holds such Munich conferences in Moscow? Everyone comes to him, so there's no point in going there; really, why would we meet with second-rank countries, why should we talk with the EU — (I'm simplifying specifically to ask the question) — when we can talk with the US that manipulates the EU through NATO anyway, and so on? Why should we talk with anyone in Europe if there's Germany and Germany has the practical interest. Nord Stream 2 is a strategic project. It's clear that we can talk with Germany and at least solve this question, but when it comes to France — why should we talk with France if Macron isn't…

Dugina: If the president is on his way out…

Shatrov: Firstly, if the president is on his way out; secondly, France isn't what it was in the time of de Gaulle, and they can't even figure Africa out. You can put pressure on them, but why should we seriously talk with them?

Dugina: It seems to me that we talk because we are very good; we are open to dialogue. We talk with all the participants of political processes. We talk with our closest partners, we talk with our more distant partners, and we talk with those on whom things depend as well as those on which things don't depend. We publish our guarantees and proposals for security guarantees, whereas American colleagues insist on not publishing them.

I think that, unlike the West, we are pursuing an open strategy, working with open cards, and we have no desire to falsify the negotiation process. We don't want to kick out Europe, which has the right to the negotiation process, and we don't want to ignore them, whereas the Americans try to hold dialogue only formally: there's black and white, friend and enemy, and they'll talk only along the lines of classic geopolitical laws. In this sense, our work is more subtle, and I think this symbolises the fact that we want peace, that Russia wants peace. We don't want war, and that's why we're trying to maximally prevent such by negotiating with everyone and showing the real picture. Vladimir Vladimirovich [Putin] once again showed everyone and demarcated the positions of the Russian Federation: we are not striving to seize regions. He told this to Macron personally, because this information simply might not reach him through his press, through his advisors.

We want to clarify, to have recorded, to show our position and to hold dialogue with subjects, not objects. We want to hold dialogue with a person who is capable of dialogue, unlike the US, which doesn't publish and doesn't say what it intends, but only promises and then backs away from these promises, as was the case in 1997 with the non-expansion of NATO to the East. We are playing openly in this process.

Shatrov: Did we help Macron with this visit? Or did it harm him?

Dugina: We helped him, of course. The only thing he could have lost were bonuses in Kiev.

Shatrov: He already lost them on the way here.

Dugina: Even if, for example, he were to have gone to Putin and then returned to France and said, "I have a position; let's do this, this, and this. Moscow is ready for peace, so come on, Anglo-Saxon colleagues, stop fanning the flames of the situation" — but he didn't say this; he went to Kiev, he spoke with Zelensky, who posed an unpleasant question, something in the likes of, "Did you have a drink after dinner; did you drink anything with Putin?" Something not very respectful, not observing diplomatic etiquette. Consequently, the points that Macron picked up in Moscow, he lost in Kiev, because there he spoke out with the thesis of "de-escalation" and called himself a peacemaker.

Shatrov: It seems to me that the last word, so to speak, will be Scholz's, because he is actually crowning the visits of European leaders. The initiative might be turned back around: they'll remember the last word that was said. How ready is Macron to handle this is what's interesting, because there are real elections coming up. Does he have the strength and time for international affairs?

Dugina: I don't think he does. His trip was purely for the media, simply a media campaign, like an interview, like a meeting with his voters.

Shatrov: The photo is still a plus.

Dugina: This photo means a lot, because even Zemmour and Le Pen positively reacted to the trip. Only they asked: "Did the telegraphist solve anything or not?" Marine Le Pen said this live on the radio station France Inter. Properly speaking, this trip didn't solve anything. Macron doesn't have the time to solve Mali, the Russian question, or the Ukraine issue. This was a media trip: he dropped by, took a picture, gained a positive media image…

Shatrov: By meeting with leaders of public opinion…

Dugina: Yes, in order to increase his own status. It's interesting how leaders raise their status by way of Putin, because he is a strong figure, and this testifies to the collapse of unipolarity. It's good that he didn't go to Biden, or else he would have taken a nosedive in ratings to 17–19%.

Shatrov: Even without visiting Biden, he still got honourable mention as being similar to de Gaulle.

Dugina: Yes, a red card, a black mark.

Shatrov: On the topic of dreams and aspirations, this is surprising, of course. On the other hand, who else does Biden have to bet on in France?

Dugina: You know what, an answer just came to mind for your question as to why Putin met with Macron: in order to tell him that the Voronezh and Rostov regions are part of Russia! For Biden, in principle, Europe is like a slice of bread, not even a player, not even a subject. The problem is that Anglo-Saxon hegemony is falling; the US has left Afghanistan, and this caused an enormous crisis and drew enormous criticism within the country. In the US itself, the situation is catastrophic. Inflation is at 8% (and higher). In general, they say that inflation on groceries is much higher, and there's also the pandemic collapse and the migration collapse. For example, Mr. Soros criticises Chinese authorities, calling into doubt their efficiency in fighting the coronavirus, but in his own country, in the US, there was a catastrophe — almost a million people dead from covid, and they keep on dying, while the healthcare system simply can't cope with such volumes of patients.

Shatrov: It's simply built differently, and it wasn't ready to cope with something of the sort.

Dugina: Yes, entirely so.

Shatrov: They need to modernise, to do things differently.

Dugina: About the migration collapse, too. When Biden became president, he said he's opening the borders and now entry into the country will be practically unrestricted — they'll be able to take in 20,000 migrants a day. In the end, everything turned into migrants starting to flood the US like covid waves, and with the most horrifying consequences — murder, theft, and it's become simply impossible to live near the border with Mexico.

Shatrov: It's simply shocking to me that in this period anyone can still look at Biden or that any leaders would try to reach an agreement on something with the United States. Perhaps in the present moment it's worth thinking about the future of Europe as a subject of international law. This will give Europe more subjectivity than the situation with the United States. It's simply astonishing that there is this long-term game and now we have such advantageous opportunities for collaborating with Europe, but the Ukrainian crisis has driven a wedge.

Dugina: The story with Ukraine is, after all, the classic geopolitical story of creating a *cordon sanitaire*, a space that is supposed to block relations between Russia and Europe. The globalists' main task now is to break off our relations, to break up our Russian-French friendship and Russian-German cooperation. The *cordon sanitaire* is a space that blocks impulses from both sides.

Shatrov: Yes, although not in the literal sense: someone might perceive the *cordon sanitaire* simply as a borderline, but it's not simply a borderline; it's a hot spot around which there are different opinions and topics for discussion. Instead of getting on with affairs, leaders are spending their time on negotiations over Ukraine; instead of ensuring global security, nuclear disarmament,, and economic cooperation, they're wasting time, year after year, on negotiations over Ukraine.

Dugina: Marine Le Pen very accurately remarked that instead of discussing Ukraine's entry into NATO, it would be better for NATO — and it really needs to — to focus on the problem of terrorism that is inside Europe as well as further off, on its horizons. In Africa as well, there is a rather critical situation when it comes to terrorism. Look at what has been created in Libya: every day there's another assassination, and the UN isn't coping with the situation at all..

Shatrov: Yes, they've forgotten all about it, and no one is bothered by what's happening in Libya. No one is talking about the situation in Yemen, the actual war going on there, where people are being killed every day. This is a point where world leaders could apply their efforts. Of course, there is a very professional and cunning game being played of shifting the subject of attention. The more they distract their attention, the more they themselves come to believe that a problem has become their problem. Why? It's a pity, of course, a waste of time, and we would like to cultivate friendship and cooperation with France by virtue of our cultural closeness. Are there any prospects for a different policy? After all, Dasha, this whole time you've often been talking about the opposition figures opposed to Macron or anyone else. But, in the end, they stick to their France within the EU, within NATO, even without the military command, and they stick with their prehistory, their inertia, which over the decades has deterred any changes of a capital, cardinal character. What's in it for us if, for example, Le Pen gets in? Then what? Will the sun rise and shine over Russian-French relations? Will the sun even rise?

Dugina: The French sociologist Emmanuel Todd says that France has 5–10 years of peaceful existence left before there'll be a revolution. France is already set up in such a way that whenever a critical amount of problems accumulates with the economy and, at the same time, with identity, both on the left front and the right front, then revolution happens. The political analyst Youssef Hindi has called the Yellow Vests a revolution and said that Emmanuel Todd greatly overestimates the 5–10 years of peace, and that everything might already start happening in these elections.

Still, it seems to me that the French, who are used to thinking revolutionarily (we can recall not only the Great French Revolution, but also 1968, which changed all the cards on the political table of France), might try to bring about a revolutionary situation. I myself took part in Yellow Vest actions and saw with my own eyes: this is an enormous amount of people going out into the streets, this is discontent, and not merely discontent with one or another party, whether right or left. The parties are no longer the ones going out into the streets. The people are going out into the streets. And I think that this people, the banner of the people, might rise up over France. I think that if Le Pen or Zemmour win, if they make it into the second round, beat Macron, break the machine of globalism and beat the candidate of nihilism, then everything can change. Moreover, Marine Le Pen has spoken, and not only once, of the need to leave the EU and reconsider relations with it.

I'm very romantically attuned, but I think that this romanticism is intrinsic to the French people, who have changed the history of France and turned it in different directions before. Therefore, I will be hoping, of course, that something very colorful will happen, whether in the elections or after them, and the sun will rise.

Shatrov: I would like to end on this, but still I'll ask one more clarifying question to conclude. It turns out that, among all the countries of the current EU, if we are to look at any country with hope, is it only France, if we take the old Europe? I won't even mention Eastern Europe — they're subjects. So, is it only France?

Dugina: It's looking like this is the case. Although earlier we saw interesting alliances in Italy, alliances between right and left, as with the Five Stars Movement and Lega Nord — two parties which represent the people, populist parties in the sense that they are…

Shatrov: Of the people…

Dugina: Of the people, yes. On the other hand, in Germany, we saw a possible alliance between AfD and Die Linke, that is between Alternative for Germany and the Left. We saw how this began to take shape and provoke new perturbations in politics. But, as it turns out, it's not Germany but France that is now in the forefront. Germany failed and there came Scholz and Baerbock, and Italy also failed, as the collaboration didn't hold out for long. As for France, there is a new horizon in which a new history really might come about, and maybe it's the Yellow Vests that will be the pioneers, and only then will all other countries follow and put on their own yellow vests.

Shatrov: Maybe Macron's visit will look differently after some time. Maybe it'll serve something, but only time will tell. Well, our programme's time has come to an end. Today we talked about the French president's visit to Russia, Russian-French relations, their past, present, and future with Daria Platonova, a political observer of the International Eurasian Movement. Thank you very much, Dasha.

Dugina: Thank you.

The Thanatology of European Politics: The French Experience of Opposing Death[1]

TODAY'S TOPIC is quite extreme. Moreover, it's at the intersection of different dimensions, including political science and thanatology. We'll also touch on the philosophical aspects of what is happening in European politics. It is entirely obvious that today we are presenting something not entirely "scientific", something hybrid. Although this is quite intrinsic to modern science — to mix together layers. Perhaps I'll be the one here to act as the postmodernist and combine different disciplines to create something that is in some sense forbidden. Therefore, let me immediately warn you that what is to be proposed here is a kind of hybrid approach to thinking through the political process in France.

I've been involved with France for a rather long time. I have the experience of living there and of political activism on French soil. I'm connected to many of the people I'll be talking about today not only by way of acquaintance via media and social networks, but by direct collaboration. In particular, in 2013, I was active in the protests against

---

1   Talk at Sun of the North in Saint Petersburg in May 2022.

gay marriage in France (the El Khomri law[2] that ended up being adopted anyway despite millions-strong protests). I also participated in a number of the Yellow Vest protests as an independent observer and sympathiser. I saw clashes with the police. For me, this was an experience of coming into contact with the soul of France, with its striking soul. Perhaps this somehow helps me to have a feel for the processes that are going on there today.

I didn't spend too long of a time in France. I don't know whether I'll be back there again, because of some sanctions[3], but let's hope that European politics will change soon and will be welcoming to those who are for Europe, not against it. Because Eurasianists, and I count myself among them, are, of course, for the flourishing of civilisations, for dialogue between civilisations, for the plurality of civilisations.

Bernard-Henri Lévy: The Empire against Kings

France today is in the vanguard of what I would call "death throes". What is happening to France, the totalitarianism that is being committed by Macron, who has been elected president for a second term on

2   The El Khomri law, named after then-Minister of Labour Myriam El Khomri, is a controversial 2016 labour reform in France that undermines workers' rights by making it easier for employers to impose longer working hours, facilitate layoffs, and weaken union power. The law faced significant opposition and protests for prioritising business flexibility over job security and labour protections, seen by many as a step back for workers' rights.

3   Daria Dugina was sanctioned by the United States government on 3 March 2022 under three Executive Orders: E.O. 13661 ("contributing to the situation in Ukraine"), E.O. 13694 ("engaging in significant malicious cyber-enabled activities"), and E.O. 13848 ("foreign interference in a United States election"). The official reasoning for the sanctions stated by the US Department of the Treasury's Office of Foreign Assets Control was that Dugina "sought contributors to write articles on UWI [United World International]", a news and analysis website which it alleged was supported by Evgeny Prigozhin, a Russian oligarch and businessman known for his close ties to Vladimir Putin and for founding the Wagner Group, a private military company involved in various conflicts and operations linked to Russian interests.

the strength of "nihilistic voting", is a curse for France and the murder of European civilisation.

For today I've prepared to speak about the death of European politics in the case of France. It was Macron's words that pushed me to think about death, especially in the context of contemporary political science. Recall that the first round of French elections was held on 10 April 2022, the second on 24 April. Between rounds, Macron gave an enormous interview to *Le Point*, the classic liberal globalist media. Much ado about nothing, it's the classic globalist narrative — but suddenly we discover a completely unique situation. In this interview, Macron said that the second round will be a battle between Thanatos and Eros. For Macron, who is rather poor in philosophical terms, even though he studied under Paul Ricoeur and was his assistant (it's strange that he didn't take in the experience of his teacher), this is something completely new. I decided to find out where he got this terminology from. It's hardly likely that these thoughts were born in his own head. I looked into the space of French thought and found out that the source of inspiration behind such thoughts is Bernard-Henri Lévy (he spoke about this in his talk in Amsterdam in 2019, the year of his debate with Alexander Dugin).[4]

Bernard-Henri Lévy is the gray cardinal of French foreign policy, the ideologist of ultra-globalism, the person responsible for the destruction of Libya in 2011, the person who brought terrorists into the Élysée Palace, the person who de facto killed Gaddafi — Gaddafi's blood is on his hands. He encouraged the separatist, anti-Gaddafist,

---

4 The debate between Bernard-Henri Lévy and Alexander Dugin, organised by the Nexus Institute for its 25th anniversary symposium, was explicitly themed as a "rematch" between Lodovico Settembrini and Leo Naptha from Thomas Mann's famous 1924 novel, *The Magic Mountain*. Settembrini embodies Enlightenment ideals, humanism, and liberal progress, while Naptha, a Jesuit with radical tendencies, champions authoritarianism, mysticism, and a rejection of modern secular values. Their debates highlight the profound struggle between rationalism and deeper spiritual conviction, reflecting the broader philosophical conflicts and existential dilemmas of pre-World War One Europe.

and terrorist groupings that were active in Libya and had the support of, among others, the US. This is the very same person, responsible for an enormous quantity of crimes, who was recently seen in Odessa. He was there supporting the Nazi criminal Marchenko, the ex-commander of the Aidar Battalion, which is banned in the Russian Federation. It's clear what side Lévy is on. When he talked about Eros and Thanatos in Amsterdam in 2018, he said that Thanatos is what is outside of "enlightened and democratic" Western civilisation, and Eros is the essence of the European and Anglo-Saxon Empire. For Bernard-Henri Lévy, "Empire" is the term that characterises the Anglo-Saxon globalist agenda. It means liberal values, liberty, free love, freedom of perversions. He treats Eros rather primitively, not as Platonism so inspiringly treats it. Lévy treats it very immanently, as the carnal satisfaction of a forbidden union. Lévy's Eros is immanentised and placed into a uterine context that is low, vulgar, and primitive.

It was Bernard-Henri Lévy who introduced the opposition between Eros and Thanatos into the most recent political discussions. He doesn't say as much about Thanatos as he does about Eros. Eros for him is the embodiment of an idea. He even has the idea of "Eros and the Talmud against the whole world". This is the centre arrayed against allegedly "destructive" anti-globalism. For Lévy, anti-globalism is unacceptable, it is a "closed society of the old type that is not ready to face changes, is extremely archaic, and is disgusting in its conservatism" (these are Bernard-Henri Lévy's expressions). For Lévy, the new Empire of Eros and the Talmud is the opposing side to the "five kings".[5] Let's name the three main ones: China, Iran, and Russia. These three kings represent the vanguard of multipolarity that needs to be harshly dealt with; it doesn't matter how. Any punitive measures can be adopted; the main point is to destroy them all.

---

5   Bernard-Henri Lévy, *The Empire and the Five Kings: America's Abdication and the Fate of the World*, trans. Steven B. Kennedy (New York: Henry Holt and Company, 2019).

This interesting remark of Lévy's, the opposition between Eros (the global Empire) and Thanatos (its opponents, the five kings), is what Macron borrows and takes up.

Macron and Death

Then I got interested in the theme of death in Macron. After all, everything that Macron names and designates is something opposite. For example, he advocates democracy and asserts that he is a democrat, yet he is a typical tyrant. Generally, you can assume the opposite of what Macron publicly states to understand his true intentions. Accordingly, if he positions himself as Eros (in fact, he tries to portray himself as Eros in photos: he has official photos with his shirt unbuttoned, which looks quite strange), then he in fact represents Thanatos.

Of course, at the outset this was only my intuition, my not entirely scientific hypothesis, something from the realm of the imagination, a kind of daydream. But then I started examining the makeup of his electorate and tried to find some basis for my view of the situation. And I discovered that approximately 70% of his electorate are people over the age of 70. No less symbolic is his spouse, who, as my friend Anton Belikov from the "After Icon" project aptly put it, can be compared to a mummy. I don't know whether you've seen the photos of Brigitte Macron (Trogneux), but she's around 70 and she doesn't look bad, but the feeling remains that it's as if you were dealing with a relic made of dust. Macron himself is much younger, the youngest ever president of France.

And so, Macron has the electorate of whoever's over 70. "Boomers" vote for Macron. "Boomers" are those born after the baby boom, the generation who are now around 70, which is now something rather "old Testament". In France, there are the "zoomers", the new "Generation Z", and the boomers, the old generation. The political analyst Dmitry de Koshko says that Macron has the votes of those for whom the future isn't important. They vote because they already have everything: they have pensions; they had a wonderful life; now they need to vote for someone young and energetic. Macron is really loved by the "grandmas" because he, so young, took such an old wife. This is a very nice indicator for elderly ladies — we can still be loved, we're in favour, so they think. That Macron has such an older audience is a very interesting point.

Next, I started examining Macron's thesis, and I understood that everything he says is about a call for death. First, there is his unprecedented and rabid support for the Kiev regime. Let me remind you that two days before the second round of presidential elections in France, he decided to supply (and to this moment is still supplying) the Armed Forces of Ukraine with CAESAR artillery systems and MILAN anti-tank missiles. This is only part, only the tip of the iceberg. He's not only delivering arms: today France's military bases are constantly training Ukrainian troops. What is this? It is not humanitarian aid. It is death.

The first batch of the 100 million euros of military aid to Ukraine announced by France's Minister of the Armed Forces, Florence Parly, consisted of tactical vests and binoculars. Fine, this could still some-how be interpreted in the spirit of playing on the side of "peace". But the subsequent batches showed matters precisely: artillery systems which shoot up to 40 kilometres are an act of supporting death. When he won the elections, he stated that he will now be even more outspoken in supporting the Kiev regime, which, in his opinion, is a "democratic regime", and that his voice will be even stronger. This is his agenda.

"No" to French Culture, "Yes" to the Global World

Now I propose to take a look at the main theses of Macron's election programme. First and foremost, this is globalism. France is declared to be part of the global world, French culture is told "no" — there is only a "European culture". Macron's teacher was Jacques Attali, the philosopher who formulated the concept of nomadic elites. The con-cept of nomadic (or mobile, constantly moving) elites says that there are no more civilisations, cultural differences, or cultural contexts in the modern world. There is only one homogenous space for producing profit, one in which there are two constantly moving types of people: migrant workers and their managers. In essence, it is unimportant where or in what part of Europe or the world you stop and reside for a moment: everything is a "hotel", uniform, faceless, "temporary stations". There is no home, no homeland. One can latch onto anything in France, in Italy, in Singapore — everything is absolutely of one type and faceless. It was Jacques Attali who found Macron as a banker and brought him into the Rothschild company. Jacques Attali is the link between Macron and the globalist agenda.

Death to Workers, the Indigenous, and Anti-Globalists

Macron is also for death when it comes to the economy: the death of the working class. Why? He proposes raising taxes and the retirement age. This means liberal capitalist economics without any social guarantees.

In migration policy as well, Macron is for death. Why? Of course, my reasoning on this topic could be seen as some kind of artistic sketch, intuition, or freehanded politological drawing. But Macron really does have a very open, loyal policy when it comes to migrants: he calls for accepting them with no restrictions; he believes that France should apologise for its colonial past. He loves to flaunt photos of himself standing and hugging dark-skinned representatives of the gay community. These pictures are meant to show that he knows no outcasts, that he accepts such "gentlemen" without reservations.

Failures in Africa

Next, let's look at his foreign policy. It is unconditional support for Kiev — a policy of death.

And then there's the monstrous neocolonialist policy in Africa. Macron, it needs to be admitted, hasn't really had a successful Africa strategy.

The first problem is with the military. When he came to power in 2017, he tried to cut the military budget; he called in the Chief of the Defence Staff and yelled at him. The Chief of the Defence Staff is not a simple person; in fact, he is a very respected military man in France: Pierre de Villiers. He represents the conservative community and is an intelligent strategist who defends France's interests and has defined them for a long time, having enormous experience in the fight against terrorism. Mr. Macron simply yelled at him in the presence of his colleagues. This incited discord and drew the fury of practically all of the military. This was impermissible behaviour on the part of the president, especially since he is "small", "young" and has no history, no party, only a hastily put-together political movement that has not proved itself in any way. And yet he opted for a rift with the military, undermining a unified military strategy, and constant disagreements with the military.

Macron's policy in Africa is also a strategy of death: a strategy of subordinating an African region to the profitable interests of France. This policy deploys troops wherever there's uranium. This is a policy of playing on inter-ethnic conflicts. If we take Mali, for example, there is an enormous amount of small ethnoi and tribes: the Azawad Tuareg (in the north), the Malinke, the Bambara, the Fulbe, the Senufo, the Dogon, and the Songhai. And what does the French army start doing? The French army starts collaborating with each of the clans, with each of these peoples, and tries to divide the tribes in order to prevent any peace negotiations. Negotiations were conducted with the Tuaregs only after the Malian government changed as a result of a coup and only thanks to the Malian people who, by the way, think of themselves as part of the Great Mali Empire that took shape in the 13th century. This is one of the most educated peoples of Africa; they exhibit astonishingly deep analyses of ongoing processes in the current situation in the country as well as in France.

The Malian people took their will and care for their country into their own hands and restored justice. The Malians carried out a *coup d'état.* They overthrew and drove out the French army in a humiliating way (Operation Barkhane). While evacuating, the French army was smart enough to leave bloody traces behind it. In Gao Bamba, a military base abandoned by the French, they found mutilated bodies. The Malian army started to investigate how the burned bodies of peasants ended up there — very strange bodies buried in the sand. Maybe the French took them to be terrorists? The army started to investigate what happened. The French themselves declared that it was a Russian and Malian provocation. They accused Russia of having some private Russian instructors do all of this. Then there began a long string of propaganda efforts to which the Malian government responded on numerous occasions. In the end, the West heard only the voice of France, and no one wants to listen to the Malians, because they are waging an anti-colonialist, anti-imperialist struggle.

In playing on these contradictions and arranging fleeting lines on the ethnic map of Africa, France precipitated these conflicts in which people are constantly killing each other. The Azawad, for example, are against the government troops. There have been many deaths. For the global community, of course, these deaths could be left unnoticed. Our consciousness is already used to death. We constantly hear about someone being killed. We have a hierarchy of deaths. For example, the life of someone killed in the Middle East is treated as more valuable than someone killed in Africa. There really is a hierarchisation. This is a separate topic for understanding death. The life of a loved one is something of the utmost importance to us. If they die, then this is a large-scale catastrophe for us. If someone of our people dies, this also hits very close to the heart. If Africans die, it's something too distant and we don't even understand it. But death has been doing its dance in this region of Africa, in Mali, and its origins lie in Macron's foreign policy.

Ukraine: A Space of Death

This death by foreign policy is also directly present in what has happened and what is still ongoing in Kiev. At the wave of Macron's hand, there are now French military personnel in Ukraine, even in Mariupol according to some data. A Turkish party has issued a statement saying that they have firm evidence and confirmation that there are 50 generals of the French army in the catacombs of Azovstal. Who are these officers? A special investigation is required to answer this question. Let's hope that we will be able to record an interview with them if they survive in the Azovstal catacombs, but this is a separate conversation. It's unclear who they are. A plane with DGSE personnel has also supposedly been shot down over Mariupol, but my sources in the French military say that they couldn't have been DGSE, which is the analogue of Russia's SVR, but more likely DMR,[6] France's analogue to the GRU.[7] In general, there's a bunch of such mystical moments. But French mercenaries are definitely in Ukraine. We won't delve into details. On the whole, Macron's foreign policy provokes death, death, and more death.

Lament for France

Now on to the opposition to Macron and to discussing who represents Eros in France. This is the most important point. You're probably thinking that I'll say that Marine Le Pen is Eros, or that Zemmour is Eros, or that there is a fire, an opposition to globalism, an opposition to death. But I have to tell you: No. There isn't any Eros. The Death

---

6   The DMR (*Direction du renseignement militaire*) is the French military intelligence agency responsible for collecting, analysing, and providing intelligence to support the operational needs and strategic objectives of the French Armed Forces.

7   The GRU (Main Directorate of the General Staff of the Armed Forces of the Russian Federation), or *Glavnoe razvedyvatel'noe upravlenie*, is the military intelligence agency responsible for handling both military and foreign intelligence operations for Russia.

of Love has overtaken the West. The West is dead. The sun has set on Europe.

So what is there? There are funerals — joyful ones, like Macron burying Europe, and grief-stricken, mourning ones. Modern civilisation cancels the sacred ritual of grief — this is extremely important. Both Zemmour and Marine Le Pen are people mourning at the funeral of their own country.

In ancient tragedy, there was the ritual of crying, of lamenting. The whole tragedy was structured around a death, around the grief over this death. A certain place was also reserved for grief in the Middle Ages. But if grief led you into complete despondency and sadness, then it was equated with sin. Hence why there appeared a special ritual for mourning, lasting 9 days or 40 days. Then, at some point, the dead are resurrected, we open the gates to the cemeteries, and so on.

In modern Western civilisation, death is displaced and taken out — there is no death. Death is to be overcome by biohacking. Biohacking is when you try to restructure your physiological processes by using various medicines and supplements as a means of extending life. One of Macron's ideologists I already mentioned today, Bernard-Henri Lévy, is a biohacker. He artificially extends his life and constantly takes pills: he brags about this, talks about it all the time, on every channel he appears on.

Marine Le Pen is an anti-globalist; Zemmour is an anti-globalist. More precisely, both Zemmour and Le Pen are the definition of grief in French culture and politics. This group is grief-stricken over dying France. They represent the dreams and rituals of mourning for long-gone Gaullism, disappearing independence, and lamenting for dead France. Therefore, in my view, there's no life whatsoever there. There is only this lament for a dying culture.

Covid Dictatorship

Examining French politics in its entirety, we can highlight several camps, but all of them are death. Zemmour, Le Pen, and Macron are something "posthumous", like palliative medicine, old age, withering away. In this vein, Macron is the one burying France but trying to remove death from the picture. Even by means of the Covid dictatorship.

What has he been criticised for? He's been criticised for his neoliberal economics, for globalism, for the foreign policy failures bound up with globalism, and for the Covid dictatorship. The Covid dictatorship is something altogether interesting. When everything is closed due to Covid, when ideas and stories about total lockdowns arrive, when ghettoisation gets underway and people are put in the ghetto of death by Covid, then all of this is an attempt to avoid death. Macron is death that doesn't recognise itself as death, death that tries to hide death from itself. Whereas Zemmour and Le Pen are aware of this death and are either going to pump adrenaline into the dying body of France or finally sing the funeral lament for the departed country.

The majority of my French friends who went to the elections and voted for Zemmour or Le Pen walked up to the ballot boxes with an utterly tragic spirit. They said: "Everything is wrong, everything is over." I protested: "How? Go and vote for Zemmour, vote for Le Pen! Let the nihilist Mr. Macron, the personification of the end of a civilisation, die! Come on!" And they would say: "We won't vote in the second round. Everything is clear: Macron has won." They sent pictures of a person sitting by a blazing fire, a huge flowing flame, simply observing and contemplating it.

Thus, from the perspective of thanatology, Macron represents the president of manifest death, death that tries hard not to recognise itself as death — death that runs away from itself. Zemmour and Le Pen represent the dying, fading, and decomposing, still grieving for something that was alive. Hence, they also opposed Covid — they believed that it would be better for everyone to get infected in order for there to then be collective immunity. This is something interesting, in fact. Because in sacred traditions, epidemics were considered something necessary to be overcome. In ancient times, there was the principle that everything needs to be got over like a sickness. The ghettoisation of disease only appears towards the onset of the modern age. In ancient times, sickness and epidemics were considered manifestations of the sacred, whether a blessing or a curse. We are already cursed, so all of us should suffer.

This is an important point about Covid. The lockdown dictatorship represents an attempt to cancel Covid, to remove the danger, to get rid of death by, as it were, kicking it out into the periphery.

Digital Immortality

Moving on, when I started investigating the topic of death—I have many more interesting things on this topic left in my notebooks, and now many things are coming to mind when I see your reactions; I see that you understand that there are some questions at hand, and I'm very attentively following your reactions and questions, so you are in many respects shaping my lecture—I noticed another important point: digital immortality is extremely important for Macron. As part of his election campaign, he created a parallel universe in Minecraft, and his election campaign was essentially built up in the artificial, virtual sphere. The users who visited his Minecraft office regretted that there was no alternative there, that it was very boring. His campaign really studied digital immortality and pointedly created a parallel reality. In *Le Figaro*, for example, an analysis of all the election campaign spectacles that were arranged and played along with by the presidential candidates indicated that the next presidential elections could be entirely virtual. There might not be any agitation efforts, where candidates ordinarily show up on site. Mr. Jean Mélenchon also believed in this digital immortality, and he went even further than Macron. Mélenchon is the left-wing candidate. I really like him for his left-wing economics: he has the idea of lowering the retirement age and he's for partial state control over the economic sphere. In general, he is a very talented orator who has actively spoken out against NATO, criticised NATO expansion to the East, and criticised the criminal Ukrainian Nazi gang. Although he only speaks of this indirectly, in hints, there is nevertheless a "geopolitical non-alignment" agenda in him. The Non-Aligned Movement arose in the time of confrontation between two blocs: the Soviet Union and Western civilisation. There were countries that didn't align with communism or liberalism. This is the geopolitical "third way" of Mélenchon, which is very interesting. But Mélenchon also has this digital immortality.

Sergei Mokhov, whose book *A History of Death: How We're Afraid of It and How We Accept It* I recently became acquainted with, says that communism generally leans towards trying to overcome death. The topic of Lenin's embalmment is very interesting here, because it illustrates a society which permits and accepts death.

Digital immortality is an element of Macronism, an element of progress, of the Western globalist "Empire". Let's recall that Jean Baudrillard, the French postmodernist philosopher, said that death is now being removed, that death is pushed out into the periphery of modern civilisation, but the cost of its discarding and attempts to ghettoise it is that it still rules over everything; it floods the whole space — everything is death. Death is everywhere precisely because of the attempt to get rid of it.

Spengler and Necropolitics

Now let's return to working through the topic and idea of death: to French necropolitics. I refer you to Oswald Spengler's idea in *The Decline of the West*. Macron once uttered in a speech that there is no French culture, only European culture. The resonance with Spengler here is obvious. Let's pay attention to the first part of the phrase. The subject of Spengler's studies on culture was the diversity of world culture (or "spiritual eras"), which he likened to living organisms going through the stages of emergence, becoming, and dying. Culture, according to Spengler, is what defines and formats an era. It is something that creates a definite unity of forms of thinking, space, and style; it is what unites the political, economic, spiritual, religious, and practical dimensions of life. The cultural-historical process is the rhythmic cycles of the birth, flourishing, and death of original, great cultures, among which Spengler counts the Chinese, Babylonian, Egyptian, Indian, antiquity, the Byzantine-Arab, Western, the Maya, as well as the young or "awakening" Russo-Siberian.

At the core of the uniqueness of each lies the special quality of their "soul". For example, the culture of antiquity was enlivened by the "Apollonian" soul, the Arab by the "magical", the Western by the "Faustian", etc. The death of any culture as a living organism leads to "culture" turning into "civilisation", that is, an ossified, immobile entity with a dead soul. According to Spengler, nine consistently evolving "cultures" on Earth in our era have undergone decline and furled up into "civilisations". Civilisation is the decline, the sunset and twilight of culture: instead of living organic forms of spiritual life, there comes something mechanical, artificial, technological, mass-oriented, and equalised. Western culture has turned into a dead civilisation. According to Spengler, the signs of this decline and collapse of culture include the "appearance of nomadic authorities" (here we can recall Jacques Attali's idea of nomadic elites) and the emergence of "wars for world domination", which we can observe today. Macron, following the Anglo-Saxon world, is vying for world domination in Kiev and in Africa. This is the main point in the profession of the tyrant. Macronism is manifest tyranny. The death of culture also entails an "oversaturation with technology", scientism and technicism, atheism and materialism, as well as nomadism and urbanisation — there's no people in the world city, only a mass.

It is interesting that the Faustian culture which Spengler discusses, the symbol of which is infinity, ends in Spengler's account with Western

Europe in the 19th century. The future, Spengler thinks, lies in the East — in Russia, in Russo-Siberian culture (the ninth culture in the world dynamic of cultures). The Russian culturologist Mikhail Epstein, seconding Spengler, speaks of an inner, sacred Siberia, of Russia as the enclave of a different spirituality — one that is not European, but rather Eastern and mystical, in the likes of what has been spoken of by writers like Yuri Mamleev.[8]

The West is Dead

To sum up, today the West is dead. European culture has died. French culture has died along with it. We have to deal with Macronism as death that ignores and doesn't accept itself.

Encountering the West today takes on the character of a clash with depraved neoliberalism, extreme individualism, toxic capitalism, frantic consumption, lies, substitutions of notions, double standards, and the desperate denial of death by decrepit Western elites who make up the concealed core of disintegrating Western mankind, in which death is presented as though it were life.

There is nothing more unnatural and obscene than when Macron says that he is the president of all of France, that he represents the majority, that he represents life — Macron has such dubious messages, and they are bound up with his excessive fascination with the environmentalist agenda and a *grivois*-like[9] attention to the life energy of young Africans.

---

8   Yuri Mamleev (1931–2015) was a Russian writer and philosopher known for his contributions to metaphysical and darkly surreal literature, often exploring themes of death, mysticism, and the grotesque. His work, particularly in *Shatuny* (The Sublimes), explores the complexities of the human psyche, blending Russian folklore with a unique existential perspective. Mamleev was one of Dugin's early teachers and inspirations in the Soviet-era dissident Yuzhinsky Circle.

9   French for "bawdy" or "risqué".

The Opposition's Dissent with Death

There is an alternative front in France: an opposition that, on the whole, represents dissent with death. But this disagreement with death does not automatically mean life. This dissent is essentially nostalgia, suffering, grief, and drama — it is like a long, dragging-on funeral for France. Zemmour has nostalgic speeches. He talks about how good things were before. His election campaign video was made in the spirit of appealing to the nation of Charles de Gaulle, perhaps even absolutely copying it. This is what the confrontation between two forces in contemporary France looks like.

I should note that the first part of my discussion on Eros and Thanatos in the political life of France was rather introductory. Or maybe for some it was bizarre and difficult. I can understand. This topic only recently came to me as a kind of targeted insight, a little inspiration that needs to be worked out in more detail. If you could share your own considerations on the idea of representing the elections through this grid of confrontation and contrast between life and death, through the prism of ontology, then I'll be very grateful.

I'll recommend you three books which can help you open up the topic of death in politics and immerse yourself in this topic:

- Henry Armand Giroux is an American sociologist who has a book entitled *Zombie Politics and Culture in the Age of Casino Capitalism*.[10] He is a left-wing analyst and professor who says that everything happening now, all of current politics, is a zombification of the population and fake news. These are fragments, broken pieces of what was once whole. Zombies flock to these pieces like users who need to build up and escalate their fill. Giroux argues that neoconservatives — of whom he is a vocal critic in America — are the ones who provoke such zombie regimes. That's why, Giroux

---

10 Henry Giroux, *Zombie Politics and Culture in the Age of Casino Capitalism* (New York: Peter Lang, 2014).

says, there are so many zombie movies on American and other TV networks. US citizens are zombies; the culture of the US is an instrument of zombification. He analyses successive eras of government, who cultivated these zombies, how and why, which he associates with neoliberalism.

- The second book that every educated person who wishes to investigate death needs to read is Jean Baudrillard's *Symbolic Exchange and Death*.[11] This is a remarkable work in which you'll find the thesis I talked about today: death spreads everywhere whenever it is denied.

- The third book, which I myself bought just recently, is Sergey Mokhov's (I have no idea who he is). I first saw his name in a bookstore. He is a contemporary author. His book *A History of Death: How We're Afraid of It and How We Accept It* has some interesting chapters, in particular the parts about how ideas of death have been transformed, how different understandings of grief have taken shape, what is now happening with the development of palliative care and gerontology, how ideas of immortality are perceived in the modern world, in modern capitalism, in modern civilisation, and how death is mythologized in contemporary culture. There are also parts on zombie politics, serial killers, black metal, how zombie-like drug addicts are being legalised, Satanism, the so-called "new romanticism", and how reburials and the fight for the rights of the dead are being cultivated. In fact, the dead play a much greater role in the modern world than we can imagine. A Party of the Dead has even been founded in Ekaterinburg. Their avantgardists come out to rallies with signs reading, "The dead are opposed!" Or "We, the dead, will always be opposed!"

---

11   Jean Baudrillard, *Symbolic Exchange and Death*, trans. Iain Hamilton Grant (Los Angeles: SAGE Publications, 2007).

Macron's Pyrrhic Victory

Let's move on to practical topics, to what has happened in France, what is about to happen, and whether there will be a revolution. This is my favourite topic that I've done many streams and speeches about.

To be brief, Macron won 58.5% with his electorate of 70+ (he has 70–80% of this electorate). His victory was absolutely nihilistic. People voted for Macron so that his rival wouldn't make it, Marine Le Pen, who has been demonised in the media for years. But Macron's victory was shaky. This is admitted not only by the political analysts who defend Le Pen or Zemmour, but by all the media. In fact, this victory for Macron was a Pyrrhic victory, it existed for only one evening, when he came out to the Champs-Élysées in front of the Eiffel Tower to celebrate his triumph to American music. Now he faces a very difficult period: social protests, citizens' increasing discontent over exorbitant prices, which are only growing as a result of the anti-Russian sanctions, rising gas prices, etc. There is a very strict system for assistance to enterprises, including the loosening of rules on firing — employees can now be fired much easier than before, and everyone knows that Macron and his neoliberal policies are behind this. Farmers have already organised an interesting action: in front of mayoral buildings they've started dumping the corresponding biological elements of what they and we use for fertiliser. Protests are expanding. The Yellow Vests protested all five years of Macron's previous reign. Judging by everything, this will spill over once again into weekly large-scale protests.

Macron is a globalist. Macron means left-wing politics (protecting minorities, unconditionally accepting migrants, globalism) and right-wing economics (neoliberalism, raw finance capitalism).

Contemporary France's Three Political Blocs

Who opposed Macron? He was opposed by two camps. These elections were interesting precisely in terms of these two camps and how they formed separate blocs. The first is Mélenchon. He is "left", advocating left-wing economics and social justice. He is a classic communist. He was joined by the Trotskyists — 1–2%. In sum, this bloc gathered 24% of votes in the elections. Mélenchon himself had 22%. Marine Le Pen, who was his rival while at the same time being almost on the same front with him in that they both represent anti-globalism, had 23% of votes in the elections. Thus, France is now divided into three blocs.

There is the globalism of Macron, who has shown his incompetence, which people have gone out to protest and which the Yellow Vests protested for his whole previous term in office. Macron is very artificial. He tries to survive by means of various strange games with Mélenchon's electorate, by means of an insane ecological agenda, and by the crisis in Ukraine. Why does Kiev need arms deliveries? In essence, it's about adrenaline. If there is a foreign enemy, if there is a foreign threat — Russia — then it is only natural that there will be consolidation, and it is largely thanks to this conflict that Macron managed to get re-elected. If the situation were milder, then I'm confident that Zemmour would have made it into the second round. He said that Russia would never go on the offensive, and that Russia is France's closest ally.

But things happened as they did. Macron won as a globalist with the 70+ electorate. In fact, he understands that he has a very elderly electorate. When he came on stage after the announcement of the second round's results, he was accompanied by youth, by children. The children were literally crowded around him and his wife. This looked weird, because in general the youth like Mélenchon, the left bloc. Le Pen is the right bloc. Zemmour can also be regarded as part of it. This confrontation has evolved from a horizontal opposition of parties into a vertical one.

Everything was quite simple in France before: Republicans vs. Socialists. Everything is also simple in France today, but the division is somewhat different: it is the people vs. the elite. Before, there was a horizontal *cordon sanitaire*: the voices of the people at the bottom were channelled into the Socialist or Republican parties in the middle, while the elites were somewhere up above. Now the *cordon sanitaire* has been taken down and all the classic parties have been knocked out of the game. There is only the people represented by two hands — the right, Le Pen, and the left, Mélenchon — and there are the elites, who are absolutely foreign to French culture and are bearers of death.

Forecasts

What is most interesting from the political point of view now is how the political space will unfold in the near future. Just ahead are the parliamentary elections, which will take place in June 2022. If Macron doesn't win, and the chances that he won't win are all there, then we'll have a situation which in French politics is called *"cohabitation"*.[12] This is when a president is from one wing, but the parliamentary majority is not from his party. This is a risky situation. It means that Macron will constantly have to put a spoke in the wheels and he'll constantly be doubted in one way or another, to the point that a parliamentary crisis might break out and Macron will be compelled to dissolve parliament. Then begins his struggle: battling against parliament instead of trying to strengthen France.

There were very interesting tendencies at the demonstrations held right after Macron's election. You could see signs with the slogans "Against liberalism" and "Against capitalism", and in Toulouse and Nantes there were signs that said "Revolution". This is left-wing France on strike. It is very decisive, irreconcilable, and it really doesn't like when it's exploited. They really don't like neoliberalism.

Mélenchon has kept his distance from Macron. In the "between rounds", despite his calls to not vote for Le Pen, he still kept his independence. He said: "Macron tried to contact me; he is speculating on us being in communication. I don't want to talk with him."

---

12   Dugina's forecast proved correct: for the first time since 1997, the current president of France did not win an absolute majority in parliament, nor did any of the other alliances, which led to a hung parliament.

Chances for Awakening

There is a new tension now — this is what needs to be followed. On the other hand, is it even worth it for us to follow a space of death? I think it's nevertheless worth it. Even if the same grieving over death and lamenting over the death of French culture persists in French politics, then this is something good, because it resembles a state of waking up. You can't talk with someone who is a harbinger of death while they deny and "ghettoise" death. But you can talk with someone who acknowledges death. For example, Zemmour says that Christian civilisation is being destroyed, is in the process of being killed, and that there is a "great replacement" going on. He took this concept from Renaud Camus. This concept says that new peoples are colonising Europe and destroying it. If we are to deal with those who are sensitive to the death underway, whether they themselves are dead or dying, then in this case dialogue between France and Russia could be more interesting and important. We'll follow how the situation unfolds. We should be sensitive and attentive to this space. After all, France is the avant-garde, the frontline of Europe. The processes unfolding there will in some time start happening in other countries as well.

Of course, there is a marked context of incoming revolution here, of *Jacqueries* breaking out across France. France thinks in cycles. They are always revolutionary. The French sociologist Emmanuel Todd recently said that the Yellow Vests have launched a new cycle in the history of France, and that after some time there might be a revolution — altogether, precisely, in 50 years. And the political scientist Youssef Hindi, who is a good friend of mine, responded to Todd: "Now time is accelerating. The time when a revolution will happen is in five or 10 years."

France on Edge

In general, Macron's coming five-year term will be interesting, revolutionary, full of protests, and completely unstable. We will see very interesting, avant-garde forms of the manifestation of the people's will. Now, after the parliamentary elections — if Macron somehow manages to keep the parliamentary majority, which I doubt — then it seems to me there will be an immense explosion. France is already on the edge. Paris is collapsing under migration. My friends say that if I were to visit, I would no longer even recognise the city.

The economic crisis is really hitting people. Ukrainian refugees who were at first accepted with great joy are now a discomfort. An article in *Le Figaro* recently cited the words of a farmer who said: "Fine, two weeks is normal, three weeks too. But they [Ukrainians] are really demanding and specific. They demand a large amount of money for sustenance."

In peaceful Paris, where Orthodox churches have never been attacked, the very beautiful Church of Seraphim of Sarov in the 15th district has been burned down. The church was set on fire by Ukrainian nationalists. An investigation is ongoing against the two suspected perpetrators.

France is a very interesting space, which needs to be followed attentively. The thanatology of French politics is a topic that deserves attention. We could go on infinitely talking about the chances of Macron's party getting re-elected in the parliamentary elections, and we could infinitely discuss whether Le Pen will win or not, or what will happen in five years. But, on the other hand, we could give an existential analysis — there's no way without such. I think that the Special Military Operation has exposed the necessity of thinking of processes in metaphysical terms and has exposed the nearness of the coming awakening. Now the time has come to wake up, no longer to remain in formal sociological analysis, and instead to head towards those ultimate things that are authentic: war, death, angst.

I think that it's not only the SMO [Special Military Operation] that needs to be studied in these terms. In fact, Sun of the North has been paying great attention to philosophical analysis of the SMO. This is necessary. It is necessary to see what sides are fighting: this is not simply a confrontation between two political models, but a confrontation between two civilisations. It is not only between Ukrainians and Russians, but between the globalist civilisation that is destroying everything, as we can see now, that is, between the civilisation of the Antichrist and Christian civilisation, the civilisation of truth, Eurasian civilisation. These topics demand being thought through.

My analysis today might be from the sphere of dreams, from a hybrid realm and interdisciplinary space. Nevertheless, I believe that it has every right to exist and that this is how we need to think now — through the prism of death, eschatology, and metaphysics.

On this note, if you'll allow, I'll end my lecture. I await your questions, reactions, and comments.

Questions and Answers

Question: Who set the Notre-Dame Cathedral on fire?

Dugina: There are different conspirological versions. Officially, it's been said that the workers' scaffolding simply caught on fire. But many people have said that it's possible that this was a jihadist attack, a special provocation, because some of the construction workers there were Arabs. By the way, what's really interesting on the note of the Notre-Dame is how Macron is trying to rebuild it. Restoration work is ongoing. Have you seen the drafts? They look completely murderous, like some kind of "attraction". On top they want to install solar panels and a garden to give food grown on the roof of the Parisian Cathedral of the Mother of God to poor migrants. They're also coming up with some kind of Disneyland entertainment sites. All of this is horrifying. When you see this, you realise just how horrifying it is that such a person, a profane atheist and puppet, has power. In one way or another, he will decide how the Notre-Dame Cathedral will be restored. I haven't seen any draft that would accurately recreate what it was before. I've seen drafts depicting a strange, transparent tower like Lakhta Centre to be built inside the cathedral. This is an utter de-sacralisation of an important symbol of French civilisation. You are right to make note of this. This is another testimony to death, to the death of the Christian culture of France.

Question: You said that Macron is about celebrating the death of France while Le Pen and Zemmour are about lamenting it. I agree with you on this. I read your blog. You've said on your blog that you like Mélenchon. How does Mélenchon fit into the fall of France?

Dugina: Here's what's interesting: Mélenchon, as a communist, works in the sphere of technology, in the sphere of progress. For him "tomorrow" means better. In this sense, Mélenchon probably also bears this death in himself, but he accepts it instead of chasing it off. Just as Lenin's embalmed body was laid down and preserved, so is Mélenchon with his holograms.

Question: That is, he takes a middling position?

Dugina: Macron is the ghettoisation of death. Mélenchon is its acceptance, but without lamenting it. Like Lenin's embalmed body, it's just there next to him, like a hologram. There were once rallies across 12 cities where they put up hologram copies [of the candidates] — "embalmed" Mélenchon. Thirdly, there is grief over the deceased, mourning. Thank you for prompting this.

Question: Daria, I completely agree with you that Europe now finds itself in the space of death. Unfortunately, these processes have been going on for a long time. For a long time time now we've been hearing about "right-wing populists" and "national conservative" forces, but they never win. They're in the position of a collective Zyuganov, who occupies a position in power but will never come to power. And the question is: do they even want to come to power? This is what I want to know. I also have a question about Mélenchon. You said that the Mélenchonists have revolutionary slogans and intend to fight. But could they become allies of the national conservatives? They're probably for migration and against family values.

Dugina: In my space of wishful thinking, my political dream, they would, of course, form a united National Bolshevik front. I thought that Marine Le Pen would reach an agreement with Mélenchon and they would play their cards together: Mélenchon would call on people to vote for Le Pen. This would have been the ideal picture: Marine is President and Mélenchon is Prime Minister or Minister of the Economy. This would have been a solution. But because all the clans, even the popular ones, are artificially fragmented, this alliance has unfortunately turned out to be impossible. I wanted this union to come out; I wholeheartedly believed in it, but it didn't happen. And it probably won't happen. They really do have different agendas, different left-wing policies and right-wing policies that are incompatible.

There are also very subtle intrigues being weaved between them. Mélenchon is a Freemason. My French conspirologist friends like Jean-Michel Vernochet often say that Mélenchon's call for "not a single vote for Le Pen" could have been influenced by his Masonic contacts. This opposition, even though it is on the whole wonderful and is, as it were, now on one and the same front in defending the people, cannot be unified, unfortunately. I said that this would be ideal, that it would be remarkable.

Konstantin Stepanov over here was at one lecture: do you remember how we dreamed that this solidarity would happen, and how much we wanted to talk about it? In all of my talks I've said that Marine Le Pen has a chance. This wasn't deceit; I didn't mislead anyone. It was my sincere wish. If you believe in something, it might come true. I personally understand that there can be no alliance between Le Pen and Mélenchon, but I will believe in this, because there should be, because this is "truthful". That's my answer. You are right, on the one hand. But I'm still going to dream.

Question: I would like to develop the following question: since last year, I've understood that Le Pen isn't big on passing. She could have given her votes to Zemmour, and she could have found some kind of agreement with Mélenchon. But everything went the other way. If we take into account that Le Pen is already old…

Dugina: You've written her off a bit too quickly. She's 53.

Question: But Le Pen is stigmatised…

Dugina: Zemmour is even farther away from Mélenchon than Le Pen, because starting in 2017, Le Pen changed her agenda and incorporated left-wing economics. During the election campaign, Le Pen's main thesis was restoring the purchasing power of French citizens. She also had an affinity with Mélenchon on the question of lowering the retirement age, whereas Zemmour says that it needs to be left as Macron changed it. What is interesting here is that Le Pen had the historic chance to create a coalition with Mélenchon, which was never possible before. Zemmour also had a chance to get elected with his sharp, grieving, lamenting rhetoric for France. But Zemmour really went after the left. He labeled them *"islamo-gauchisme"* ("Islamo-leftism"). He really doesn't like Mélenchon. It was Le Pen who had all the chances to unite with Mélenchon.

Question: When it comes to the next elections, is there any figure with prospects who is not too well known at the present? Who could make it to the top and unify with Mélenchon or someone like him?

Dugina: I think that this person is dead. He's gone. But he existed in the past. Actually no, I know one wonderful person who could do so: Alain Soral, the leader of the Égalité et Réconciliation movement, who is now locked up in a Swiss prison after being driven out of France by an endless amount of criminal proceedings. His main slogan is "left in economics, right in politics." He is beyond any single agenda. He has a wonderful book, which has been translated into Russian and published by Academic Project: *Understanding the Empire*. Read it; it is really interesting. Soral is in many respects a representative of the Fourth Political Theory which Alexander Gelyevich Dugin is developing. Unfortunately, in this situation Soral can't run in the elections.

Marion Le Pen will never conclude an alliance with Mélenchon. For her, there is no question of left-wing politics. Marion is from the "Future Leaders" series, a personage who has now returned to politics. She is the niece of Marine Le Pen and the granddaughter of Jean-Marie Le Pen. She is on her way back. She will work with Zemmour's election campaign. She is now the vice president of Zemmour's Reconquête [Reconquista] movement. But she will never unite with Mélenchon. The people who could do so are either dead or have been subjected to total ostracism to the point of imprisonment. One of Alain Soral's friends, Dieudonné, a black comedian of Cameroonian origin, is now being persecuted for his jokes about Macron. He has to pay fines and is now sitting in prison. Does this seem like an act of racism? No, he is against Macron — and it doesn't matter what skin color he has. The fact that he is against Macron is the weightiest argument.

Comment from the audience: This is completely Orwellian.

Dugina: Yes. I see my Sinologist friends are here, including a wonderful lecturer who in her book discusses the Chinese school of "the changing of names". This impressed me: Europe needs a renaming of things, a rectification of names. You've just mentioned Orwell: "Peace is war, war is peace." They really do have everything completely confused, turned on its head. Here we need a Great Renaming, a Change of Names, which is what we'll be doing in our Sun of the North lecture cycles.[13] I invite you to follow this. Sun of the North will be presenting an important deconstruction of the Special Military Operation. It's already started. It's a philosophical conceptualisation of what's going on. There are different lecture courses. I recommend you Andrei Korobov-Latyntsev's course on the philosophy of war and death, on Russian philosophy of war. This is very important, because war and conflict always have an important existential dimension which we need to pay attention to.

Question: How does Macron get along with Biden?

Dugina: They're good friends. Biden called him and wanted to congratulate him immediately after the elections, but Macron at the time could be found in Versailles, where I think he had a closed party. The next day they called each other. Biden said that he really supports Macron and is very happy about his re-election. They had

---

13   Published as *Velikoe russkoi ispravlenie imen. Sbornik po itogam zasedanii filosofskogo sobora v 2022 godu* (Saint Petersburg: Solntse Severa, 2023).

a lengthy conversation and they immediately came to the Ukrainian question. They have close, good contact. They're friends. When he was a presidential candidate in 2016, he invited Hillary Clinton to visit him. Macron was minister of the economy from 2014 to 2016. He has good, friendly relations with the neoconservative clan and globalists. In general, he came out of the American environment. He has work experience in banks and he's hired political consultants from the American McKinsey & Company. There was a loud affair around this. Under him, the country has been handed over to external management. The scandal with McKinsey was before the first round: Macron had hired this American consulting company, which had previously consulted the CIA on how to restructure its departments. Macron hired them and ordered them to work out healthcare legislation. They worked everything out. The company hasn't paid taxes in France for 10 years. They were caught for this after they worked out the law. They started to bury everything. In the end, some senators even said that when they analysed how Macron's friendship and collaboration with this consulting agency operated, they understood that Macron had practically destroyed the country's sovereignty and given up the country to external management. This report was released on March 16th. It's interesting that before the first round all the newspapers were talking about this, but as soon as the "in-between rounds" started, no one talked about McKinsey. This is very bad and very telling.

Thank you, friends!

France before the Elections: The Special Military Operation Changes Plans[1]

Vadim Egorov: How has it happened that the Special Military Operation is now influencing the elections in France? In general, how influential is it in your opinion?

Daria Dugina: The Special Operation has, of course, brought certain adjustments to the course of the election campaigns. You've discussed Zemmour on here, and Zemmour really was compelled to pull in the reigns, take a back seat, and apologise for his raging agenda. He had to apologise for when he claimed that there would be no Special Operation, that Russia wouldn't start combat operations. On the other hand, the Special Operation and attitudes towards it are not the priority question in France today.

If yesterday you were attentively observing the debates or my commentary on my Telegram channel, then you know that the debates over Ukraine came out to 15–20 minutes. The debates on purchasing power, on Marine Le Pen and Macron's economic agenda, and on diverse other topics, such as ecology, took up much more time. To summarise, we could say that Ukraine really has introduced some adjustments into the election campaign, particularly by de facto sending Zemmour to

---

1   A transcript of Dugina's appearance on the stream *Russkii muzhichok Govorun*, hosted by Vadim Egorov with Valentin Khoroshenin on 21 April 2022.

the sidelines, but it can't be said that it has overturned the political landscape.

Now they're talking about the formation of three new blocs. The French sociologist Emmanuel Todd says that France has been split into three countries. The first country is the Macronists, the 65+ audience, people who live in big cities. By the way, there's one really interesting and cool topic that I heard in the debates yesterday: if we analyse Macron's rhetoric, then there are many old French words and expressions in his speech. He is essentially speaking the language of his spouse, his teacher, who is of quite a decent age. Yesterday he used practically five or six very old phraseologisms, like *ripoliner* — this verb means "to varnish a surface, give something a shiny appearance". Macron's audience, or bloc #1, treats Ukraine in the following way: "Ukraine is a democracy; democracies shouldn't be bombed, so we should stand on Ukraine's side." This is the ultra-globalist agenda that operates in the wake of the main American globalist trend, the key front of movement of the world financial elite which asserts the world hegemony of Anglo-Saxon civilisation.

The second audience are Marine Le Pen's voters. Here it's very important to emphasise that the Marine Le Pen of 2022 is not the Marine Le Pen of 2017. She has made some serious corrections to her programme, and we can find a rather strong tilt towards left-wing economics. At the present moment, she's paying great attention to issues like purchasing power and reducing VAT (all of this could be seen in the debates). She shares many narratives that are dear to the traditional "left", despite her being stuck with the party label of the National Front, which supported "right-wing" strategies in the economy, so today she is attracting more and more sympathy from the "left", or she's at least neutralising the old antipathies towards her, such as those held by the "left" which has been declining in recent time. In fact, at Le Pen's rally in Paris last Saturday, which brought together different political movements opposed to Macron, you could also hear speeches by representatives of the left. One of my friends who was there considers herself a partisan of Mélenchon's left-wing movement, the *Front de gauche* of "Méluche", since she was 14 or 16, and in the current catastrophic conditions of the globalist elites' offensive she understands the need for a "right-left" alliance. She says, "Yes, Marine Le Pen is not exactly 100% what I'm for, but Le Pen would be better than Macron, because Macron is neoliberalism, capitalism in the worst, inhuman form, while Le Pen means an agenda that is essentially oriented towards working-class interests."

Studies show that peripheral France prefers Méluche and Marine Le Pen. These are very serious shifts. Of course, popular France, the France of Marine Le Pen, is cautious about Russia's Special Operation. Yesterday, Le Pen naturally expressed solidarity with the Ukrainian people, but her and her bloc are thinking first and foremost about the need to preserve their own economy in the conditions of a complex and difficult geopolitical confrontation. The main thing here is pragmatism and realism. This is expressed in her formulation that "the French and France shouldn't commit harakiri and shouldn't craft a mindless sanctions policy that will ruin the French economy". This is sober realism. Therefore, delivering arms to Kiev is, in her point of view, fanning the flames of the conflict, and what is needed is a peacekeeping mission.

By the way, what's interesting from this camp is that Marine Le Pen really competently attacked Macron in the debates when she argued that Macron is the one responsible for the Russian-Ukrainian conflict because he failed in his own mission. After all, he came to Moscow and Kiev and then claimed that he was proud to have convinced the president of the Russian Federation not to start the operation, and then, a few days later, everything turned around and didn't go according to Macron's scenario. This is all naïveté, cunning, incompetence, a lack of understanding of the laws of geopolitics, formalism, bragging, arrogance, self-confidence, and the desire to easily add points to his score in the upcoming elections, and nothing more.

On the accusations that Marine Le Pen has made, there's another interesting point. Macron tried to play it safe, so that there wouldn't be any more accusations of this kind, and dismissed the head of the DGSE, France's military intelligence, Éric Vidaud. In fact, Éric Vidaud was an anti-NATO-oriented general and there was a colossal intrigue behind his firing that was fomented by a powerful clash inside the French intelligence community. There were so many intrigues that one could write a whole detective novel about how two intelligence directorates, the DGSE and DRM, are clashing with each other, setting up each other's officers and scribbling denunciations. What's most interesting is the answer to the question: how is the current conflict in Ukraine connected to the activities of each of these units? But that's a different story.

The third clan is "Méluche", the Mélenchonists. They are also a movement with very significant prospects. In fact, I like them. I'll immediately say that I have a biased position. Naturally, I have greater sympathy for Marine Le Pen, especially her new "white-red", "right-left", or we could even say "National Bolshevik" agenda (which elegantly combines "right" elements in politics with "left" ones in economics), but I also have great sympathy for Méluche for his socio-economic agenda plus his radical criticism of NATO and his agenda for France to be non-aligned. Méluche is the third candidate who constitutes the "third bloc". Here we can see the following attitude towards the Ukrainian conflict: NATO is to blame for the conflict, because Russia needed to be presented with the guarantees that were promised and that Russia itself has sought, in essence, the capitalist world. NATO is fanning the flames of tension on Europe's borders, leading towards a long-term war, and all of this is in fact to the detriment of France. Of course, he also has some contradictions, particularly his active calls for accepting Ukrainian refugees.

And so, we have three blocs: Macron with his absolute support for the Kiev regime, which he calls a "democracy", Marine Le Pen with her political realism, critique of NATO, and demand that "France not commit harakiri" and that the French economy "not shoot itself in the foot", and the third bloc of Méluche. Méluche is obsessed with

"non-alignment". It's very often been common for left-wing movements in France to declare this non-alignment. Non-alignment during
the Cold War meant not joining either NATO or the Soviet Union. This
position of Mélenchon's is very interesting. In general, Méluche is one
of the rising stars of the French elections despite the fact that these are
likely the last elections in which he'll run. He is a colourful personality
and a very convincing speaker. Of course, there are some issues with
him which are completely unacceptable to me: in the very least, there's
the left-wing politics — the migration question, questions of values,
questions of minorities and so on. But, nevertheless, he's charismatic,
optimistic, and he didn't opt to ally with Macron. Although on 10 April
he called for not a single vote to go to Marine, he did not call for voting
for Macron. When Macron tried to speculate on holding talks with
Méluche just a few days ago, Méluche said: "I'm not going to talk with
this monsieur; the president is speculating on the fact of us having a
correspondence."

Accordingly, these are the three blocs. The Mélenchonists have
probably the most active and lively audience: the rebellious youth.
May is waking up, crazy May, and the lycées in the centre of Paris are
now blockaded. Children aged 14–16 are camped around the fences,
blocking entrances, laying out picnics, partying, and drawing pictures
of a bloody Macron and aggressive Le Pen. And strikes are starting at
the Sorbonne.

Marine Le Pen's camp is rather patchy, but she is wonderful when
it comes to how stoically she is leading this campaign and speaking up
for the people. You could just feel this at the debates yesterday when
she said: "Macron, you're accusing us of having a loan in a Czech bank,
but we're a poor party, and our French banks wouldn't give us loans."
This was, in fact, something deep, as if she was speaking in the name
of the whole people: "We're poor, we don't have money." She used the
word *pauvres*, and the expression on her face was so cool!

But, of course, Marine Le Pen is not the fire in these elections. The
fire of these elections is Zemmour. In fact, it needs to be said that he

hasn't given up. He's now actively sitting with his beloved Sarah Knafo, his love. They've decided to go with Marine Le Pen and the so-called "Generation Z". It's really called "Generation Z", which is very funny given that this "generation" arose before the beginning of the Special Operation — maybe they knew something!

The drive, the existence, the life of the French is now beating in the ranks of Mélenchonists, in the ranks of the Zemmourists, but it isn't too strong in Le Pen's camp. She's been left by some of whom are probably the best cadres in this period of the election campaign. They're still calling for voting for her, but they've left her. In Macron's milieux, meanwhile, there's an audience of "dead" people. These are existentially dead people who are in an absolute neoliberal coma, people who represent the past, the people of the "unipolar moment". Look at his wife — what a symbol of a departing cadaver! On the other hand, he has these "old words" I mentioned, which is also very important — that such a young president speaks in old-fashioned phrases. Yesterday, to be honest, I think he quoted Gérard Majax. Majax is an illusionist that the generation born in the 1990s doesn't know. He's an illusionist that the 60- and 70-year-old voters know from back when he did shows. I don't know, but maybe he's like Kaspirovsky[2] — maybe he would be the counterpart. What a strange quote.

In short, Macron has a "dead" audience; the "dead" vote for Macron. The semi-alive who are coming back to life vote for Marine Le Pen. The revolting fiery leftists, the high school students and kids, are for Méluche.

This is how things look. Accordingly, there are three attitudes towards Ukraine. Marine Le Pen and Méluche are closer, they have similar understandings of the conflict. Everything is different with Macron: he's the representative of the "dead" clan of globalists.

---

2   Anatoly Kaspirovsky (b. 1939) is a Russian psychotherapist and television personality, famous in the 1980s and 1990s for his televised "healing" sessions, which captivated millions across the Soviet Union, although his methods were often controversial and drew skepticism.

Valentin: You mentioned the high school students. I hope they're playing chess on their strikes, because otherwise it wouldn't look good. When it comes to Marine Le Pen's peacekeeping mission, I'm simply wondering: what's it all about? Because I associate French peacekeeping missions with altogether strange things, like with how they're extremely militarised, no?

Dugina: You mean what would her peacekeeping mission look like if she becomes president?

Valentin: I heard that she proposed, or in the very least her rhetoric mentioned, a peacekeeping mission instead of supporting the military conflict by supplying weapons. In this case, what would this peacekeeping mission consist of? A no-fly zone over Ukraine?

Dugina: In fact, this isn't fully clear, because they touched on this question only in passing, and all of it lasted around 15 minutes. Macron acted repulsively yesterday: he made faces and said phrases like "oi-oi-oi" to Marine Le Pen's face. *Le Figaro* today even initiated a massive investigation of what he meant when he said *"oi-oi-oi"*[3] — was it *"oi-oi-oi"* in the sense of a condemnation or was it something like quoting "Oi!" skin punk style? This is remarkable and very substantive journalism, is it not? But seriously, I'm not making any of this up. *Le Figaro* is really investigating what Macron meant.

But about Marine Le Pen, it's not really clear. I don't know what such a peacekeeping mission is in her understanding. I think that the Le Pen version of a peacekeeping mission would be sitting everyone down, holding real Minsk negotiations, and insisting on an actual resolution to the conflict, not on formal promises but on some concrete decisions with the real signatures of responsible persons. Just how implementable this would be now is unclear. It is clear that she accuses Macron of not being able to persuade and force NATO to provide written guarantees on the Minsk Agreements before the start of the conflict. That is, the charge she levels against Macron is that before all

---

3   "*Oi-oi-oi*" in French is an expression of surprise, dismay, or exasperation, similar to the English "oh dear" or "oh no".

of this started, he should have compelled NATO, insisted on providing some written guarantees. He didn't do this. He's not a peacemaker.

And about the "Oi! Punk", *Le Figaro* says that he probably meant "*oi-oi-oi*" as in the onomatopoeia expressing pain, irritation, or anxiety. But the "*oi-oi-oi*" thing is such a fun little embellishment to yesterday's debates.

Egorov: What do you think: why did Marine Le Pen once again right now decide to mention her position on Crimea? Didn't this push European French voters away from her?

Dugina: No, in fact, the situation is the following. The French are in the stage of waking up. They don't believe the propaganda that is constantly poured on them. There exists an enormous, developed network of information agencies, among them TV Libertés, France-Info, and different portals like Stratégica, Breizh-info, and many platforms where an alternative point of view is expressed and there's no aggressive propaganda. Even on the channels held by Zemmour's sponsors (like Vincent Bolloré), like CNews, Anne-Laure Bonnel went on and said that Donbass was bombed for eight years by the Nazi Kiev regime.

The French are distinguished for their political thinking. In America — and this is generally visible in the media — the mentality accepts whatever is "convenient" and "useful", that is, it practises pragmatism in the spirit of Peirce,[4] and the truth is whatever leads to subsequent use: "It doesn't matter whether something is true or false; what matters is that it can lead to something profitable. And if it leads somewhere into these spheres, then okay, let's keep going." But the French philosophical picture of the world is based on the philosophy of the Enlightenment. They have a very strong idea of checking, of verifying, of critically perceiving one or another direction of thought,

---

4   Charles Sanders Peirce (1839–1914) was an American philosopher, logician, and mathematician, often regarded as the founder of pragmatism. He defined pragmatism as a method for clarifying concepts by considering their practical effects, asserting that the meaning of an idea or proposition lies in its observable consequences.

so for them, of course, the story that "Russia is bombing cities and peaceful civilians" draws a sense of distrust. Therefore, Le Pen's statements on Crimea, on Russia's reunification with Crimea, and Macron's screeching about Russia bombing democracy—all of this provokes thought and requires verification. In fact, Crimea is met with moderate understanding among the French; it doesn't draw protest in principle. As for Macron's statements about Ukraine being a democracy—this is still dubious to the French.

I've immersed myself in studies done on the Kiev Nazi regime and Nazi groups and I discovered that in 2016 there was a semi-closed document in French agencies. It passed through the Ministry of Foreign Affairs and also circulated in journalistic circles and then made its way right to me. This document says that there is a bloc taking shape in Ukraine which might be dangerous for Europe. It is a bloc of radical Nazism. Accordingly, in 2016, diplomats in the French Ministry of Foreign Affairs and French journalists touched on this topic in one way or another.

In fact, it needs to be said that the French don't have the unambiguous picture that "Russia is bad" and "Ukraine is good". The French simply think that there is aggressive propaganda being deployed and that this is bad. Macronism and the Macron regime say that "Ukraine is good", "Russia is bad", and the French think: "Well, fine, but this is the Macron regime, the same one that pushed us down onto our knees, that is to blame for inflation, that made us lose our jobs, that made gas expensive and prices rise so much that we had to turn down the temperature in our homes." And a healthy judgment prevails: "Maybe this isn't how things are; maybe they're different?" This is a very important point.

Therefore, when it comes to "Crimea is Russia" for Marine Le Pen, her statements don't scare off voters. And Zemmour, in fact, was gaining popularity by virtue of his positions. He simply came up with one rhetorical point that very intensively and offensively worked until the Special Operation began. He had a very convincing campaign, but at one moment, when the Special Operation began, he started to slightly try to justify himself — saying that he had something else in mind. These justifications came at the cost of his aggressive tone being lowered. He is good when it comes to energetic offensive with his fury. He really is a very interesting political thinker. And he added a unique dimension to these elections. Have you ever seen a contemporary European politician say, "Carthage is the Anglo-Saxon world", "Rome is France", "Europe is France", or "Europe is Rome"? Or who says *"Carthago delenda est"* ("Carthage must be destroyed") and in so doing is actually proclaiming eternally relevant geopolitical laws? This is very serious; it is very strong. He is considering the whole history of France. I once had a book somewhere which discusses these types of questions like deconstructing French history through the prism of geopolitical laws and blocs. The author shows where on the temporal axis we find the period of rise, the time of fall, the moment of subordination to globalist doctrine and the point of the ruin of Rome. He argues that our modern situation is repeating the history of the fall of Rome.

To get back to your original question on Ukraine, it needs to be noted that no, neither the annexation of Crimea nor the SMO push French voters away, although they do not have a definitive decision on the Ukrainian question — they leave it open under a question mark, as a sign that something has yet to be said.

Egorov: Well, in this case, it really looks odd that Zelensky in an interview is calling for voting for Macron, and Navalny on Twitter, or rather some people from Navalny, have been writing rather dubious analyses and also ultimately called for voting for Macron. This is quite a dubious step in present circumstances. If the French really are so critical towards such imposed propaganda, then what's interesting is who would be accepting such a decision from the likes of Zelensky and Navalny?

Dugina: You know, this can't, in fact, be deemed anything other than meddling in the internal affairs of the state of France. Because, in essence, this interview was not only published, and not only contained words in support of Macron, but was aired on television screens right ahead of the debates. This was, in fact, a kind of programming and social engineering upon the audience that was supposed to watch the debates afterwards. When I saw the news, I understood that the masks have been taken off and just how dishonest the election strategy is. What could have been done in this instance? What about Le Pen? Even if she had won in terms of votes, they still wouldn't let her into the presidency because the propaganda and machine of globalism is so strong and so furiously tramples over and annihilates any manifestations of sovereignty, common sense agendas, and the manifestation of the people. It's not only Navalny or Zelensky who act this way, but hundreds of other representatives of the international clan of the world's globalist elites. By the way, presentations like these are a black mark on Macron, because when the head of a failed state — I have in mind Zelensky — says that he supports Macron but won't find a common language with Marine Le Pen, then this is all the worse for Macron and all the better for Marine Le Pen.

The heads of government of Germany, Scholz, Spain, Pedro Sanchez, and Portugal, Antonio Costa, also today indirectly called on the pages of *Le Monde* for voting for Macron against Marine Le Pen. They didn't name names, but they said: we stand for the candidate of the democratic party. Democratic? Uff! Well, in general, sure, Macron really is almost Biden, maybe only a bit younger. And then they stated that they call for voting against the "extreme right" candidate. I wonder who that could be! In fact, this "extreme right" here is funny because François Asselineau, one of the 12 candidates in the elections, as soon as the results of the first round were announced and Marine and Macron made it into the second round, called for voting against the "terrible candidate from the ultra-right bloc". Who would this be? François Asselineau had Macron in mind. He said that Macron is now bringing out his ultra-right, fascist-Nazi agenda by supporting the Kiev regime, the junta, and therefore he poses a danger. So paradoxical are the worlds of Postmodernity — in the sense that liberalism today expresses itself in Western hegemony and the American agenda supporting a Nazi regime. And in what version? This is, in some sense, the Nazi regime of Dmytro Dontsov.[5] It is the idea of extreme nationalism, of establishing the exclusive supremacy of a Ukrainian nation, of will dominating over reason, and justifying any deeds. This is "integral nationalism". If we read Dmytro Dontsov, then we'll see that his works are the original, dangerous firepit out of which the xenophobic, Russophobic movement that we now see on Kievan lands developed, which is now supported by the "fascisising" liberals of the whole world, including Bernard-Henri Lévy, who visited the fascist Marchenko[6] and paced around Odessa with him.

I'd like to go back to the interesting topic that we touched on when we were talking about the electorate, about the Ukrainian regime and the three blocs of voters in France. Macron is the cadaver candidate, the candidate of the "dead". All the "ballot stuffing" and the machines used to count votes in accordance with the US election schemes will be used for him. Macron is dead France, a continuation of the idea of Jacques Attali, who insisted that all the differences between cultures should die, that there will be a global world in which only different types of nomadic communities remain. These will be societies of migrant workers and the very mobile managers administrating them. Macron, as I already noted, is the production of a cadaver world; he is the lead driver of dying France. That's why he has an older wife: she is his psychopomp[7] into the world of decrepitude and death. Macron's

---

5   Dmytro Dontsov (1883–1973) was a Ukrainian writer, philosopher, and political theorist, known for developing an influential, radical form of Ukrainian nationalism.

6   Serhiy Marchenko (b. 1981), Ukraine's Minister of Finance since 2020, has played a key role in securing international financial aid, including a $50 billion loan supported by frozen Russian assets.

7   A psychopomp is a mythical or spiritual figure responsible for guiding souls to the afterlife or escorting them between realms.

world is the order of the old globalism we know and liberalism living out its old age, now represented by senile old men like the dying Soros, Rothschilds, Rockefellers, the old Jacques Attali and shabby Bernard-Henri Lévy. Marine Le Pen has the intermediate age component of the electorate, the voters that are 25, 35, 45. Finally, the Zemmourists are younger. The Mélenchonists are the life of the youth, the future. This is what's interesting from the point of view of an existential analysis of voters' temperaments. But this is a digression.

Valentin: I wonder: when Macron goes home to his wife, does he treat her like Baba Yaga[8] and ask her and her hut to turn around to face him? Anyway, to get back to the Spanish authorities, it's noteworthy that they seem to be playing with the recent news that Spain intends to stop supplying energy to France. I think that Spain can't do this, as it would mean unilaterally violating agreements, but, nevertheless, as far as I understand, in this case words and deeds diverge.

Dugina: Yes, in fact, if you check how things stand with logic and necessity among Western leaders, they have very low ratings. Their words and deeds are different. Even Macron declares: "I want to make peace", but then he sends weapons worth 100 million dollars to Kiev. Also binoculars and tactical vests, fine. Ok, maybe this too, and then peace. But we'll still deliver some CAESAR artillery systems! Oops! And then it's uncovered that French soldiers might be hiding in Mariupol, in Azovstal, and not just any ordinary mercenaries. There are mercenaries there — I already clarified this question, as I have contacts in France who told me that there are mercenaries who have been killed there. It's possible that there aren't only mercenaries there.

They're doing a really wonderful job covering this on the Zvezda channel: they're very consistently conducting investigations live on air on a special programme which hosts various journalists who present

---

8   Baba Yaga is a powerful witch-like figure in Slavic folklore, often portrayed as an ambiguous, sometimes malevolent character who dwells deep in the forest. Her hut, a small wooden house standing on chicken legs, can rotate or move at her command, adding an eerie, magical element to her mysterious presence.

their ideas and inquests. But I haven't really delved into this topic; I didn't verify it until I went to Mariupol and went down into the Azovstal catacombs.[9] It seems that there could have been instructors tied to the DRM, France's military intelligence directorate, there.

In general, everything here is shrouded in secrets and mystery, because deeds and words are not identical. This is a world of "wandering meaning". This is a world in which one word has three meanings. A world where when we say the Russian word *mir*, this word has three meanings. In Old Church Slavonic, there were two ways of writing it: мир and мiръ. The first meant the world as it's given, world in the sense of "we're in the world", while the other meant the world as a task, "world" as "peace", as a state opposite to that of war. Every war has the aim of establishing the "peace-world", but without war the "peace-world" is impossible. War is an absolutely necessary topic for establishing order, for establishing the мiръ that is above what's ordinarily given.

You know, Spain is also now starting enormous weapons deliveries. I think it was just today that there was a massive portion of arms — I think I wrote about it on my Telegram channel. There were 200 tonnes of military equipment, which is twice the volume of military aid that Madrid has sent to Kiev to date. This has been announced by the prime minister of Spain, Pedro Sanchez.

Valentin: What's funny is that Zelensky has demanded 7 billion dollars a month. This really interestingly correlates with Zelensky being ready to fight for 10 years. This is a colossal quantity of money.

Dugina: Look at just how interesting the character of this conflict is. After all, from our side, we see some kind of strange, modified version of ourselves. For example, I think they could fight for 10 years: they have Slavic stubbornness and we also have Slavic stubbornness. Only this stubbornness is mixed up with obsession. In general, this situation, this conflict is interesting in the dimension of its confrontation,

---

9   Dugina visited Lugansk, Donetsk, Mariupol, Melitopol, and Kherson as a journalist in June 2022.

its glowing heat. This is a very frightening but interesting clash with ourselves. Because we are de facto looking in the mirror and seeing something completely frightening, some kind of hybrid.

This is the time of the Great Awakening. I think this is a chance for us to wake up. It seems to me that now all of history or, in the very least, the whole history of my life has been split into "before" and "after" the Special Operation. Simply the world has taken a radical turn and radically changed. All the cards have been re-dealt and, indeed, all the masks have flown off.

I don't know about you, but among those around me there have been one or two people who have spoken critically of the SMO. And there was one person who said, "We're going too slowly", "We're moving forward too slowly for some reason." This person has something to do with the military, and he said this on the third day of the Special Operation. He became the third person I blocked after the first two, who completely rejected the Special Operation, or more accurately, spoke negatively about it. This is a special type of armchair experts who after three days had already concluded that "we're going too slow to take Kiev".

It seems to me that the Special Operation has really strongly shown people as they are and really strongly fused people together. All the protests that arose right after the operation began and kept up the tension instantaneously dissipated. It became clear that you're either for or against, either for the Russian World, for us, for Eurasian civilisation, or you're an enemy. I'll emphasise that this isn't simply the Russian World, but Eurasian civilisation. The Kadyrovtsy[10] are fighting alongside Russians, hand in hand, and today there was even an absolutely insane episode on a Telegram channel where girls who were sitting in a basement in Mariupol, hiding from bombings, suddenly uttered such words: "I hear 'Allahu Akhbar' and I understand that this

---

10 The Kadyrovtsy are pro-Russian paramilitary forces from Chechnya, loyal to Chechen leader Ramzan Kadyrov, known for their role in enforcing his rule and participating in Russian military operations, particularly in Ukraine.

means 'the Russians are coming.'" The word "Russian" has become something supra-ethnic: Russians have become something universal. The Kadyrovtsy are fighting as Russians, we accept them as such, and they've accepted our Russian World. In general, this is a remarkable situation which the Special Operation has really brought out in a cool way, like a litmus test, like some kind of scan. The Special Operation has unveiled the sources of light, the sources of warmth, like an infrared light, like thermal imaging. And I see this in everything. The Special Operation began and now it's obvious who is a friend and who is an enemy.

The bookstore Listva is doing amazing things with its *Tyl'* ["Rear", "Behind Lines"] project. I call on everyone watching us to pay attention to this project, to donate to it. If you don't have money, at least donate 100 rubles, or 200, or 300 — I don't know, maybe 500 or borrow 1,000 from someone or, if you really don't have any money, go make some! Or if you don't have money, go and work there yourselves, because even the smallest help contributed to humanitarian projects like this is important. Buy a book in Listva about a white officer, sign it, and write a letter. Any contribution from any point is very needed.

In fact, it's also very important to pray, to sincerely pray. It doesn't matter what your faith is. If you're Russian, you should simply go and start believing in the Russian Orthodox God. Today is Holy Thursday, so we still have some time left to repent.

When we talked with Father Andrei Tkachev about the Special Operation, he told us that once after he had given a sermon, an old man came up to him and said: "Father, I kneel down to pray once a day, and I feel a bullet flying past a Russian soldier." Kneel down in prayer — this is very important.

Now I'd like to turn to our listeners: sorry, esteemed listeners, for adding the religious angle to the Special Operation, but without a religious interpretation and religious understanding we won't understand all of these conflicts and clashes between civilisations. In France, which we're talking about today, Ukrainians set fire to the Church of

St. Seraphim of Sarov in Paris' 15th district. It burned to the ground. A judicial inquiry is ongoing. This is a real confrontation: they didn't just burn down a Russian cultural centre, they burned down a church, a wooden church, one of the most beautiful churches in Paris. It was so cozy that when I visited it, I had the feeling as if I were somewhere in Kostroma. Although, of course, in Kostroma the church is made of stone, but nevertheless, the feeling arises that you're in the depths of the Yaroslav or maybe Tver region, yet even Tver has stone churches. I don't know how to compare it, but I've seen such churches near Tver.

The battle that is going on in Ukraine is, in fact, a clash between Christian and anti-Christian civilisations. You can argue as much as you want that there are Orthodox people and believers in Ukraine. Yes, there are believers. But the model that dominates there is an obsession that is utterly anti-Christian, a completely mad eschatological Darkness — Darkness with a capital "D". From our side, it is an absolutely luminous struggle.

By the way, France doesn't see this conflict as a conflict of civilisations at all. It doesn't take into account the religious dimension at all. In France, even the conservative Marine Le Pen isn't religious. The conservatives like Zemmour have even criticised Marine Le Pen for constantly talking about secularism. She talks about *laïcité*.[11] For many of my French friends, Le Pen is missing the religious dimension.

I know a number of people who have come to Orthodoxy and who are now interested in this dimension that is new to them. They were the ones who sent me the information about the Church of Seraphim of Sarov — one of the priests, a French national, came there from the New Right movement. He was in the New Right movement, was a pagan, and then amazingly came to Orthodoxy.

What am I talking about? We need to pray; we need to pray for Russian soldiers, for our victory, for us to have success on all fronts.

11   *Laïcité* is the French concept of secularism, which mandates the strict separation of religion from public institutions and ensures that the state remains neutral regarding religious beliefs, promoting equality and freedom of conscience.

And, in this sense, of course, the Special Operation is something very important, really important for such an awakening. If we don't seize this chance, if we don't wake up from hibernation, from indifference, from idleness, then woe to us, woe to us! If this Special Operation doesn't touch us and affect us deep down, then it's time to think about who we are — maybe we're absolutely abandoned, God-forsaken people. Sorry for this inadvertent *pathos* which might have slipped out. I'm simply really, sincerely concerned about this situation, and it seems to me that what is happening now is an event of the greatest scale. I feel that whenever sorrow or some kind of eschatological pessimism takes over, I simply force myself to understand how our soldiers and heroes are moving forward for 50–60 days, how they're going on the offensive, how they set their watches at every post. Therefore, I think this is a very important aspect. We need to not forget about it.

Egorov: Does it also seem to you that the Special Operation, and everything that's happening in the world in connection with it, is increasingly less like Postmodernity, and more like, God forgive me, "meta-Modernity", whose existence I've always denied until this all started? The grand narratives and meta-narratives that Postmodernity fought against are returning, and the irony and scepticism towards everything is going away. People are starting to perceive everything more sincerely, all the while as they dig through tons of things in which it is impossible to figure out what is true and what is not true. And some things, roughly speaking, are falsified even more than, say, in the case of the the war over Libya and how it was covered.

Dugina: On the matter of irony, whether it's going away or not — after all, the figure of Zelensky is the figure of the jester. In the Middle Ages, the jester personified the Antichrist. The devil stood behind him, and he appeared exclusively during rare periods of the annual cycle and personified the enemy of mankind. Irony, jokes, and buffoonery are all attributes of an impure spirit. On the stage of history, Zelensky is the lying jester, the embodiment of dubiousness and mockery, the Satanic tempter of Ukraine, the agent of the Prince of Darkness.

But I agree with you: a meta-narrative really is growing. Once again, the same division that existed in traditional societies is coming about: the forces of light against the forces of evil. The jester and the anti-Christian vs. Christian, Russian civilisation. This is the return of the grand narrative. If we go back to the French topic, then in these presidential elections there were very strong moods around the return of grand discussions. First and foremost, thanks need to be given to Zemmour for reviving grand narratives and starting to talk about how French civilisation is dying. Zemmour is holding rallies which have astonished me. He's gone to the monument to the Archangel Michael in Vendée, which was supposed to be removed for building new housing. He went out with the French conservative Philippe de Villiers, and in front of a gathering of conservatives, Catholics, and nationalists he proclaimed: "Let's save the Archangel Michael!" This is the serious return of meta-narratives, of generally grand, great narratives, a return to the French agenda. And it is thanks to this "Zemmourism", it seems to me, that there was an injection of adrenaline into the whole, rather stale election campaign, in which the "dead" Macron fought against the "semi-dead", "dying" Marine, who has been gradually disintegrating under the influence of political cadavers and zombies. The West as a whole is inclined towards slumber; it tends towards fading away into micro-narratives. In essence, the fact that words diverge from deeds is connected to the fact that words are uttered with no responsibility. They don't have the link between "word" and "meaning", and this is the classic sign of Postmodernity. The same goes for "fake news", meaning a deliberately false information agenda which rapidly unwinds, changes, and is forgotten in a moment, which is also a sign of Postmodernity.

In any case, we can say that the meta-narrative of the new great tale is coming from the East. We, Russia, and also China, India, Iran, Pakistan, the Arab countries, and the countries of Africa — to the degree that they have kept to their positions — are the meta-narrative. This means the preservation of great historical meaning, upholding classical politics, including the notions of "friend" and "enemy" and respectful attitudes towards the religious traditions of populations.

In the Chinese political lexicon, for example, there are the notions of "friend", "enemy", and "Chinese dream" — these are all points in Xi Jinping's speeches. He is of the military clan — the great Russian Sinologist Nikolai Vavilov has written about this in his book *The Uncrowned Kings of China*, where he talks about how how diverse Chinese politics is.[12] There are also clans in China just as there are in Russia: the military clan, the Deep State, the clear-cut one that formulates everything on the grounds of Carl Schmitt's ideas of "friend" and "enemy", "land" and "sea", "good" and "bad". There are also globalists oriented towards the Western world who have settled into China's Komsomol organisation. There is the intermediary Shanghai group which balances between the two.

Today the world is divided. There is the world of anti-Postmodernity with its deep, clear-cut, maximally grand narrative. There is the world of Postmodernity, which is represented by the West with its minimal narrative and lack of responsibility for its words. Look at how insatiably the West gobbles up stories about mass killings. Remember the tempo of events between Bucha, the "row [*bucha*] in Bucha", the provocation set up by the Ukrainian obsessors, as well as Kramatorsk. After all, there was a very small interval of time between these events. People require new injections of emotions, new adrenaline — this is zombie politics. And this is a sign of Postmodernity. In fact, Henry Giroux, an American sociologist, characterises the contemporary structure of the world as a zombie-apocalyptic world, and he explains how zombie politics is about orienting people to see, get, and "need" something "living", even if only in the media sphere — to be sent in search of a "living" person or fact and hastily swallow it up to then continue chasing after the "living".

---

12 N.N. Vavilov, *Nekoronovannye koroli krasnogo Kitaia* (Moscow: Karpe Diem, 2023).

Despite the fact that Postmodernity is completely dominant in the West today, the grand narrative of anti-Postmodernity is starting to build up an alternative campaign to the West, an alternative pole to the West, which is already contained in the formula "the West and the rest". The "rest" today is starting to wake up and return to the grand classical narrative.

Valentin: One funny politician said that he would emigrate to Europe only for retirement, because there's nothing for youth to do there.

Dugina: Yes, I think that we need to build some arks and airships for those who don't agree with the regime that reigns there. And we need to do something avant-garde, something beautiful, something in Alexei Belyaev-Gintovt's style,[13] some kind of immense ethereal ships that would fly over from the old world to the new world, form the world of Postmodernity to our world, to our Russian world. And we'll accept them and hold enormous choral dances [*khorovody*].

You know, I recently clashed with a person who suddenly said: "Now they'll probably ban Western music." And suddenly such joy came over me that I asked: "And what would happen with our consciousness if we stopped listening to Western music for a few days — if we just didn't listen to it?" Well, of course, we could listen to classical music. I recently went to a Wagner show, by the way. Literally a few days after the Special Operation began, I went to *The Valkyrie* and to *Siegfried*, and I listened to their performance by the Gergiev orchestra — it probably lasted six hours. I was amazed at how this music sobers up and can actually fully resurrect a person. We listen to the too ordinary rhythms of Western music, even if someone listens to punk, dark rave, new wave, experimental, or something else. Well, experimental of some sort, like

---

13   Alexei Belyaev-Gintovt (b. 1965) is a Russian artist known for his neo-imperial-themed works, often inspired by Soviet iconography and Russian history. He is closely associated with Alexander Dugin and his Eurasianist ideology, as Belyaev-Gintovt's art reflects themes of Russian cultural revival and resistance to Western influence, aligning with Dugin's anti-liberal, Traditionalist views.

Aidan Baker[14] — I was just reminded of him for some reason. We listen to this music and our consciousness gets simplified. Listen to Wagner and you'll break in the third hour — it's a very complex narrative, an incredible gamma of emotions.

Therefore, it seems to me that we are presented with a great chance: we have all the prerequisites to restore and develop ourselves, fantastically and aspiringly, like we've never dreamed of. We have such a majestic history full of meanings, such a wonderful religious and theological tradition, such a delightful musical heritage, the understudied Silver Age[15] and everything of the sort. We have the most extraordinary possibilities to be intelligent and thoughtful, elevated and practical, traditional and avant-garde, deep and fashionable Russian people. In fact, so much has already been thought of and written down, and there are all the prerequisites. An organic Russian fashion exists among us. And here I see that you're wearing the traditional Russian *kosovorotka* shirt.[16] In Listva I saw *kosovorotka* shirts as well as *kokoshnik* headdresses,[17] and it doesn't look "cringe" at all, but graceful, elegant, and delightful. In general, Russian fashion produces a very organic and festive impression. It all resembles the iconic, picturesque dawn of our soul, and it looks very cool — very meaningful, thoughtful, and

14 Aidan Baker (b. 1974) is a Canadian musician, composer, and author known for his work in ambient, experimental, and drone music, particularly as a member of the band Nadja.

15 The Russian Silver Age, spanning from the 1890s to the 1920s, was a period of extraordinary cultural vibrancy in Russia, marked by innovation in poetry, philosophy, and the visual arts. Influential figures like poets Anna Akhmatova, Osip Mandelstam, and Marina Tsvetaeva; philosophers Vladimir Solovyov and Nikolai Berdyaev; and artists Mikhail Vrubel and Kazimir Malevich explored themes of spirituality, symbolism, and existentialism.

16 A *kosovorotka* is a traditional Russian shirt with a high collar and a diagonal, off-center closure, typically worn by men and often associated with rural, peasant clothing.

17 A *kokoshnik* is a traditional Russian headdress worn by women, featuring a fan-shaped, often jewelled or embroidered, crest that arches over the head and is typically tied with ribbons under the chin, symbolising Russian folk heritage.

artistic. Therefore, I think that a great opportunity has appeared before us now.

Valentin: We wish success to the whole orchestra performing Wagner's music.

Dugina: Thank you for the invitation to your stream. I once again call on all of our listeners: donate, go wherever things are difficult and wherever your help is needed, and in general help our Russian World, or else it'll be too late. We need to help and get involved now. All the best!

OTHER BOOKS PUBLISHED BY ARKTOS

OTHER BOOKS PUBLISHED BY ARKTOS

OTHER BOOKS PUBLISHED BY ARKTOS

OTHER BOOKS PUBLISHED BY ARKTOS

P R Reddall	Towards Awakening
Claire Rae Randall	The War on Gender
Steven J. Rosen	The Agni and the Ecstasy
	The Jedi in the Lotus
Nicholas Rooney	Talking to the Wolf
Richard Rudgley	Barbarians
	Essential Substances
	Wildest Dreams
Ernst von Salomon	It Cannot Be Stormed
	The Outlaws
Werner Sombart	Traders and Heroes
Piero San Giorgio	Giuseppe
	Survive the Economic Collapse
	Surviving the Next Catastrophe
Sri Sri Ravi Shankar	Celebrating Silence
	Know Your Child
	Management Mantras
	Patanjali Yoga Sutras
	Secrets of Relationships
George T. Shaw (ed.)	A Fair Hearing
Fenek Solère	Kraal
	Reconquista
Oswald Spengler	The Decline of the West
	Man and Technics
Richard Storey	The Uniqueness of Western Law
Tomislav Sunic	Against Democracy and Equality
	Homo Americanus
	Postmortem Report
	Titans are in Town
Askr Svarte	Gods in the Abyss
Hans-Jürgen Syberberg	On the Fortunes and Misfortunes
	of Art in Post-War Germany
Abir Taha	Defining Terrorism
	The Epic of Arya (2nd ed.)
	Nietzsche is Coming God, or the
	Redemption of the Divine
	Verses of Light
Jean Thiriart	Europe: An Empire of 400 Million
Bal Gangadhar Tilak	The Arctic Home in the Vedas
Dominique Venner	For a Positive Critique
	The Shock of History
Hans Vogel	How Europe Became American
Markus Willinger	A Europe of Nations
	Generation Identity
Alexander Wolfheze	Alba Rosa
	Globus Horribilis
	Rupes Nigra

www.ingramcontent.com/pod-product-compliance
Lightning Source LLC
Chambersburg PA
CBHW020526270326
41927CB00006B/459